P5

Advanced Performance Management
Study Manual

For Exams until June 2016

ACCA

British Library Cataloguing-in-Publication Data
A catalogue record for this book is available from the British Library

Published by InterActive World Wide Limited
Westgate House, 8-9 Holborn
London EC1N 2LL

www.iaww.com/publishing
www.studyinteractive.org

ISBN 978-1-78480-057-4

Fifth Edition 2015

We are grateful to the Association of Chartered Certified Accountants (ACCA) for permission to reproduce syllabuses, study guides and pilot/specimen papers.

We are grateful to the Chartered Institute of Management Accountants (only where applicable) and the Institute of Chartered Accountants in England and Wales (only where applicable) for permission to reproduce past exam questions. The answers have been prepared by InterActive World Wide.

Foreword

Thank you for choosing to study with the London School of Business and Finance.

During the last 10 years LSBF has gone from a start-up to one of the major providers of exam training for ACCA. We have managed that by offering the highest standard of exam training towards the ACCA qualification.

You now have the opportunity to take advantage of the accumulated knowledge of the ACCA tutor team in this Study Manual. We have developed the new books to reflect what you need to know to pass the exam. They are comprehensive and map the syllabus whilst at the same time emphasising those parts of the syllabus that are most likely to be examined.

The books take account of current academic theory on how you learn best. They are designed to be easy to read and to assimilate knowledge from. Further reflecting LSBF's commitment to cutting edge technology, they are supported by a wide range of interactive and recorded content. I believe that we are offering the best study text available.

I wish you the very best of luck in your studies.

Aaron Etingen

ACCA (first time passer), FRSA, MSI, BSc (Accounting & Economics)

Founder and Executive Chairman

Contents

London
School of Business
& Finance
shaping success in business and finance

London
School of Business
& Finance
shaping success in business and finance

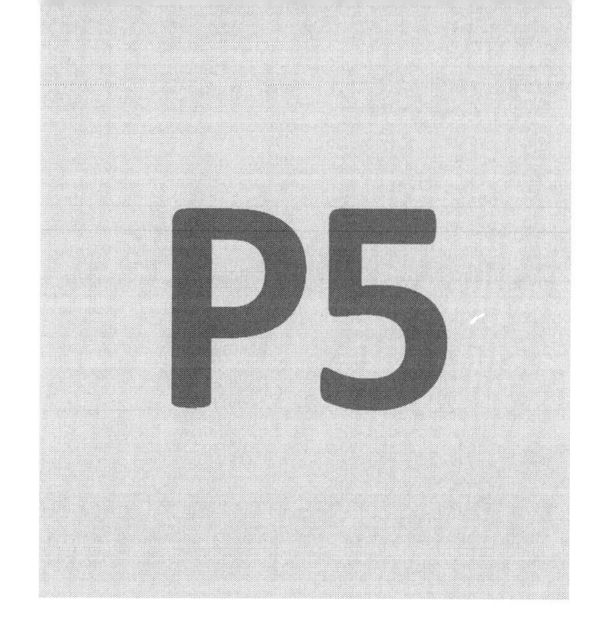

Getting Started on P5

London
School of Business
& Finance
shaping success in business and finance

Aim of the paper

To apply relevant knowledge, skills, and exercise professional judgement in selecting and applying strategic management accounting techniques in different business contexts and to contribute to the evaluation of an organisation and its strategic development.

Outline of the syllabus

A. Strategic planning and control
B. External influences on organisational performance
C. Performance measurement systems and design
D. Strategic performance measurement
E. Performance evaluation and corporate failure
F. Current developments and emerging issues in performance management

Format of the exam paper

The syllabus is assessed by a three hour paper-based examination.

The examination consists of:

- Section A – one compulsory question comprising 50 marks
- Section B – two out of three questions comprising 25 marks each

Efficient and effective studying with LSBF

1. Study in a good environment

There are so many potential distractions you need to avoid. Your studies require you to gain enough depth of knowledge. E-mail, mobile phones, social networking sites act as threats to you. For example, seeing that you have a new e-mail in your Inbox distracts you and it is hard not to respond to its existence, even if it is only spam e-mail. Get away from all of these and you'll have a far better retention of the knowledge you have gained. You'll stay alert if you sit at a desk so long as you don't have your PC/Mac on!

2. Get an overview of the subject early

Knowing the big picture of the subject you are about to study is a great way to study efficiently. This is hard for you to gain without knowledge of the subject, so use the knowledge of your provider of material for the exam, like the Overview given in this Study Manual.

3. Study when best for you in the day

Many people can double their reading speed and improve their concentration by studying early in the day. Also it has been shown that revision in the evening without major distractions afterwards (avoid late-night parties, for example!) allows your brain to work on the material once you are asleep and can significantly improve your memory.

4. Skim the chapter first for the main ideas

Read the Chapter Context and scan the structure of the main chapter sections. You'll improve your reading speed and comprehension if you understand the structure of the chapter first.

5. Form a question or questions

Boost your reading comprehension, reading speed, and concentration by formulating your own questions (write them down if it helps) and/or using the ones that we have provided. Read the chapter to obtain the answers. Your reading speed improves by doing this, and you become far more focused on your material so you will retain more. Use the following questions – **what, when, why, who, which, where, how** – and the main section titles in the chapter.

6. Take notes

Improve your overall study effectiveness by jotting brief notes immediately after reading each section of the chapter. Linking your points together, using a mind map for example, helps memory. Refer back to your notes later to test your understanding (and see point 7 below).

7. But avoid highlighting

Although some readers believe that highlighting in yellow (or any other colour, for that matter) improves their reading speed and comprehension, the reverse is actually

true. Highlighting simply means they don't bother learning the material right now. The result: they end up reading the material twice, and possibly not understanding or remembering it either time! Similarly, using material that has been highlighted by the publisher is ineffective for your learning.

8. Repetition, repetition, repetition

We learn by repeating. It can be shown that if you don't repeat knowledge almost immediately then you have no chance of remembering it. We also need to repeat that knowledge again within the next 90 to 120 minutes or we will forget it. So build in time to your studies to do this, it will be very effective for you. How do we learn?

9. What's the story?

At the end of each chapter, try to generate your own story for what you have just been reading. Use the Questions at the start of the Chapter and the Key Learning Points at the end of the Chapter to help here. Making your **own** story is a very powerful way of helping you remember. It can have a start a middle and an end, just like a normal story!

LSBF material – how we help you

- ✓ **Our authors are all experienced at producing targeted material for your exam. So you will gain from that wealth of knowledge, for example by understanding the Overview of the syllabus at the start of your studies and reviewing your knowledge in line with it as you progress.**
- ✓ **Our material is based on knowledge of how your brain works to help you study better.**
- ✓ **We pose you questions at the start of each chapter to assist your learning and boost your interest and retention. Look for the '3 Questions' that we have at the start of each chapter. These help you become engaged with the material and will mean you can answer the three questions better as well as the other material in the chapter. For example:**

3Q

1. Can you describe each of the key three decisions?
2. What aim in a company is 'a fundamental aim' and hence key to this paper?
3. What types of government policy can come into conflict?

- ✓ **You will be advised where you should stop and spend time learning/memorising key facts or knowledge. Look out for the 'Learn's to help your repetition of important knowledge.**

Learn

- ✓ **Similarly if you have to be familiar with the principles behind a few paragraphs (such as a calculation) then we will prompt you with 'Principle' plus guidance on what to go back for. Take time to stop yourself and check that you are happy with these, they are key for the exam. For example:**

Principle

Learn the steps above so you can apply them in the exam

- ✓ **You will find when a formula or other information is given in the exam. Look out for the 'Given's.**

Given

- ✓ **We want you to build up a 'story' based on the material to help you remember it better. When you see the 'What's the Story' at the end of each chapter, take time to link the chapter together and also link to any relevant previous chapters.**

What's the story?

Stop and think through the 'story' of this chapter and how it links with other chapters (use the Overview to help).

- ✓ **Importantly, we don't bloat our material with extra unneeded features (for example in the margins of the page, which are inefficient for students to learn from). All the reminders to learn are in the centre of the page.**
- ✓ **You will leave with 'Key learning points' to go away with that will help you build up that story.**
- ✓ **We are interested in your feedback – please complete the Feedback Form at the end of studying this paper and have the chance to win a prize!**

Overview

The ACCA P5 paper, Advanced Performance Management, helps you develop your knowledge of issues and techniques that are required to make a business operate well. This develops from papers that you have already seen, such as F5 and P3.

The syllabus states that the aim of the paper is 'apply relevant knowledge, skills and exercise professional judgement in selecting and applying strategic management accounting techniques in different business contexts and to contribute to the evaluation of the performance of an organisation and its strategic development'.

Let's see how this is reflected in this Study Manual and its chapters. There are chapters on the strategic planning and risk, performance management, measures and systems, organisational structure and current developments.

Strategic planning and risk
Strategic Planning and Control (Chapter 1) covers the bigger picture for an organisation, how they can be successful over time. This involves both your Paper P3 knowledge and also looking at the control aspects. Risk and Uncertainty as Part of Strategic Planning (Chapter 4) looks at what can change externally and internally for organisations and how that can be taken into account as much as possible.

Performance management, measures and systems
Firstly you will see Performance Management and Control (Chapter 2) to understand how an organisation can try to set up its performance systems so that it achieves its objectives. We then look at Financial Measures of Performance Evaluation (Chapter 5) so that we can understand the sources of financial information and how they can be used to assess how well the organisation is doing. Financial and management accounts are both useful here as well as other longer-term methods, such as project appraisal. Non-financial Measures of Performance Evaluation (Chapter 8) takes other measures of performance to assess an organisation. These measures can often be more useful than financial measures of performance as they are often show the underlying causes of the final financial effects we see. We then look at Performance Systems Issues (Chapter 9) which shows how things can go wrong within a performance system and what we might do to address these problems. We finish by looking at Corporate Failure (Chapter 10) which is an extreme case of a strategy or performance system not working well. Here you will see ways to measure and prevent this.

Organisational structure
We then look at how businesses can set themselves up. Organisational Structure and Business Integration (Chapter 3) looks at the possibilities for the structures of a business and then the way that a business can integrate its various parts. Divisionalisation (Chapter 6) explains methods of dealing with an organisation that has various parts, whether relating to different fundamental businesses or other aspects such as the overseas divisions. Transfer Pricing (Chapter 7) looks at how the divisions of organisations transact with one another and how they set transfer prices for these transactions. This affects the profits in both divisions as well as the other issues like the tax the organisation pays.

Current developments

Current Developments and Emerging Issues in Performance Management (Chapter 11) looks at new issues in performance management within an organisation as well as other issues such as accounting for the environment, public sector organisation and how the role of the management accountant is changing as organisations progress.

Take a look at the overview diagram for P5. You can see the diagram covers the strategic planning, performance management, financial and non-financial measures, performance systems, organisational structure and divisionalisation and current developments.

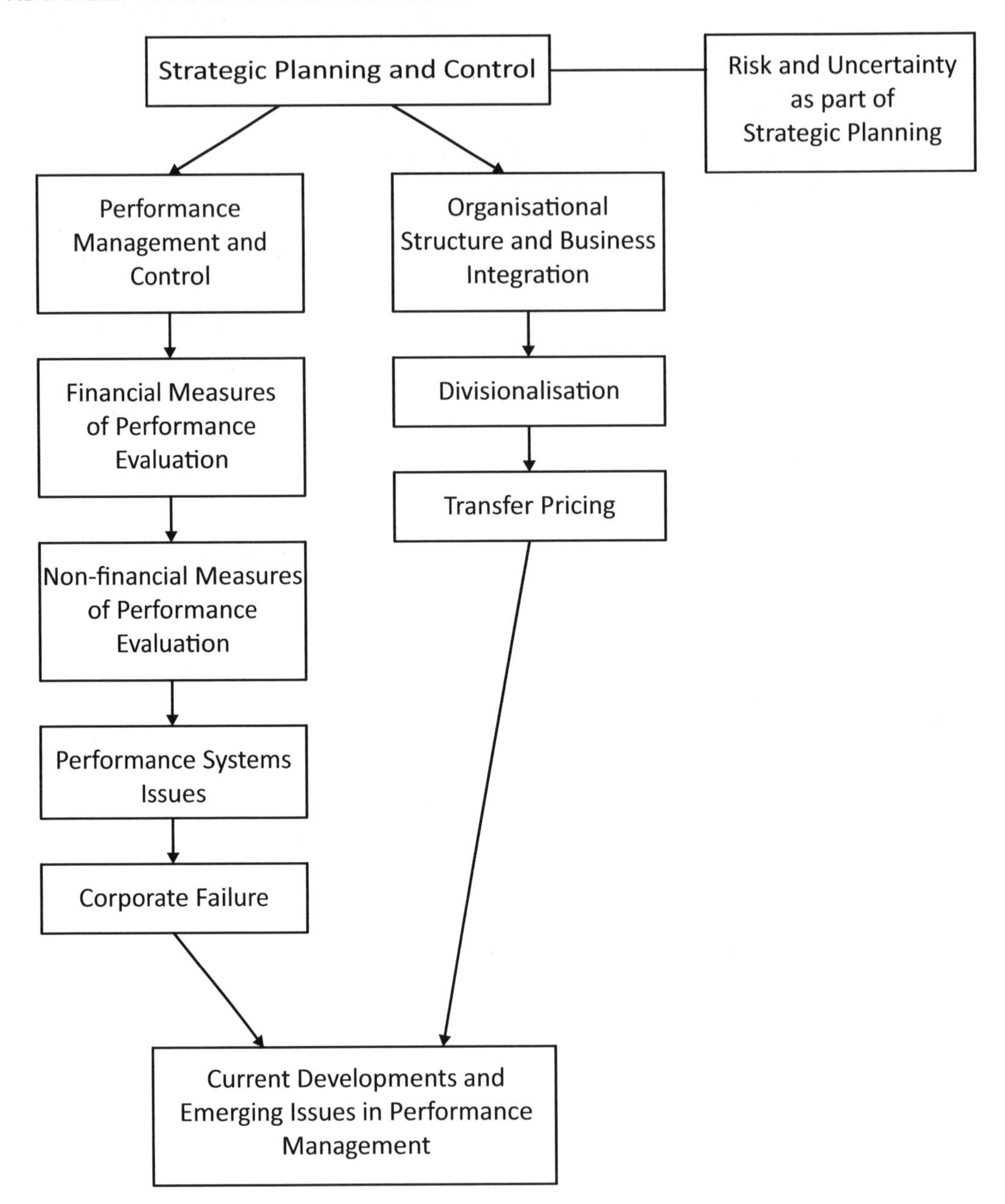

Learn this diagram so that you can see where the subjects you have learnt fits in. It will be useful to come back to during your studies so that you can see the 'big picture' for the paper.

Finally look around at your own organisation and others that you come into contact with to observe your studies in real life. You will see differing organisational structures and the way companies have become divisionalised as well as current developments in performance management as above. In this way you will help your learning and make the subject more interesting and useful.

Syllabus and Study Guide

ADVANCED PERFORMANCE MANAGEMENT (P5)

SEPTEMBER 2015 TO JUNE 2016

This syllabus and study guide is designed to help with planning study and to provide detailed information on what could be assessed in any examination session.

THE STRUCTURE OF THE SYLLABUS AND STUDY GUIDE

RELATIONAL DIAGRAM OF PAPER WITH OTHER PAPERS

This diagram shows direct and indirect links between this paper and other papers preceding or following it. Some papers are directly underpinned by other papers such as Advanced Performance Management by Performance Management. These links are shown as solid line arrows. Other papers only have indirect relationships with each other such as links existing between the accounting and auditing papers. The links between these are shown as dotted line arrows. This diagram indicates where you are expected to have underpinning knowledge and where it would be useful to review previous learning before undertaking study.

OVERALL AIM OF THE SYLLABUS

This explains briefly the overall objective of the paper and indicates in the broadest sense the capabilities to be developed within the paper.

MAIN CAPABILITIES

This paper's aim is broken down into several main capabilities which divide the syllabus and study guide into discrete sections.

RELATIONAL DIAGRAM OF THE MAIN CAPABILITIES

This diagram illustrates the flows and links between the main capabilities (sections) of the syllabus and should be used as an aid to planning teaching and learning in a structured way.

SYLLABUS RATIONALE

This is a narrative explaining how the syllabus is structured and how the main capabilities are linked. The rationale also explains in further detail what the examination intends to assess and why.

DETAILED SYLLABUS

This shows the breakdown of the main capabilities (sections) of the syllabus into subject areas. This is the blueprint for the detailed study guide.

APPROACH TO EXAMINING THE SYLLABUS

This section briefly explains the structure of the examination and how it is assessed.

STUDY GUIDE

This is the main document that students, learning and content providers should use as the basis of their studies, instruction and materials. Examinations will be based on the detail of the study guide which comprehensively identifies what could be assessed in any examination session. The study guide is a precise reflection and

breakdown of the syllabus. It is divided into sections based on the main capabilities identified in the syllabus. These sections are divided into subject areas which relate to the sub-capabilities included in the detailed syllabus. Subject areas are broken down into sub-headings which describe the detailed outcomes that could be assessed in examinations. These outcomes are described using verbs indicating what exams may require students to demonstrate, and the broad intellectual level at which these may need to be demonstrated (*see intellectual levels below).

LEARNING MATERIALS

ACCA's Approved Content Programme is the programme through which ACCA approves learning materials from high quality content providers designed to support study towards ACCA's qualifications.

ACCA has three Approved Content Providers, Becker Professional Education,

BPP Learning Media and Kaplan Publishing.

For information about ACCA's Approved Content Providers please go to ACCA's Content Provider Directory.

The Directory also lists materials by other publishers, these materials have not been quality assured by ACCA but may be helpful if used in conjunction with approved learning materials or for variant exams where no approved content is available. You will also find details of Additional Reading suggested by the examining teams and this may be a useful supplement to approved learning materials.

ACCA's Content Provider Directory can be found here –

http://www.accaglobal.com/uk/en/student/acca-qual-student-journey/study-revision/learning-providers/alp-content.html

Relevant articles are also published in Student Accountant and available on the ACCA website.

INTELLECTUAL LEVELS

The syllabus is designed to progressively broaden and deepen the knowledge, skills and professional values demonstrated by the student on their way through the qualification.

The specific capabilities within the detailed syllabuses and study guides are assessed at one of three intellectual or cognitive levels:

Level 1: Knowledge and comprehension

Level 2: Application and analysis

Level 3: Synthesis and evaluation

Very broadly, these intellectual levels relate to the three cognitive levels at which the Knowledge module, the Skills module and the Professional level are assessed.

Each subject area in the detailed study guide included in this document is given a 1, 2, or 3 superscript, denoting intellectual level, marked at the end of each relevant line. This gives an indication of the intellectual depth at which an area could be assessed within the examination. However, while level 1 broadly equates with the Knowledge module, level 2 equates to the Skills module and level 3 to the Professional level, some lower level skills can continue to be assessed as the student progresses through each module and level. This reflects that at each stage of study there will be a requirement to broaden, as well as deepen capabilities. It is also possible that occasionally some higher level capabilities may be assessed at lower levels.

LEARNING HOURS AND EDUCATION RECOGNITION

The ACCA qualification does not prescribe or recommend any particular number of learning hours for examinations because study and learning patterns and styles vary greatly between people and organisations. This also recognises the wide diversity of personal, professional and educational circumstances in which ACCA students find themselves.

As a member of the International Federation of Accountants, ACCA seeks to enhance the education recognition of its qualification on both national and international education frameworks, and with educational authorities and partners globally. In doing so, ACCA aims to ensure that its qualifications are recognized and valued by governments, regulatory authorities and employers across all sectors. To this end, ACCA qualifications are currently recognized on the education frameworks in several countries. Please refer to your national education framework regulator for further information.

Each syllabus contains between 23 and 35 main subject area headings depending on the nature of the subject and how these areas have been broken down.

GUIDE TO EXAM STRUCTURE

The structure of examinations varies within and between modules and levels.

The Fundamentals level examinations contain 100% compulsory questions to encourage candidates to study across the breadth of each syllabus.

The Knowledge module is assessed by equivalent two-hour paper based and computer based examinations.

The Skills module examinations F5-F9 are all paper based three-hour papers containing a mix of objective and longer type questions. The *Corporate and Business Law* (F4) paper is a two- hour computer based objective test examination which is also available as a paper based version from the December 2014 examination session.

The Professional level papers are all three-hour paper based examinations, all containing two sections. Section A is compulsory, but there will be some choice offered in Section B.

For all three hour examination papers, ACCA has introduced 15 minutes reading and planning time.

This additional time is allowed at the beginning of each three-hour examination to allow candidates to read the questions and to begin planning their answers before they start writing in their answer books. This time should be used to ensure that all the information and exam requirements are properly read and understood.

During reading and planning time candidates may only annotate their question paper. They may not write anything in their answer booklets until told to do so by the invigilator.

The Essentials module papers all have a Section A containing a major case study question with all requirements totalling 50 marks relating to this case. Section B gives students a choice of two from three 25 mark questions.

Section A of both the P4 and P5 Options papers contain one 50 mark compulsory question, and Section B will offer a choice of two from three questions each worth 25 marks each.

Section A of each of the P6 and P7 Options papers contains 60 compulsory marks from two questions; question 1 attracting 35 marks, and question 2 attracting 25 marks. Section B of both these Options papers will offer a choice of two from three questions, with each question attracting 20 marks.

All Professional level exams contain four professional marks.

The pass mark for all ACCA Qualification examination papers is 50%.

GUIDE TO EXAMINATION ASSESSMENT

ACCA reserves the right to examine anything contained within the study guide at any examination session. This includes knowledge, techniques, principles, theories, and concepts as specified.

For the financial accounting, audit and assurance, law and tax papers except where indicated otherwise, ACCA will publish *examinable documents* once a year to indicate exactly what regulations and legislation could potentially be assessed within identified examination sessions..

For paper based examinations regulation ***issued*** or legislation ***passed*** on or before 31st August annually, will be examinable from 1st September of the following year to 31st August t of the year after that. Please refer to the examinable documents for the paper (where relevant) for further information.

Regulation issued or legislation passed in accordance with the above dates may be examinable even if the ***effective*** date is in the future.

The term issued or passed relates to when regulation or legislation has been formally approved.

The term effective relates to when regulation or legislation must be applied to an entity transactions and business practices.

The study guide offers more detailed guidance on the depth and level at which the examinable documents will be examined. The study guide should therefore be read in conjunction with the examinable documents list.

SYLLABUS

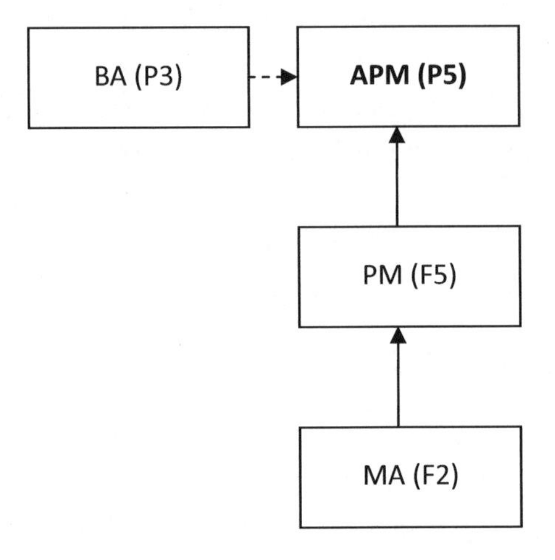

AIM

To apply relevant knowledge, skills and exercise professional judgement in selecting and applying strategic management accounting techniques in different business contexts and to contribute to the evaluation of the performance of an organisation and its strategic development.

MAIN CAPABILITIES

On successful completion of this paper, candidates should be able to:

A. Use strategic planning and control models to plan and monitor organisational performance

B. Assess and identify relevant macro economic, fiscal and market factors and key external influences on organisational performance

C. Identify and evaluate the design features of effective performance management information and monitoring systems

D. Apply appropriate strategic performance measurement techniques in evaluating and improving organisational performance

E. Advise clients and senior management on strategic business performance evaluation and on recognising vulnerability to corporate failure

F. Identify and assess the impact of current developments in management accounting and performance management on measuring, evaluating and improving organisational performance

RELATIONAL DIAGRAM OF MAIN CAPABILITIES

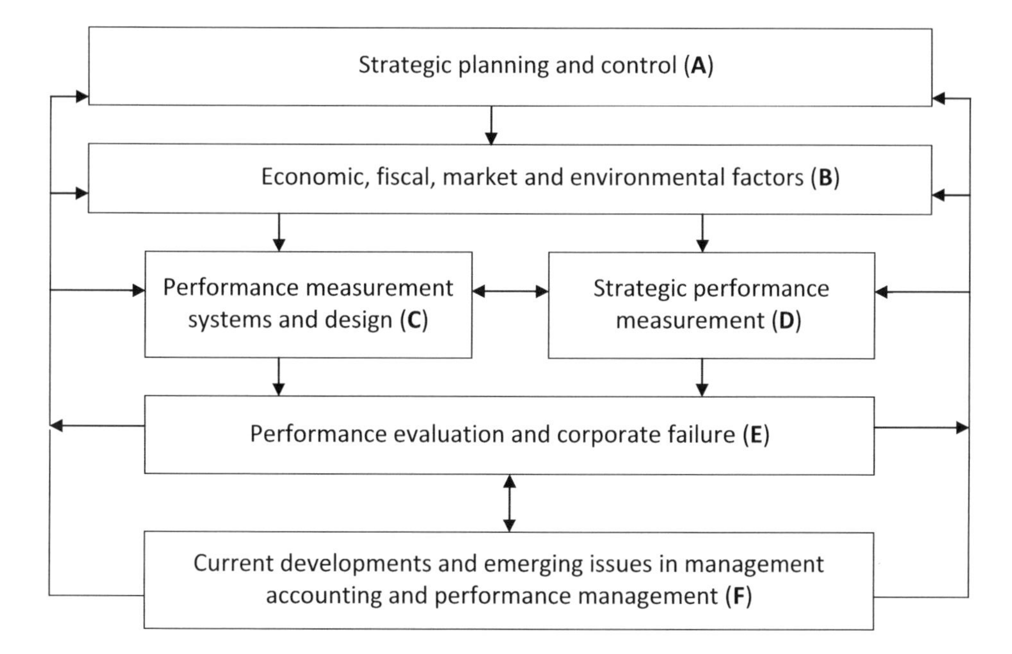

RATIONALE

The Advanced Performance Management syllabus further develops key aspects introduced in Paper F5, *Performance Management*, at the skills level and draws on aspects of the material covered from a more strategic and operational planning perspective in Paper P3, *Business Analysis*.

The syllabus introduces candidates to the strategic role of management accounting as a discipline for planning and controlling performance so that strategic objectives can be set, monitored and controlled. It also covers the impact of external factors on strategic management issues, such as macro economic, fiscal, market and environmental impacts on performance. From appreciating the strategic context of performance management and the impact of wider factors, the syllabus examines, at an operational level, the issues relating to performance measurement systems and their design.

The syllabus then moves from performance management systems and their design to the scope and application of high-level performance measurement techniques in a variety of contexts, including not-for-profit organisations and multi-national businesses. Having covered the strategic aspects of performance management and operational systems for the measurement and control of performance in a variety of contexts, candidates are then expected to synthesise this knowledge in the role of an advisor to senior management or independent clients on how to assess and control the performance of an entity, including the recognition of whether a business is facing difficulties or possibly failure.

Finally, the syllabus deals with current developments in performance management and with emerging issues as they might affect or influence the management of performance within organisations.

DETAILED SYLLABUS

A. Strategic planning and control

1. Introduction to strategic management accounting
2. Performance management and control of the organisation
3. Changes in business structure and management accounting
4. Effect of Information Technology (IT) on strategic management accounting
5. Other environmental and ethical issues

B. External influences on organisational performance

1. Changing business environment
2. Impact of external factors on strategy and performance

C. Performance measurement systems and design

1. Performance management information systems
2. Sources of management information
3. Recording and processing methods
4. Management reports

D. Strategic performance measurement

1. Performance hierarchy
2. Strategic performance measures in private sector
3. Divisional performance and transfer pricing issues
4. Strategic performance measures in not-for-profit organisations
5. Non- financial performance indictors
6. The role of quality in management information and performance measurement systems
7. Performance measurement and strategic human resource management issues
8. Performance measurement and the reward systems
9. Other behavioural aspects of performance measurement

E. Performance evaluation and corporate failure

1. Alternative views of performance measurement and management
2. Strategic performance issues in complex business structures
3. Predicting and preventing corporate failure

F. Current developments and emerging issues performance management

1. Current developments in management accounting techniques
2. Current issues and trends in performance management

APPROACH TO EXAMINING THE SYLLABUS

Paper P5 builds on paper F5, *Performance Management*, and candidates are expected to have a thorough understanding of the paper F5 syllabus. In addition, candidates

will also be required to apply the principles and techniques covered in paper F2, *Management Accounting.*

Paper P5 has a link with Paper P3, *Business Analysis*, in the areas of strategic planning and control and performance measurement

EXAMINATION STRUCTURE

The examination will be a three hour paper in two sections:

Section A

Section A will contain one compulsory question comprising of 50 marks

Section B

In section B candidates will be asked to answer two from three questions comprising of 25 marks each

Total 100 marks

STUDY GUIDE

A. STRATEGIC PLANNING AND CONTROL

1. Introduction to strategic management accounting

(a) Explain the role of strategic performance management in strategic planning and control.[2]

(b) Discuss the role of corporate planning in clarifying corporate objectives, making strategic decisions and checking progress towards the objectives.[2]

(c) Compare planning and control between the strategic and operational levels within a business entity.[2]

(d) Assess the use of strategic management accounting in the context of multinational companies.[3]

(e) Discuss the scope for potential conflict between strategic business plans and short-term localised decisions.[2]

(f) Evaluate how SWOT analysis may assist in the performance management process.[2]

(g) Apply and evaluate the methods of benchmarking performance.[3]

2. Performance management and control of the organisation

(a) Evaluate the strengths and weaknesses of alternative budgeting models and compare such techniques as fixed and flexible, rolling, activity based, zero based and incremental.[3]

(b) Assess how budgeting may differ in not-for-profit organisations from profit-seeking organisations.[3]

(c) Evaluate the impact to an organisation of a move beyond budgeting[3]

3. Changes in business structure and management accounting
(a) Identify and discuss the particular information needs of organisations adopting a functional, divisional or network form and the implications for performance management.[2]
(b) Assess the influence of Business Process Re-engineering on systems development and improvements in organisational performance.[3]
(c) Discuss the concept of business integration and the linkage between people, operations, strategy and technology.[2]
(d) Analyse the role that performance management systems play in business integration using models such as the value chain and McKinsey's 7S's[3]
(e) Identify and discuss the required changes in management accounting systems as a consequence of empowering staff to manage sectors of a business.[3]

4. Effect of Information Technology (IT) on strategic management accounting
(a) Assess the changing accounting needs of modern service orientated businesses compared with the needs of traditional manufacturing industry.[3]
(b) Discuss how IT systems provide the opportunity for instant access to management accounting data throughout the organisation and their potential impact on business performance.[2]
(c) Assess how IT systems facilitate the remote input of management accounting data in an acceptable format by non-finance specialists.[2]
(d) Explain how information systems provide instant access to previously unavailable data that can be used for benchmarking and control purposes and help improve business performance (for example, through the use of enterprise resource planning systems and data warehouses).[2]
(e) Assess the need for businesses to continually refine and develop their management accounting and information systems if they are to maintain or improve their performance in an increasingly competitive and global market.[3]

5. Other environmental and ethical issues
(a) Discuss the ways in which stakeholder groups operate and how they affect an organisation and its strategy formulation and implementation (e.g. using Mendelow's matrix).[2]
(b) Discuss the ethical issues that may impact on strategy formulation and business performance.[3]
(c) Discuss the ways in which stakeholder groups may influence business performance.[2]

B. EXTERNAL INFLUENCES ON ORGANISATIONAL PERFORMANCE

1. Changing business environment

(a) Assess the continuing effectiveness of traditional management accounting techniques within a rapidly changing business environment.[3]

(b) Assess the impact of the different risk appetites of stakeholders on performance management[3]

(c) Evaluate how risk and uncertainty play an important role in long term strategic planning and decision-making that relies upon forecasts of exogenous variables. [3]

(d) Apply different risk analysis techniques in assessing business performance such as maximin, maximax, minimax regret and expected values.[3]

2. Impact of external factors on strategy and performance

(a) Discuss the need to consider the environment in which an organisation is operating when assessing its performance using models such as PEST and Porter's 5 forces, including areas:[2]
   (i) Political climate
   (ii) Market conditions
   (iii) Funding

(b) Assess the impact of governmental regulations and policies on performance measurement techniques used and the performance levels achieved (for example, in the case of utility services and former state monopolies).[3]

C. PERFORMANCE MEASUREMENT SYSTEMS AND DESIGN

1. Performance management information systems

(a) Discuss, with reference to performance management, ways in which the information requirements of a management structure are affected by the features of the structure.[2]

(b) Evaluate the compatibility of management accounting objectives and the management accounting information systems.[3]

(c) Discuss the integration of management accounting information within an overall information system, for example the use of enterprise resource planning systems.[2]

(d) Evaluate whether the management information systems are lean and value of the information that they provide.[3]

(e) Highlight the ways in which contingent (internal and external) factors influence management accounting and its design and use.[3]

(f) Evaluate how anticipated human behaviour will influence the design of a management accounting system.[3]

(g) Assess the impact of responsibility accounting on information requirements.[3]

2. Sources of management information

(a) Discuss the principal internal and external sources of management accounting information, their costs and limitations.[2]

(b) Demonstrate how the information might be used in planning and controlling activities e.g. benchmarking against similar activities.[2]

(c) Discuss those factors that need to be considered when determining the capacity and development potential of a system.[2]

3. Recording and processing methods
(a) Demonstrate how the type of business entity will influence the recording and processing methods.[2]
(b) Discuss how IT developments e.g. unified corporate databases, RFIDs and network technology may influence management accounting systems.[2]
(c) Discuss the difficulties associated with recording and processing data of a qualitative nature.[2]

4. Management reports
(a) Evaluate the output reports of an information system in the light of[3]
    (i) best practice in presentation;
    (ii) the objectives of the report/organisation;
    (iii) the needs of the readers of the report; and
    (iv) avoiding the problem of information overload

D. STRATEGIC PERFORMANCE MEASUREMENT

1. Performance hierarchy
(a) Discuss how the purpose, structure and content of a mission statement impacts on business performance.[2]
(b) Discuss the ways in which high-level corporate performance objectives are developed.[2]
(c) Identify strategic objectives and discuss how they may be incorporated into the business plan.[2]
(d) Discuss how strategic objectives are cascaded down the organisation via the formulation of subsidiary performance objectives.[2]
(e) Discuss social and ethical obligations that should be considered in the pursuit of corporate performance objectives.[2]
(f) Explain the performance 'planning gap' and evaluate alternative strategies to fill that gap.[3]
(g) Apply critical success factor analysis in developing performance metrics from business objectives.[3]
(h) Identify and discuss the characteristics of operational performance.[2]
(i) Discuss the relative significance of planning as against controlling activities at different levels in the performance hierarchy.[3]

2. Strategic performance measures in private sector
(a) Demonstrate why the primary objective of financial performance should be primarily concerned with the benefits to shareholders.[2]
(b) Justify the crucial objectives of survival and business growth.
(c) Discuss the appropriateness of, and apply different measures of performance, including:[3]
    (i) Return on Capital Employed (ROCE)
    (ii) Return on Investment (ROI)
    (iii) Earnings Per Share (EPS)
    (iv) Earnings Before Interest, Tax, Depreciation and Amortisation (EBITDA)
    (v) Residual Income (RI)
    (vi) Net Present value (NPV)
    (vii) Internal rate of return and modified internal Rate of Return (IRR, MIRR)
    (viii) Economic Value Added (EVA ™)
(d) Discuss why indicators of liquidity and gearing need to considered in conjunction with profitability.[3]
(e) Compare and contrast short and long run financial performance and the resulting management issues.[3]
(f) Explore the traditional relationship between profits and share value with the long-term profit expectations of the stock market and recent financial performance of new technology companies.[3]
(g) Assess the relative financial performance of the organisation compared to appropriate benchmarks.[3]

3. Divisional performance and transfer pricing issues
(a) Describe, compute and evaluate performance measures relevant in a divisionalised organisation structure including ROI, RI and Economic value added (EVA).[3]
(b) Discuss the need for separate measures in respect of managerial and divisional performance.[2]
(c) Discuss the circumstances in which a transfer pricing policy may be needed and discuss the necessary criteria for its design.[2]
(d) Demonstrate and evaluate the use of alternative bases for transfer pricing.[3]
(e) Explain and demonstrate issues that require consideration when setting transfer prices in multinational companies.[2]

4. Strategic performance measures in not-for-profit organisations
(a) Highlight and discuss the potential for diversity in objectives depending on organisation type.[3]
(b) Discuss the need to achieve objectives with limited funds that may not be controllable.[2]
(c) Identify and discuss ways in which performance may be judged in not-for profit organisations.[2]
(d) Discuss the difficulties in measuring outputs when performance is not judged in terms of money or an easily quantifiable objective.[2]
(e) Discuss how the combination of politics and the desire to measure public sector performance may result in undesirable service outcomes.[3]
(f) Assess 'value for money' service provision as a measure of performance in not-for-profit organisations and the public sector.[3]

5. Non-financial performance indicators
(a) Discuss the interaction of non-financial performance indicators with financial performance indicators.[2]
(b) Discuss the implications of the growing emphasis on non-financial performance indicators.[3]
(c) Discuss the significance of non-financial performance indicators in relation to employees.[2]
(d) Identify and discuss the significance of non-financial performance indicators in relation to product/service quality e.g. customer satisfaction reports, repeat business ratings, customer loyalty, access and availability.[3]
(e) Discuss the difficulties in interpreting data on qualitative issues.[2]
(f) Discuss the significance of brand awareness and company profile and their potential impact on business performance.[3]

6. The role of quality in management information and performance measurement systems
(a) Discuss and evaluate the application of Japanese business practices and management accounting techniques, including:[3]
  (i) Kaizen costing,
  (ii) Target costing,
  (iii) Just-in-time, and
  (iv) Total Quality Management.
(b) Discriminate between quality, quality assurance, quality control and quality management.[2]
(c) Assess the relationship of quality management to the performance management strategy of an organisation.[3]
(d) Advise on the structure and benefits of quality management systems and quality certification.[3]
(e) Justify the need and assess the characteristics of quality in management information systems[3]
(f) Discuss and apply Six Sigma as a quality improvement method using tools such as DMAIC for implementation.[2]

7. Performance measurement and strategic Human Resource Management issues
(a) Explain how the effective recruitment, management and motivation of people are necessary for enabling strategic and operational success.[3]
(b) Discuss the judgemental and developmental roles of assessment and appraisal and their role in improving business performance.[3]
(c) Advise on the relationship of performance management to performance measurement (performance rating) and determine the implications of performance measurement to quality initiatives and process redesign.[3]

8. Performance measurement and the reward systems
(a) Explore the meaning and scope of reward systems.[2]
(b) Discuss and evaluate different methods of reward practices.[2]
(c) Explore the principles and difficulty of aligning reward practices with strategy.[2]
(d) Advise on the relationship of reward management to quality initiatives, process re-design and harnessing of e-business opportunities.[3]
(e) Assess the potential beneficial and adverse consequences of linking reward schemes to performance measurement, for example, how it can affect the risk appetite of employees.[3]

9. Other behaviour aspects of performance measurement
(a) Discuss the accountability issues that might arise from performance measurement systems.[3]
(b) Evaluate the ways in which performance measurements systems may send the wrong signals and result in undesirable business consequences.[3]
(c) Demonstrate how management style needs to be considered when designing an effective performance measurement system.[3]

E. PERFORMANCE EVALUATION AND CORPORATE FAILURE

1. Alternative views of performance measurement and management
(a) Apply and evaluate the 'balanced scorecard' approach as a way in which to improve the range and linkage between performance measures.[3]
(b) Apply and evaluate the 'performance pyramid' as a way in which to link strategy, operations and performance.[3]
(c) Apply and evaluate the work of Fitzgerald and Moon that considers performance measurement in business services using building blocks for dimensions, standards and rewards.[3]
(d) Discuss and apply the Performance Prism.[2]
(e) Discuss and evaluate the application of activity-based management.[3]
(f) Evaluate and apply the value-based management approaches to performance management.[3]

2. Strategic performance issues in complex business structures
(a) Evaluate the use and the application of strategic models in assessing the business performance of an entity, such as , Boston Consulting Group and Porter.[3]
(b) Discuss the problems encountered in planning, controlling and measuring performance levels, e.g. productivity, profitability, quality and service levels, in complex business structures.[3]
(c) Discuss the impact on performance management of the use of business models involving strategic alliances, joint ventures and complex supply chain structures. [3]

3. Predicting and preventing corporate failure
(a) Assess the potential likelihood of corporate failure, utilising quantitative and qualitative performance measures and models (such as Z-scores and Argenti).[3]
(b) Assess and critique quantitative and qualitative corporate failure prediction models.[3]
(c) Identify and discuss performance improvement strategies that may be adopted in order to prevent corporate failure.[3]
(d) Discuss how long-term survival necessitates consideration of life-cycle issues.[3]
(e) Identify and discuss operational changes to performance management systems required to implement the performance improvement strategies.[3]

F. CURRENT DEVELOPMENTS AND EMERGING ISSUES IN PERFORMANCE MANAGEMENT

1. Current developments in management accounting techniques
(a) Discuss the ways through which management accounting practitioners are made aware of new techniques and how they evaluate them.[3]
(b) Discuss, evaluate and apply environmental management accounting using for example lifecycle costing, input/output analysis and activity-based costing.[3]
(c) Discuss the use of benchmarking in public sector performance (league tables) and its effects on operational and strategic management and client behaviour.[3]
(d) Discuss the issues surrounding the use of targets in public sector organisations.[3]

2. Current issues and trends in performance management
(a) Assess the changing role of the management accountant in today's business environment as outlined by Burns and Scapens.[3]
(b) Discuss contemporary issues in performance management.[2]
(c) Discuss how changing organisation's structure, culture and strategy will influence the adoption of new performance measurement methods and techniques.[3]
(d) Explore the role of the management accountant in providing key performance information for integrated reporting to stakeholders.[2]

SUMMARY OF CHANGES TO P5

ACCA periodically reviews its qualification syllabuses so that they fully meet the needs of stakeholders such as employers, students, regulatory and advisory bodies and learning providers.

There are changes to the syllabus to reflect the latest business and educational developments affecting this paper. These are summarised in the table below.

Section and subject area	Syllabus content
A1 Strategic planning and control	A1g amended to; Apply and evaluate the methods of benchmarking performance
C1 Performance management information systems	C1b amended to; Evaluate the compatibility of management accounting objectives and the management accounting information systems
E1 Alternative views of performance measurement and management	E1a amended to; Apply and evaluate the 'balanced scorecard' approach as a way in which to improve the range and linkage between performance measures E1b amended to; Apply and evaluate the 'performance pyramid' as a way in which to link strategy, operations and performance E1c amended to; Apply and evaluate the work of Fitzgerald and Moon that considers performance measurement in business services using building blocks for dimensions, standards and rewards
E2 Strategic performance issues in complex business structures	E2a; Ansoff has been deleted

London
School of Business
& Finance
shaping success in business and finance

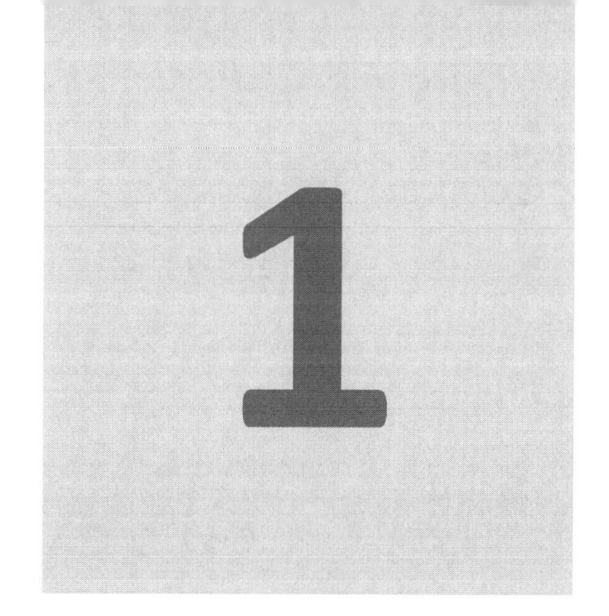

1

Strategic Planning and Control

Context

We look at strategic planning firstly to start to understand its use for performance management. In order to do this we need to make sure that we are up to speed with strategic planning and then see how we can start to apply what we know to the control of an organisation.

Issues like the environment and the stakeholders involved are very important here.

3Q

1. Can you give examples of SMART objectives?
2. What is SWOT analysis and what is its purpose?
3. Why is it difficult to forecast the long-term impact of exogenous variables?

1.1 What is strategy?

Definition

Strategy can be defined as the direction and scope of an organisation over the long term, which achieves advantage for the organisation in a changing environment through its configuration of resources and competences with the aim of meeting the needs of the markets and fulfilling stakeholder expectations.

Key phrases in relation to strategy include:

'Long-term direction...'

'A course of action aimed at allowing an organisation to achieve its objectives and satisfy its mission...'

'A means to achieve a sustainable competitive advantage'

'The core of a company's strategy concerns its markets and its products and is about choosing:

1. where to compete – which business segments
2. how to compete – on what basis to compete

1.2 Types of strategy

Corporate strategy
This looks at the industries in which the organisation operates. This may mean deciding to leave existing areas or enter new ones. This is particularly true if the organisation has a number of divisions.

In the P5 exam, you as the management accountant might be asked to prepare information to assist in a decision such as whether to leave or to join an industry.

Business strategy
This looks at how the organisation (or subsidiary/division) competes. This tends to be mean either:

- The division is trying to win customers by being better than rivals in some way; or
- The subsidiary is trying to win customers by being cheaper than rivals.

Operational strategy
This looks at how resources are used to carry out the strategies noted above.

Principle

Differences among the strategy levels

1.3 The principal internal and external sources of information

In order to plan, we need to look at where the information will come from to make decisions, the costs of getting the information and any limitations. One major source will be the management accounting system of the organisation, which should provide information, including the trends of the information, on internal issues such as:

- Materials costs incurred in each part of the business
- Revenues and prices
- Staff hours and costs incurred, performance of each member of staff
- Overheads
- Ideally, customer data, such as purchasing patterns and satisfaction ratings

Much of this data will be relatively cheap to obtain if the system is set up to gather it. The limitations will be where data isn't collected, despite, in hindsight, being important. For example, if customer feedback isn't obtained then problems in the business may not be found, or opportunities missed. Similarly if information is mis-recorded this limits its use.

External data is important but usually more expensive to obtain. Market information, such as market size and growth data is very difficult to obtain by most businesses directly and immediately, so it may be necessary to use a market research company to help, though at a cost. This data, if a standard report, may be out of date and may not focus on the detail the business wants.

So it is worth noting that most businesses, when they are making their strategic plans, are using information that could be improved. Finally, it is worth considering that a lot of data is backward-looking, rather than forward-looking. Most strategic decisions involve looking forward to decide what strategy will work in the future.

Levels of strategic decision-making

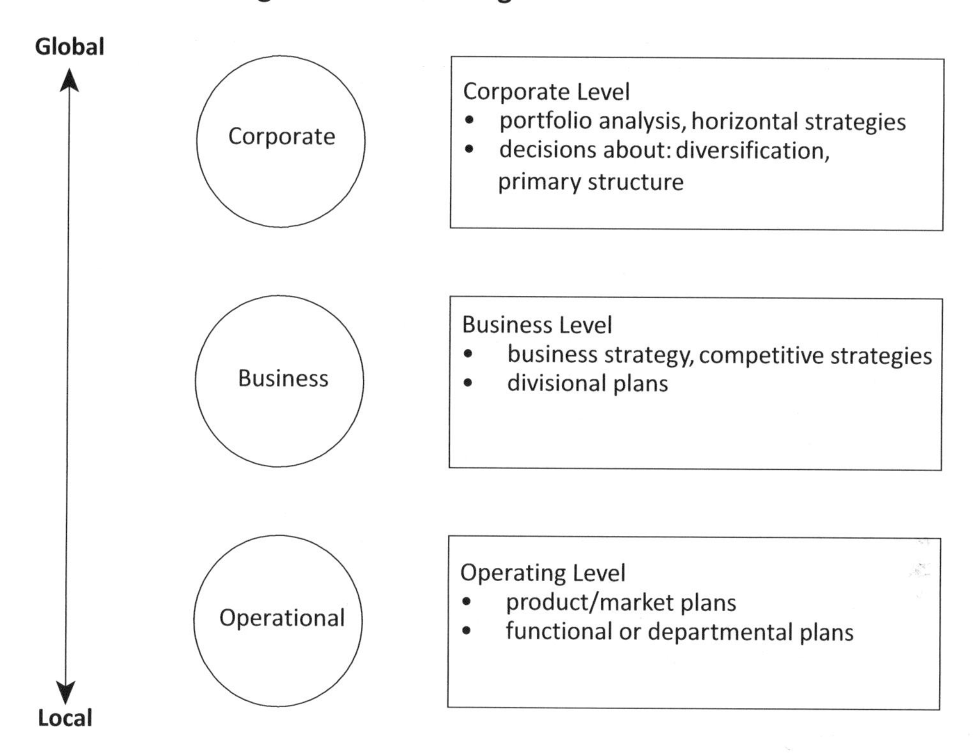

1.4 Corporate planning

Corporate planning refers to the formal process which facilitates the three-stage framework above.

Corporate planning supports senior management in making decisions to ensure corporate objectives are met. Its main roles are to:

- Manage the business planning process through which the objectives of individual departments and support services are agreed
- Compile and publish the annual plan for the organisation
- Monitor performance against the targets set in the business planning process
- Monitor performance compared with other similar organisations
- Undertake specific strategic projects.

Corporate objectives

A strategy analysis will generate a range of objectives:

- Maximisation of shareholder wealth (usually via maximising profit)
- Maximisation of sales (whilst earning an acceptable level of profit)
- Growth (in sales, asset value, number of employees)
- Survival
- Research and development

- Quality of products and service
- Employee motivation and welfare
- Environmental concerns

Two of the most important objectives are survival and growth.

Survival
A business is like a living thing in that it employs people, has premises that it is based and interacts with other businesses and its customers. Hence the employees of the business will be keen to continue with the business as long as possible. Some businesses have upturns and then downturns and through those downturns the business is likely still to have hope that it can improve and progress. So survival is an aim of most businesses.

Growth
Growth is a means for a business to be survive – if a business is static or declining the chances are that it won't survive long. However it is also a means for the business to be successful. Fast rates of growth are attractive as they mean increasing revenues, potentially increasing profits, more employment and overall success. So growth is a main objective of all businesses and, for quoted companies (ie quoted on a stock market), is the focus each time they report to the stock market.

Each objective will create competition for scarce resources within the organisation, giving rise to conflicts which need to be resolved, eg profit versus environmental concerns or profitability against liquidity.

IE Illustrative example 1.1

Profit is important for a business to be successful. However most ventures require some cash to be spent upfront before any cash is returned. Hence indicators of liquidity and gearing need to be considered in conjunction with profitability. Looking at two businesses, a construction company and a training company, let's consider the likely cash flows and problems:

Construction company – is likely to have large cash flows before it generates any returns, either from the sale of a building or from rents from that building. There are lots of costs upfront and the company will probably have to gear up, by borrowing from banks in order to survive though this period. Often building costs overrun, so a buffer has to be built in and cash flow managed over time.

Training company – may well receive course fees in advance of a course and incur costs, like the salaries of lecturers, though the course. So there are less cash flow issues, though the period of time recruiting students is important as, if there aren't enough students on the course and hence fees collected, it will be difficult to sustain the costs relating to the courses later.

To facilitate implementation and control and to reduce potential conflict, objectives need to be translated into SMART (specific, measurable, achievable, relevant and time bound) targets.

Examples of SMART objectives include:

- Achieve a growth in EPS of 3% pa over the coming five-year period.
- Obtain a turnover of £50 million within three years.
- Develop at least two new markets within five years.

The achievement of these objectives has to be compared against stated objectives to assess the organisation's performance. This is an essential activity as it highlights any weakness in the organisation's corporate plan or its execution. Action can then be taken to remedy any shortfalls in performance.

Objectives must be continually reviewed, because as the environment changes so plans and objectives will need revision.

Corporate planning is an ongoing process which must react quickly to the changing circumstances of the organisation.

For the organisation operating in a single competitive environment, the corporate plan will focus on business-level strategy, that is, how best to compete based on the threats and opportunities of its industry environment. Such an organisation may be a single business enterprise or a strategic business unit (SBU) within a larger group. Each SBU or single business will direct functional area strategy, the plan as to how each function (eg R&D, production, marketing/distribution, finance, human resources, management information systems) will contribute to support the overall business-level strategy.

The relationship between strategic objectives and business activity

Strategic objectives are cascaded down the organisation via the formulation of subsidiary performance objectives. The objectives developed by individual business units or areas should be:

- vertically consistent ie all parts of the business should be operating in a goal congruent way – the behaviour of individual business units and staff should be consistent with the objectives of the organisation as a whole
- horizontally consistent ie different parts of the business should support each other rather than act in a way which advances one part of the business at the expense of another

Secondary objectives may relate to individual products, departments, individuals or business units.

A hierarchy of objectives can be summarised as follows:

1. Mission
2. Objectives
3. Strategy
4. Tactical plans
5. Operational plans

Objectives are informed by the Critical Success Factors (CSFs) identified by the organisation and will give rise to Key Performance Indicators (KPIs) used to measure organisational performance.

Critical success factors (CSFs) are those areas in which an organisation needs to perform best if it is to achieve overall success.

Corporate planning process

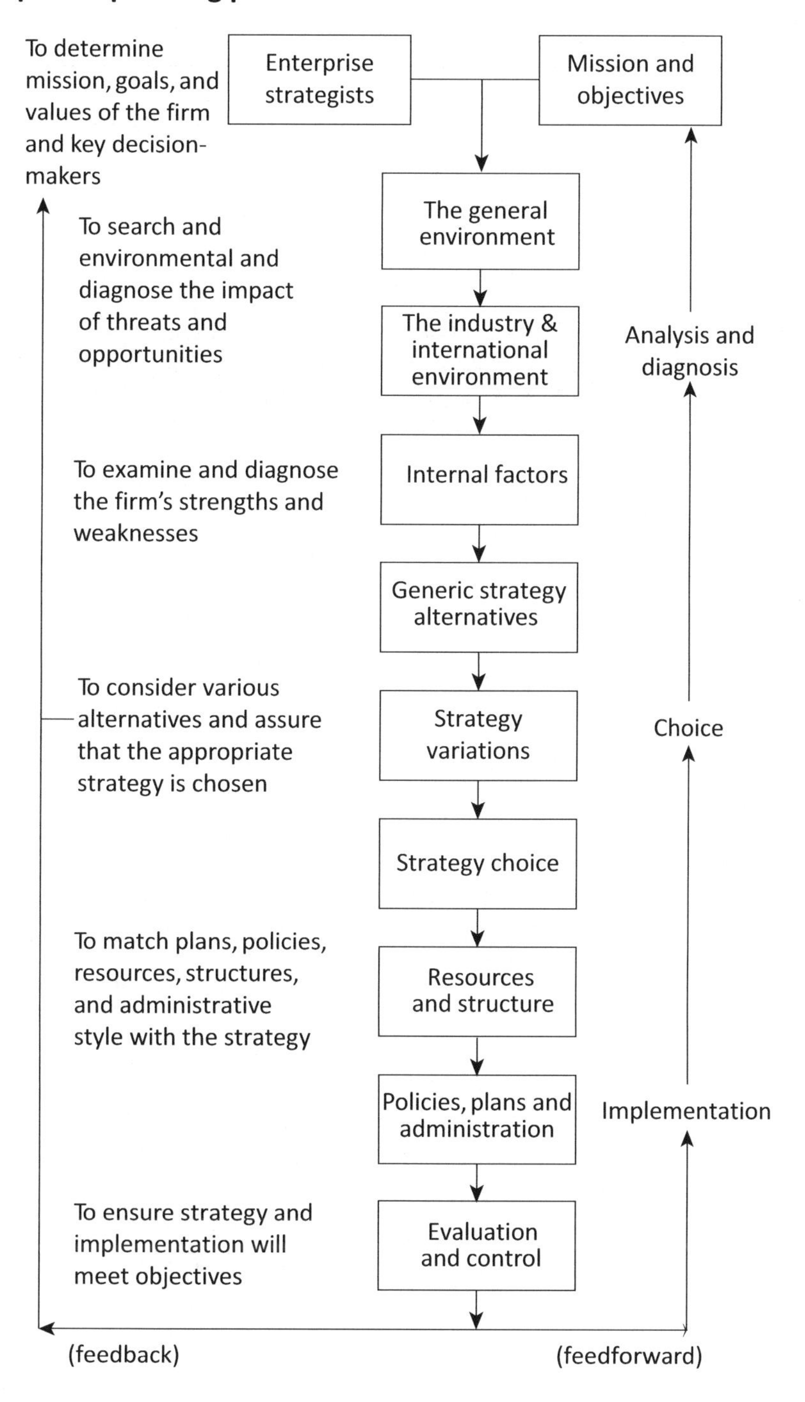

Principle

Role of strategic performance management in strategic planning and control

1.4.1 Planning and control

Planning and control are often portrayed as distinct processes. They are, however, closely related. Planning is concerned with identifying where the organisation wants to be (usually expressed in terms of objectives) and how it will get there (strategies).

Control activities are concerned with monitoring achievement of objectives and suggesting corrective action, which may include modification of objectives. Management control also ensures that resources are obtained and used effectively and efficiently.

Planning is characterised by the following:

- Long-term focus
- Considers the whole organisation as well as individual Strategic Business Units (SBUs)
- Matches the activities of an organisation to its external environment
- Matches the activities of an organisation to its resource capability and specifies future resource requirements
- Will be affected by the expectations and values of all stakeholders, not just shareholders
- Distinguishes strategic management from other aspects of management in an organisation because it involves a high degree of uncertainty, it requires an integrated approach to management and it may involve major change in the organisation.

Although planning is concerned with long-term goals it often involves short-term action. For example, the acquisition of a new company is made in order to fulfil a long-term objective but requires a series of short-term operational planning and control decisions.

Such decisions:

- are usually based on a given set of assets and resources
- do not usually involve the scope of an organisation's activities
- rarely involve major change in the organisation
- are unlikely to involve major elements of uncertainty and the techniques used to help make such decisions often seek to minimise the impact of any uncertainty
- use standard management accounting techniques such as cost-volume-profit analysis, limiting factor analysis and linear programming.

Control can be strategic or operational.

Strategic control is concerned with monitoring the implementation of the organisation's strategy to ascertain how well the strategic objectives are being achieved, eg managing shareholder expectations.

Operational control is concerned with the management of existing assets and resources, given the existing strategic direction.

Operational control will not lead to changes in that strategy.

1.4.2 Strategic planning vs local decision-making

The distinction between strategic planning (long term) and localised decision-making can create conflicts. In summary, a strategic business plan:

- Supports major business changes through a programme of projects
- Tends to have a relatively long time scale over several years or financial periods
- May require a specific strategy support team reporting to high level management and the co-ordination of many staff in different geographic locations, departments and projects
- Required budgets may be expressed in forecast outline terms
- Objectives may be expressed in wide terms perhaps reflecting aspirations rather than specific targets eg maximising shareholder wealth
- Is likely to be reported on half yearly or yearly cycles, although monthly reporting is not uncommon

Whereas a short-term business plan:

- Tends to support a specific business process over a short timescale, perhaps no longer than one financial year
- Usually focuses on the activity of a specific location, department, cost centre or project
- Likely to be expressed in measurable specific objectives or targets
- Likely to be managed by a single manager with supporting staff
- Likely to have to be reported on monthly, weekly and perhaps even daily.

The potential sources of conflict between strategic business plans and its short-term component business plans include:

- Departments or cost centres may not be financed or resourced to meet the need of the overall strategic business plan.
- Lack of alignment of local business objectives with strategic objectives and local objectives may not support the strategic business plan.
- Departmental or cost centres may not be designed to deliver the strategic business plan.
- Localised decisions by managers are likely to maximise results to meet their localised objectives rather than support the strategic business plan.
- Meeting the strategic business plan might only be through the removal of aspects of the business that will deliver it eg through planned redundancy leading to reduced commitment to deliver the strategic plan.
- Strategic business plan may not be designed to solve local problems or support local processes.

- The purpose of the strategic business plan may not be communicated clearly to lower level managers, leading to confusion eg higher level management may not be prepared to release commercially sensitive information to lower level managers.

This has some important implications in the following areas:

- Developing consistent strategies. Overall strategic objectives should be broken down into compatible objectives at local level, so that conflicts can be avoided. The strategic planning process has to be multi-layered.
- Deciding between strategic options. Strategic business plans should be carefully evaluated and the impact of unintended consequences considered.
- Development of appropriate performance measures. Localised performance measures need to be articulated in strategic planning terms.

The strategy support team should ensure that all lower level managers understand the terms of the strategic plan so supporting local objectives and performance measures can be designed.

1.4.3 Strategic planning model

Johnson and Scholes' model of strategic planning is a useful framework for examining performance management and strategic management accounting issues.

This is a model that you have seen in your P3 studies encompassing:

1. Mission and objectives
2. Environment analysis
3. Position (internal) analysis
4. Strategic options
5. Strategic choices
6. Implementation of strategy

Within this framework, the role of Key Performance Indicators (KPIs) is central to performance management.

The stages of strategic analysis
Stage 1: Vision (also known as mission) gets turned into:

Stage 2: Goals (to satisfy key stakeholders) which are turned into:

Stage 3: Objectives which are compared with current performance to produce:

Stage 4: Gap analysis (difference between what we expect to achieve and what stakeholders require)

Gap analysis

Gap analysis is useful for showing how strategies will enable the organisation to meet targets for key objectives (or at least those that can be easily quantified).

For objectives to serve as a tool for stretching an organisation to reach its full potential, they should be challenging but achievable. Thus, the gap BC in the figure below should be just the right size to be significant enough to excite interest, because

closing it would benefit the company greatly, but it should not be so large a gap that no matter how hard the company tries it would be impossible to close.

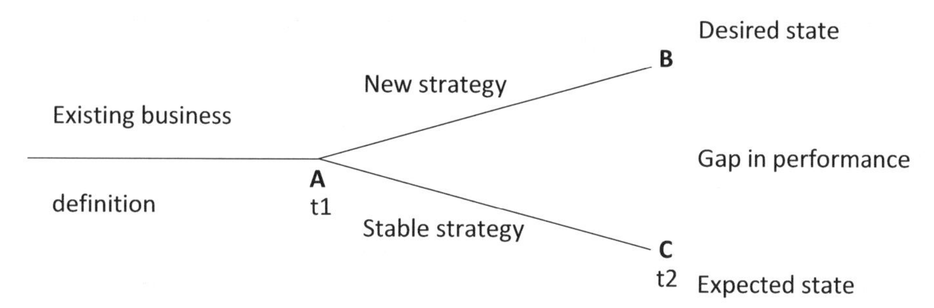

To close this gap:

Develop new options which can be evaluated using the suitability, feasibility and acceptability parameters (sensitivity analysis) which allow strategies to be chosen:

- Suitability – analyses whether the options are adequate responses to the assessment of the organisation's strategic position
- Acceptability – considers whether the options meet and are consistent with the organisation's objectives and are acceptable to the stakeholders
- Feasibility – assesses whether the organisation has the resources it needs to carry out the strategy

1.4.4 SWOT analysis and performance management

To assist in closing the gap between predicted and desired performance, the organisation's strengths, weaknesses, opportunities and threats need to be ascertained. This is often done using a SWOT analysis.

The purpose of SWOT analysis is to provide a summarised analysis of the company's present position in the market place. Based on the SWOT analysis, the organisation can develop strategies to address the gap between the current position and where it wants to be. It can also be used to help identify Critical Success Factors (CSFs) and Key Performance Indicators (KPIs).

The work involved draws on the data obtained about objectives, current position, extrapolated position, gaps and environmental forecasts, and is sometimes called corporate appraisal.

Critical Success Factors (CSFs) are the major determinants of financial and competitive success in a particular industry. Critical success factors highlight the things all firms in the industry must pay close attention to - the functions and skills that are crucial to success and profitability eg in brewing, the CSFs are utilisation of capacity to keep costs low, a strong network of wholesale distributors to gain access to as many retail outlets as possible and clever advertising to induce beer drinkers to buy a particular brand and pull the product through the channels.

CSFs can serve as cornerstones on which business strategy is built. Frequently, a company can win a competitive advantage by concentrating on being distinctively better than rivals in one or more of the industry's CSFs.

IE Illustrative example 1.2

Hewlett-Packard might concentrate on the support technology activity as a CSF because of its enormous potential for value creation in the form of innovative products, but it would not be that worried about inbound logistics. On the other hand, Toyota with its just-in-time system would regard inbound logistics as a CSF because this produces great value in the form of lowering costs.

A SWOT analysis is often defined as:

Strengths	**Weaknesses**
Positive factors or distinctive capabilities or core competencies that provide a significant competitive advantage that the organisation can build on.	Negative aspects in the organisation, such as deficiencies in the present competencies or resources, or its image or reputation, which limit its effectiveness and which need to be corrected.
Opportunities	**Threats**
Favourable conditions that usually arise from the nature of changes in the external environment, such as new markets, improved economic factors or a failure of competitors.	Negative conditions that usually arise from the nature of changes in the external environment and developments.

The SWOT analysis can be used to identify the extent to which the organisation has managed to obtain a fit with its environment and can suggest possible strategies to close the resulting performance gap.

- SO strategies pursue opportunities that are a good fit to the organisation's strengths.
- WO strategies overcome weaknesses to pursue opportunities.
- ST strategies identify ways in which the organisation can use its strengths to reduce its vulnerability to external threats.
- WT strategies establish a defensive plan to prevent the organisation's weaknesses from making it highly susceptible to external threats.

EG Learning example 1.1

Recommend Key Performance Indicators (KPIs) that can be used by a business to support the given CSFs:

CSF	KPI
Maintain overall gross profit percentage of 40%	
Increase customer satisfaction each year	
Be the most innovative company in the market	

1.4.5 Benchmarking

Performance is often assessed in relation to benchmarks. Benchmarking requires gathering information that can be used to generate targets so that current levels of performance can be evaluated and improved. Benchmarking can particularly help organisations to improve the performance of aspects of their business which are currently underperforming.

Benchmarking targets can be based on data from within the organisation (internal benchmarks) or from outside the organisation, for example from other businesses in the same industry, competitors, or other businesses which engage in the same or similar processes (external benchmarks).

External benchmarks might include:

- Targets based on the market performance of comparable companies
- Industry averages

Internal benchmarks might include:

- The best-performing divisions within the company
- Targets based on improvements from last year's performance

IE Illustrative example 1.3

Benchmarking is associated with the Rank Xerox organisation, which had started to lose market share after many years of market dominance. They used the benchmark of 'best in class' to compare performance, which then provided the target for the organisation to aim for.

Rank Xerox identified critical areas where it was failing and found a supermarket chain (Walmart) that had similar business processes in those areas. This chain of supermarkets was renowned as being the best and Rank Xerox used the supermarket approach to redesign their own approach and improve their performance.

There are three types of benchmarks:

Internal

- This is where another department of the organisation is used as the benchmark because conformity of service is critical
- Although easily arranged it is unlikely to provide innovative solutions

Competitor

- Uses a direct competitor with the same or similar process because the competitor is the threshold benchmark
- Problem is whether the competitor will really be keen to hand over information on their basis for success.

Process or activity

- Focuses upon a similar process in another company which is not a direct competitor (the example above) to look for new innovative ways to create advantage, as well as solving threshold problems
- Such an approach takes time and is expensive but resistance is likely to be less and can provide a new basis for advantage.

Learn

A typical benchmarking process is likely to include:

- Identifying what is wrong within the current organisation and the criteria that will be used to assess success, selecting the approach and type of benchmarking and identifying best practice elsewhere.
- Collecting data and information developing with partners a mutual understanding and benchmarking protocol, agreeing terminology and performance measures to be used, undertaking information and data collection, collation of findings.
- Analysing the findings review of findings, gap analysis, seeking explanation for the gaps in performance, ensuring comparisons are meaningful and credible, communicating the findings and identifying realistic opportunities for improvement.
- Implementation of recommendations, examining the feasibility of making improvements with respect to organisational constraints and preconditions, obtaining the support of key stakeholders for making the changes needed, implementing action plans, monitoring performance, keeping stakeholders informed of progress.
- Monitoring and reviewing evaluate the benchmarking process and the results of improvement initiatives against business objectives, documenting the lessons learnt, periodically reconsidering the benchmarks in the light of changes.

The potential benefits to be obtained from a benchmarking exercise are:

- Identifying gaps in performance by comparing an organisation's own performance with the performance of the organisation acting as the benchmark

- Putting the company's resources and performance into perspective, reflecting the fact that it is the relative position of a company which matters in assessing its capabilities
- Reducing costs and making efficiency-related savings
- Learning and applying best practices
- Learning from the success of others
- Minimising complacency with your own performance
- Encouraging continuous improvement
- Delivering products and services to specified standards
- Providing information about sources of competitive advantage and competitive disadvantage
- Providing assurance that targets are reasonable, achievable and suitable
- Being effective as a way of implementing changes in business processes

There are a number of difficulties and issues facing organisations wishing to undertake a benchmarking exercise.

- Benchmarking exercises can be costly and time consuming – it is necessary to consider whether the value of the exercise is sufficient to justify its cost.
- Other organisations may be unwilling to share information.
- It may be difficult to obtain accurate information, particularly non-financial information, about competitors.
- The business functions being benchmarked must be similar enough to allow meaningful comparison.
- Companies need to be as specific as possible when identifying areas to benchmark. For example, if a company is interested in studying customer service, it needs to determine what specific area or activity within customer service needs to be examined.
- Success will hinge on the level of commitment from top managers who must be prepared to make changes in response to the results of benchmarking.
- Benchmarking information must be interpreted carefully to ensure that organisations are being compared on a similar basis, and account must be taken of differences in the way data is produced, such as differences in accounting treatment, and external factors which influence performance in the area being benchmarked.
- Benchmarking assumes that there is a single best standard to achieve or a single best way of carrying out an activity.
- It is based often on historic performance and so may not be relevant for future strategic development.
- It may create unwanted side effects and dysfunctional behaviour (eg managers' focus on the measure rather than the long-term objectives of the business).
- Organisations should concentrate on areas that: tie up most cash, significantly improve the relationship with customers and impact on the final results of the business.

1.4.6 Making strategic choices

Strategic options can be evaluated using the suitability, feasibility, acceptability framework. The strategic management accountant will contribute to the acceptability and feasibility aspects in particular.

Aspect	Key concerns	Financial analysis
Acceptability	Returns to stakeholders'	Cash flow forecasts to ensure dividend growth requirements can be met NPV analysis ROCE Valuation of real options Shareholder value analysis Economic value added Cost benefit analysis Ratio analysis (eg dividend yield, growth)
Suitability	Risk	Sensitivity analysis Breakeven Ratio analysis (eg gearing, dividend cover) Expected values
Feasibility	Resources	Cash flow forecast to identify funding needs Budgeting resource requirements Ability to raise finance needed Working capital implications Foreign exchange implications

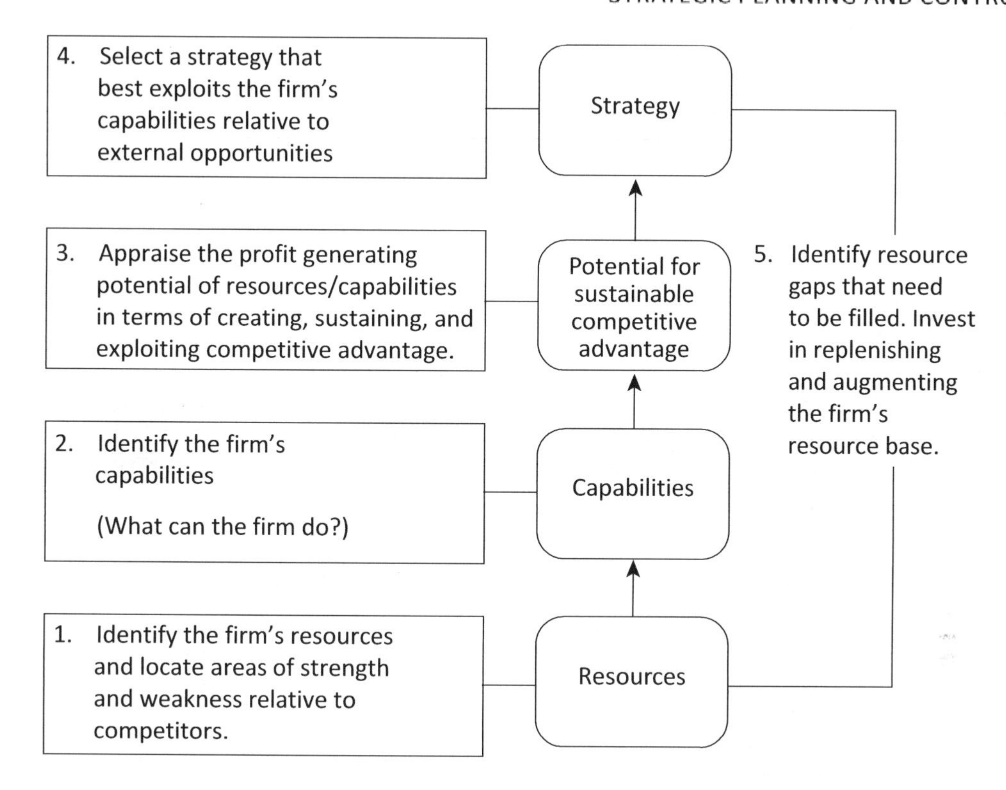

1.5 What is Strategic Management Accounting (SMA) and why is it needed?

Many organisations are facing business environments that are changing in some or all of the following ways:

- Greater globalisation and increasing competition
- More rapid change (dynamism) and increasing complexity
- Greater perceived risk
- A switch to more emergent styles of strategic planning
- A greater awareness of the need for a clear, sustainable competitive strategy
- A greater emphasis on quality (eg the adoption of six sigma methodologies)
- A drive for cost reductions (eg through outsourcing to countries with lower wage costs)
- The use of greater automation in manufacturing systems and an increase in the strategic significance of IT and IS
- A need for greater flexibility and a switch to more flexible organisational forms

These developments have required the introduction of new management accounting practices and the modification of old ones.

Ken Simmonds defined SMA as "a form of management accounting in which emphasis is placed on information which relates to factors external to the firm, as well as non-financial information and internally generated information."

Simmonds saw SMA as the collection of management accounting information about a business and its competitors for use in developing and monitoring the business strategy. The emphasis was placed upon relative levels and trends in real costs and prices, volume, market share, cash flow and stewardship of the resources available to the business.

Michael Bromwich pointed out that adding the strategic perspective to traditional management accounting required the role of accounting to extend in two directions. First, costs need to be integrated into strategy through strategic cost analysis, and thus align costs with strategy. Secondly, to ascertain, albeit in a fairly general way, the cost structure of competitors and to monitor the changes over time. In achieving this, Bromwich also sees two distinct approaches:

- costing product attributes provided by the company's products
- cost the functions in the value chain which are perceived as giving value to the customer

Historically the role of the management accountant was often limited to the measurement of financial information in retrospect with a focus on operational budgeting, target setting and control.

These measures tend to be

- Short-term
- Backwards looking
- Focused at individual departments
- Able to be produced in standard reports
- Able to be produced at regular intervals
- Produced by junior staff for senior staff to review.

These characteristics are useful for *control* purposes but we saw that strategy is concerned with big decisions, such as whether:

- to acquire a new company
- to launch a new product
- to close down a division.

Traditional management accounting will not help with these decisions. Instead we need to use strategic management accounting.

The term 'strategic management accounting' (SMA) has come into common use more recently. It refers to the full range of management accounting practices used to provide a guide to the strategic direction of an organisation.

SMA gives a financial dimension to strategic management and control, providing information on the financial aspects of strategic plans and planning financial aspects of their implementation.

It supports managers throughout the organisation in the task of managing the organisation in the interests of all its stakeholders.

SMA places an emphasis on using information from a wide variety of internal and external sources in order to evaluate performance appraise proposed projects and make decisions.

It focuses on the external environment, such as suppliers, customers, competitors and the economy in general as much as on the organisation itself.

Strategic management accounting monitors performance in line with the organisation's strategic objectives in both financial and non-financial terms.

SMA is an approach in which financial information is used to develop superior strategies as a means of achieving sustainable competitive advantage.

The SMA process involves asking

Where are we now?	Start
Where do we want to be?	End
How might we get there?	Means
Which way is best?	Evaluation
How can we ensure arrival?	Control (Then go back to Start)

Any strategic choice will need to be justified using the criterion of:

- Suitability
- Feasibility
- Acceptability

SMA information can assist with making strategic choices because its main features are that it is:

- Externally focused
- Forward looking
- Aimed at achieving the goals of the entire organisation
- Produced when needed
- Not in a standard form

It is also important to note that this externally focused and forward looking perspective means that different information systems will need to be developed to provide:

- Product profitability – Why is one product making more profit than another?
- Customer profitability – Why are some customers worth more than others?
- Pricing decisions – Including looking at customers and competitors
- Brand values – How much should be invested in a brand?
- Shareholder wealth – What choices will increase it?
- Possible acquisition targets
- Expected synergistic gains
- Decisions on entering new industries or markets
- Decisions on launching new products
- Decisions on whether to expand certain parts of the business
- Decisions on whether to close or sell-off various parts of the business

The last two points are particularly important. Senior management will need to identify which parts of the business are performing well and which are under-performing.

Note that many of the tools and techniques studied in F5 (and some in F9) are still examinable in P5, including the following:

1. Costing methods, eg target costing, life cycle costing
2. Limiting factor analysis
3. Relevant costing
4. Risk techniques, eg expected values, minimax regret, maximin, maximax
5. Budgeting, eg flexed budgets
6. Forecasting techniques, eg hi–low, time series, learning curves
7. Standard costing

Senior management will need to introduce a set of performance measures, using techniques such as those above, which can be used to summarise the performance of the business.

Much of the P5 exam will be concerned with:

- What the business is trying to achieve
- What performance measures would be useful
- How these measures can be calculated
- What the results might mean
- The effect of these measures on the behaviour of departmental managers.

IE Illustrative example 1.4

A company selling a range of wooden garden sheds in UK is facing a number of problems: demand is seasonal, the market is becoming more fashion conscious and there is a growth in the use of non-traditional materials such as plastics.

As a result the company finds itself with high inventory levels of some items which are not selling, and is unable to meet demand for others. A decision is needed on the future strategic direction and possible options which have been identified are to use temporary staff to manufacture products on a seasonal basis in response to fluctuations in demand, or to concentrate on producing premium products which are smaller volume but high priced and less dependent on fashion.

How could strategic management accounting help with the decision-making?

George Brown wrote that the achievement of long-term goals will require strategic planning which is linked to short-term operational planning. If there is no link between strategic planning and operational planning the result is likely to be unrealistic plans, inconsistent goals, poor communication and inadequate performance measurement. In order to create this link, strategic management accounting helps to provide the operational information that supports the strategic objectives. This will

enhance the decision-making involved as the decisions will be founded upon useful information that helps management decide if they are following a good strategy or if they are failing and need to re-assess their direction.

1.6 Key models used in strategic management accounting

There are a number of useful models used in strategic management accounting, some of which you will have seen in P3. Make sure you learn the parts of the model and know why you are using each one.

1.6.1 The BCG Matrix

The BCG Matrix attempts to analyse the products that a company currently offers. The matrix can then be used to suggest what to do with each product. The model looks at two measurements – market share and market growth and divides products into four categories.

Because the model uses market growth it can be combined with the Product Life Cycle model.

The categories are:

BCG Matrix	Stages in the Product Life Cycle model
Question marks: High market growth, Low market share	Introduction
Stars: High market growth, High market share	Growth
Cash: cows Low market growth, High market share	Maturity
Dogs: Low market growth, Low market share	Decline or extension

Boston Consulting Group Growth/Share Matrix

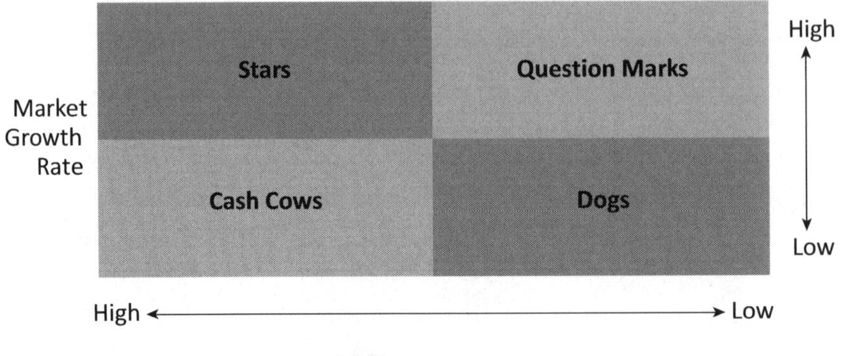

Learn

In the exam you may have to calculate the market share of a product. If the information is available it would also be useful to calculate profit margins for each product.

High or low market share is calculated by taking the organisation's own market share and comparing it to the market leader. The closer this is to 1.0 the higher the market share (a score of 1.0 would mean that the organisation is the market leader).

'Question marks' have a lot of potential due to the high growth. The decision is whether to:

- Spend money to build up market share
- Spend money to hold market share
- Leave the market.

'Stars' also have a high market share:

- The market is growing (introduction or growth stage of the life cycle), so new competitors will be attracted into the market.
- Prices may need to be kept low to maintain market share.
- Marketing costs might also need to be high to keep sales growing.
- Profits may not be high.

'Cash cows' are in the mature or decline stage of the life cycle:

- The threat of new competitors is low and the high market share makes the threats from substitutes and existing competitors low as well.
- This product should be earning reasonable profits.
- The product cannot grow any further (since the market is already mature).

'Dogs' have low market share and low growth. They should be closed unless needed by one of the other products.

The company should aim to have a balanced portfolio, with cash cows funding the growth of stars and question marks.

The Product Life Cycle (PLC)

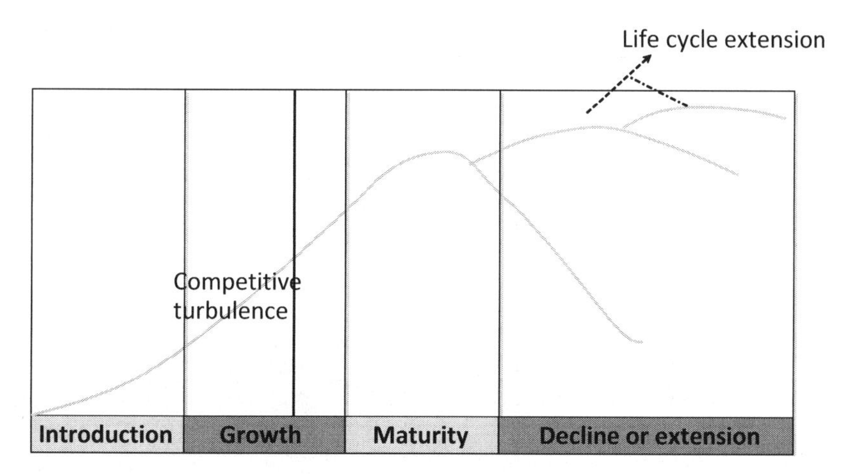

The BCG model (and the Product Life Cycle model) can also be used to look at the industries a company operates in. Again, the company should aim to have a balanced portfolio.

1.6.2 Porter's Five Forces model

One of the main exponents of strategic management accounting is Michael Porter. Porter takes a two-pronged approach. First he assesses different industries in terms of their long-term profitability. He sees five competitive forces that will contribute to a strategic equation.

1. The threat of new entrants into the market
   This is influenced by the cost of entry into a market and the opportunity to make a profit. In principle, the larger the organisation and the more investment required, the less likelihood of any competition.
2. The threat of substitute products or services
   For example, competition from Internet marketing affecting newspapers that rely on advertising revenues.
3. Rivalry amongst existing organisations within the industry
   For example, supermarkets and the food market being threatened by discount providers.
4. The bargaining power of suppliers
5. The bargaining power of buyers

 **Learn**

Prices are influenced by the bargaining power of buyers and the threat of substitutes. Costs are influenced by the bargaining power of suppliers and the rivalry between competitors.

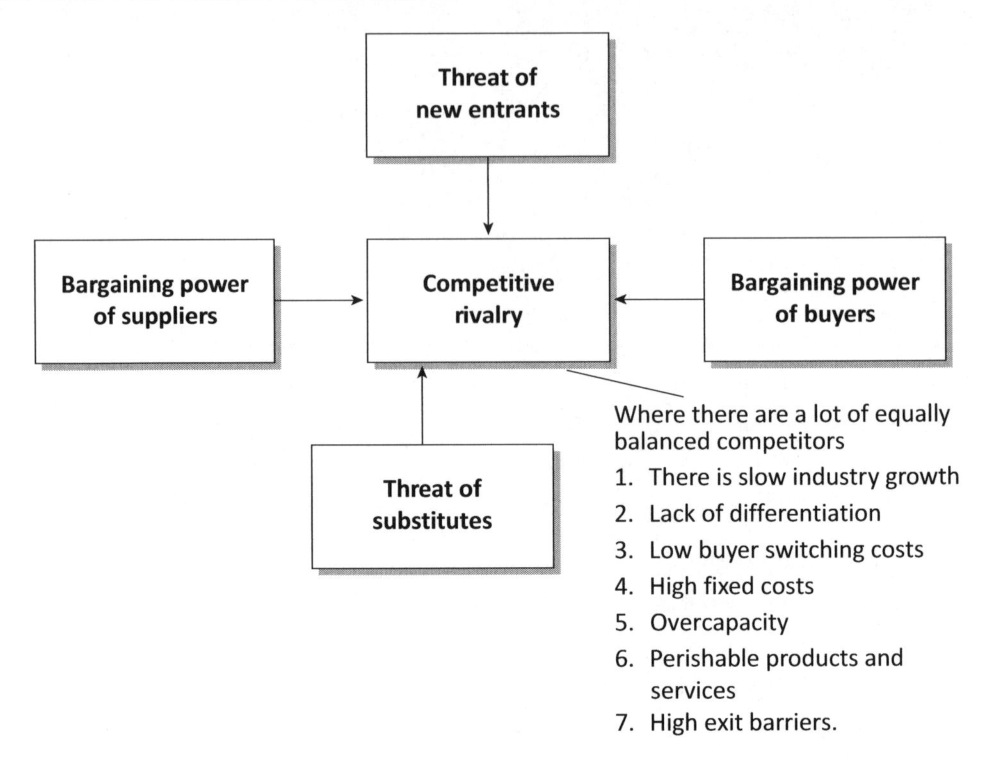
Threat of new entrants
Bargaining power of suppliers
Competitive rivalry
Bargaining power of buyers
Threat of substitutes
Where there are a lot of equally balanced competitors
1. There is slow industry growth
2. Lack of differentiation
3. Low buyer switching costs
4. High fixed costs
5. Overcapacity
6. Perishable products and services
7. High exit barriers.

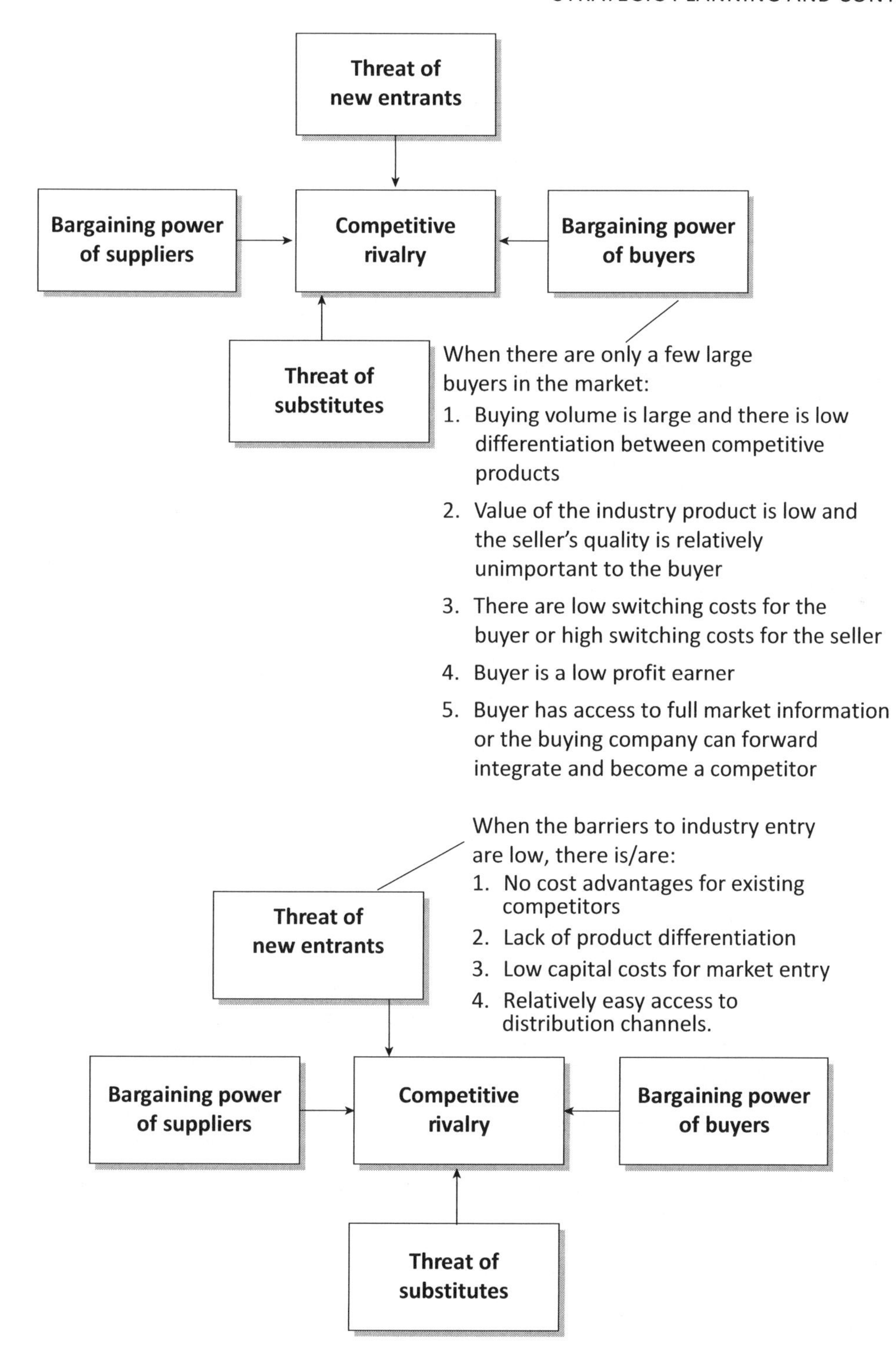
Threat of new entrants
Bargaining power of suppliers
Competitive rivalry
Bargaining power of buyers
Threat of substitutes
When there are only a few large buyers in the market:
1. Buying volume is large and there is low differentiation between competitive products
2. Value of the industry product is low and the seller's quality is relatively unimportant to the buyer
3. There are low switching costs for the buyer or high switching costs for the seller
4. Buyer is a low profit earner
5. Buyer has access to full market information or the buying company can forward integrate and become a competitor
When the barriers to industry entry are low, there is/are:
1. No cost advantages for existing competitors
2. Lack of product differentiation
3. Low capital costs for market entry
4. Relatively easy access to distribution channels.
Threat of new entrants
Bargaining power of suppliers
Competitive rivalry
Bargaining power of buyers
Threat of substitutes

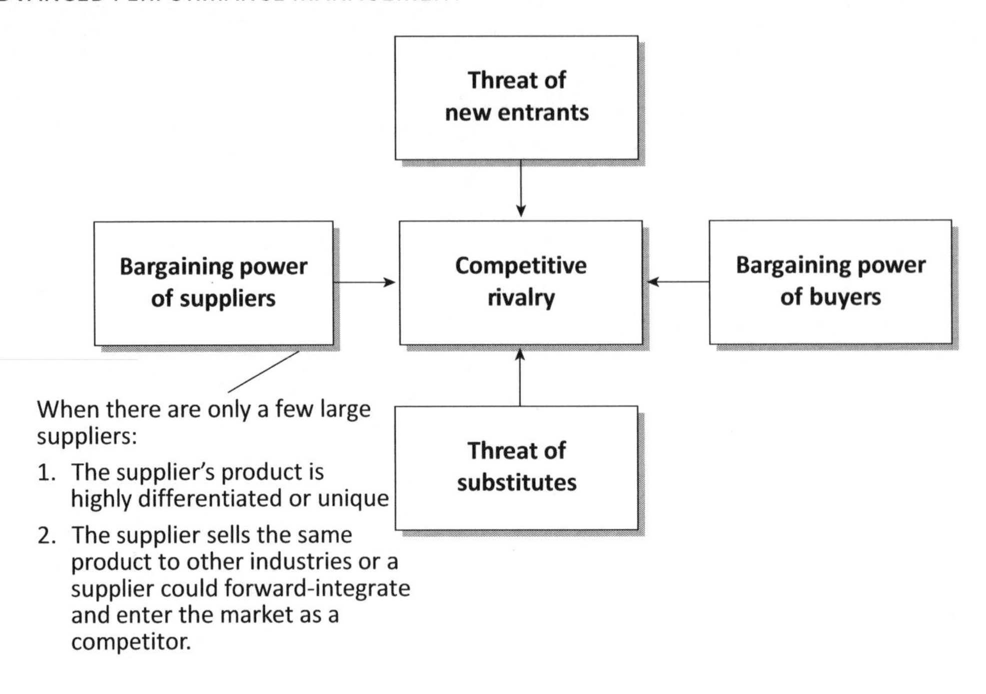

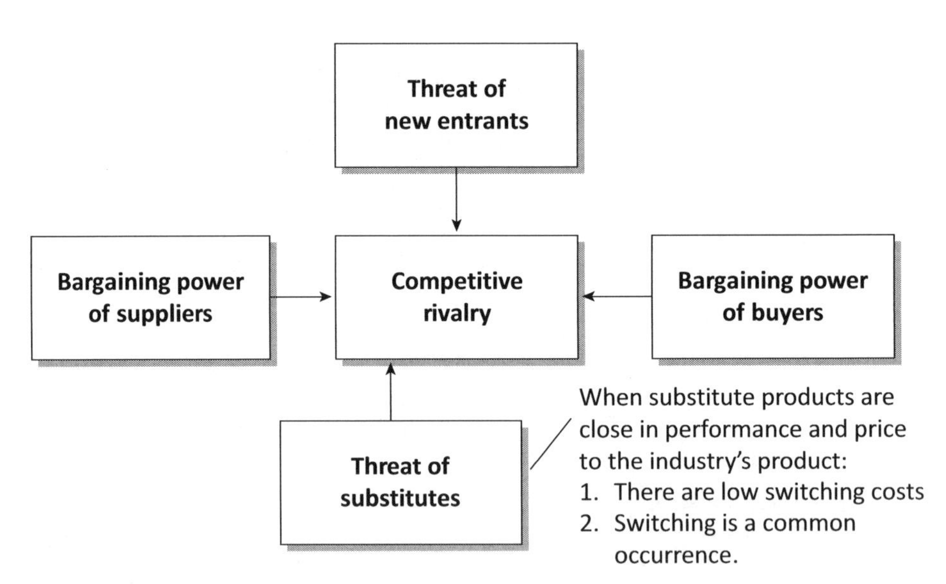

Saturated markets seem to be dominated by global players and customer retention becomes increasingly important, as it is difficult to create a sustainable competitive advantage, as most innovations can be copied by rivals and cost advantages are difficult to obtain given the size of firms.

Five Forces analysis: Key questions and implications

- Are some industries more attractive than others?

- What underlying forces in the macro environment drive the competitive forces?
- Will competitive forces change?
- What are the strengths and weaknesses of the competitors in relation to the competitive forces?
- Can competitive strategy influence competitive forces? (eg build barriers to entry).

Key aspects of Five Forces analysis

- We use the analysis at the level of strategic business units (SBUs).
- We need to define the industry/market/sector.
- We can't just list the forces: we need to derive the implications for the industry/organisation.
- We should note connections between competitive forces and key drivers in the macro environment.
- We have to establish interconnections between the five forces.
- Note that competition may disrupt the forces rather than accommodate them.

EG Learning example 1.2

Explain briefly the use of the Five Forces model within a strategic business environment.

1.6.3 Porter's generic strategies

Two 'generic' strategies that are frequently distinguished are 'price leadership' and 'differentiation'. Price leadership implies low prices combined with a standardised offering. The strategic effort goes into developing a customer proposition that appeals to large numbers of customers and can be provided at low cost. Product variation or even tailoring products to individual customers' wishes is then not usually part of the product offering. Budget airlines are a fairly extreme example of this strategy.

By contrast, 'differentiation' emphasises the satisfaction of individual customer's wishes as closely as possible, be it with respect to quality of manufacture, ease of use, flexibility of application or delivery, product variety, reliability or any combination of these. An example would be luxury motor vehicle manufacturers. Product cost is also a concern for organisations that pursue this strategy, but not to the same extent as for those that pursue price leadership.

Even though the strategy literature often portrays price leadership and differentiation as strategic opposites, in practice one usually finds combinations of the two, for example, in the various markets for electronic consumer goods.

There are different reasons for this. In large organisations some divisions may tend towards one strategy and some towards the other. During their life cycle, certain products may start out as differentiated products that are tailored towards the high price segment (perhaps because they are innovative), and later they may be marketed to compete mainly on price (perhaps because many competitors have entered this market, production volumes have increased and high quality is no longer a differentiating factor).

The strategic relevance of management accounting would depend on the extent to which it supports management in finding out which strategy is most promising for an organisation. Here one would expect management accountants to prepare alternative scenarios together with marketing, product, and production managers, who assess the long-term profitability of operating in different markets, offering different price–value combinations to different customer segments. In target costing, value engineering and life cycle costing, the experience has been that such efforts are best placed in the development and design stages of a new product, because here a large percentage of a product's cost is built into its design.

The role of management accountants can be to advise on the cost implications of certain design choices and calculate the added revenue that can be expected from additional product attributes (eg reliability, functionality, appearance, etc).

Michael Porter also poses the question about the enterprise's relative position within its industry. The question of position is important because it influences the ability of a business to generate profits greater or less than the industry average. Above average returns may be achieved by sustainable competitive advantage. This is achieved by three basic generic strategies.

	Cost advantage	*Differentiation*
Market wide	**Cost leadership**	**Differentiation**
Focus	**Cost focus**	**Differentiation focus**

Competitive advantage

Cost leadership

An enterprise aims at being the lowest cost producer in the industry. This is achieved by economies of scale, capitalising on experience curve effects, tight cost control and cost minimisation in such areas as R&D, service and advertising.

This is also known as a 'no frills' strategy, adopted because the enterprise deals with:

- Commodity-like products or services
- Price sensitive customers
- High buyer power and/or low switching costs
- Small number of providers with similar market shares
- Major competitors it wishes to avoid.

Differentiation

An enterprise seeks to offer some different dimension in its products/services that is valued by its customers and may command a premium price. This can be achieved by image, superior customer service solutions, dealer network and support and product design.

Enterprises adopting this strategy operate within highly competitive markets where customer attrition rates are high. The key to delivering this competitive strategy is supporting high level of customer service and marketing through quality with a detailed system of target setting in place to ensure compliance. When choosing a differentiation strategy, an organisation will take into account the following factors – reputation, size, financing ability, command of technology, economies of scale and the ability to deliver geographical coverage.

Focus

This has two variations – cost focus and differentiation focus. Strategies that are based upon focus concentrate on narrow segments to the exclusion of others. For example, the focus strategy of Millenium & Copthorne has been to deliver only five star hotels in particular geographical areas.

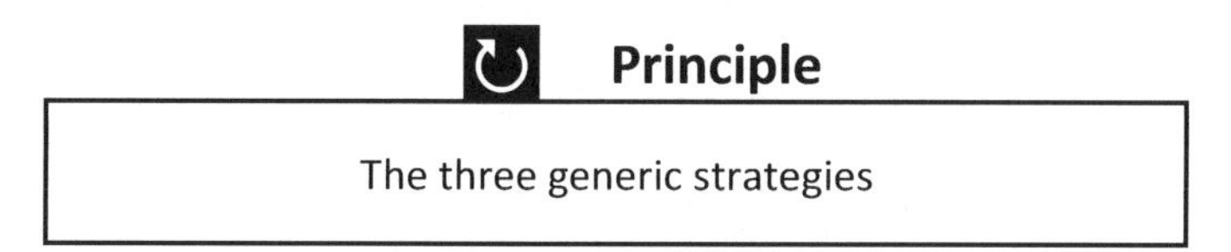

1.6.4 Porter's value chain

Modern writers such as Hammer and Davenport argue that successful organisations do not have departments and functions that try to maximise their own performance and efficiency at the expense of the whole; but have business integration, which means that all aspects of the business must be aligned to secure the most efficient use of the organisation's resources, so that it can achieve its objectives effectively.

The main framework for understanding integrated processes and the linkages within them is Porter's Value Chain model. Value is what the customers are prepared to pay, and this is a function of the image of the product.

Porter says that the ability of an organisation is often judged by the consumer or users of the product or service.

Processes need to be viewed as complete entities that stretch from initial order to final delivery of a product. IT needs to be used to integrate these activities.

The model has nine elements and the value chain concept identifies the links between activities and the value of these activities, each with operating costs and allocated assets driven by one or more cost drivers. Some of these cost drivers may be controllable.

The processes in the value chain need to be viewed as complete entities that stretch from initial order to final delivery of a product.

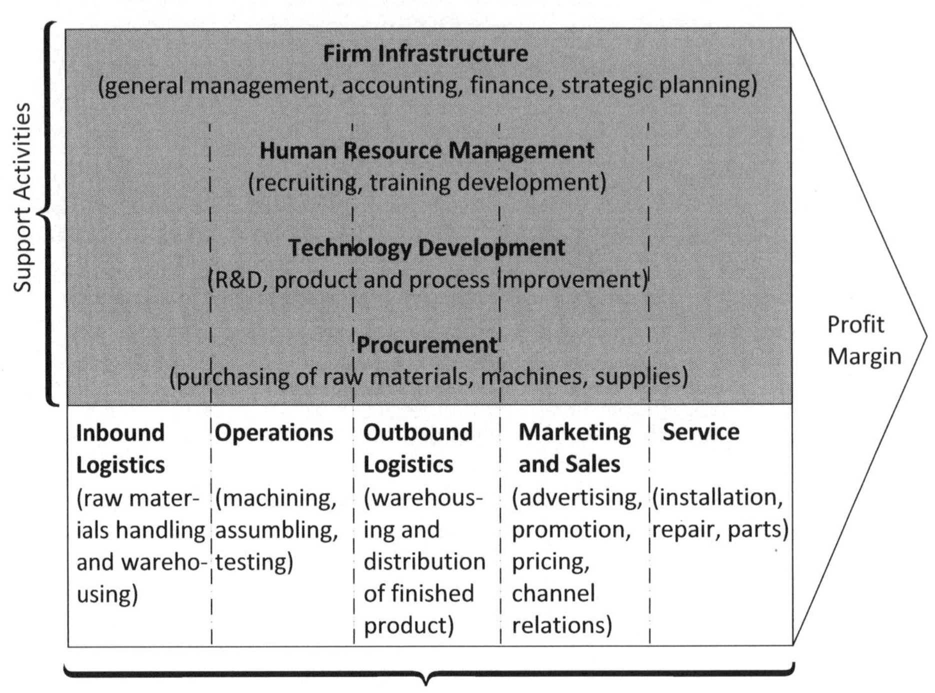

Primary activities

1. Inbound logistics
   Activities concerned with receiving, storing and distributing the inputs to produce the product/service
2. Operations
   The process of transforming the inputs into final products or services (assembly and packaging)
3. Outbound logistics
   Collection, storage and distributing the product to the customer
4. Marketing and sales
   Informing the customer/consumer of the product
5. Service
   All activities which enhance or maintain the product or service (product repairs, guarantees)

Each of these groups of primary activities are linked to **support activities.**

Support activities

1. Firm infrastructure/management systems
   Involves planning, finance and quality control
2. Human resource management
   Involves recruiting, training, development and rewards of all staff
3. Technological development
   Associated with research and development and product design
4. Procurement

Learn

Strategic issues related to value chains for manufacturing organisations

Inbound logistics	Operations	Outbound logistics	Marketing and sales	Service
		Procurement		
Transport Warehousing Capital	Machines Consumables	Transport Warehousing	Product/Service Patents Licences Brand names Market research	Franchises Credit facilities
		Technology development		
Know-how Design Technology Transfer (in)	Process development	Shipments	Network of contacts Information systems	Fault diagnosis
		Human resource management		
Recruitment Supplier vetting Shareholders Creditor relations Image with investors	Team spirit Job satisfaction Subcontractors	Subcontractors	Agents Sales force Distributors Merchandisers Goodwill	After-sales staff Reputation Maintenance staff
		Management systems		
Purchasing Systems Vehicle Scheduling Materials handling	Production Planning Quality control Cash management Stock control Facilities layout	Delivery scheduling	Order processing Debtor control	Customer service system

The model is useful for:

- Assessing the available resources within an organisation
- Being part of a strategic analysis to identify strengths or weaknesses
- Analysing those processes responsible for designing, producing, marketing and delivering the product to the end user

- Analysing resources to establish how competitive differences are achieved
- Analysing external relationships which the organisation has with suppliers and distribution systems.

In making the analysis, attempts must be made to assess the impact of the cost drivers on each of the elements. Also, the cost of the nine elements must produce a satisfactory overall margin.

Once this exercise is complete, an attempt must be made to analyse one's competitors in the same way. Strategic advantage will then be identified if the total cost of the elements is less than that of the competitors. Taking a more positive approach, assess if the margins are better than those of the competition. If they are not, then a strategy must be developed to achieve a lower cost position through controlling the cost drivers. This may mean cost savings by cost cuttings, or improving productivity.

The value chain model is particularly useful for:

- focusing on how each activity in the process adds to the firm's overall competitive advantage
- emphasising CSFs within each activity and overall
- examining both primary activities (eg production) and support activities, such as HRM, which may otherwise be dismissed as overheads
- ongoing performance management, as targets can be set and monitored for different activities, enabling the performance of the overall process to be assessed and managed.

1.7 Strategic implementation

This is concerned with the translation of strategy into organisational action through organisational structure and design, resource planning and the management of strategic change.

Successful implementation of strategy is likely to be dependent on the extent to which these various components are effectively integrated to provide competences which other organisations find it difficult to match.

The implementation process can be thought of as having several parts:

- Resource planning and the logistics of implementation. This process will address the problem of the tasks that need to be carried out and also the timing of them. There may need to be changes in the mix of resources required to implement the strategy and decisions will need to be taken about who is to be responsible for the changes.
- The organisational structure may need to be changed, eg, from hierarchical to matrix or from centralised to decentralised.
- The systems employed to manage the organisation may need to be improved. These systems provide the information and operational procedures needed in the organisation. It may be that a new information management system is required to monitor the progress of the strategy. Staff may need to be retrained or new staff recruited.

1.8 Mission

The mission statement (also known as the vision) is a statement that describes the basic purpose or what an organisation is trying to accomplish.

According to Peter Drucker, there are a number of fundamental questions that an organisation will need to address in its search for this purpose:

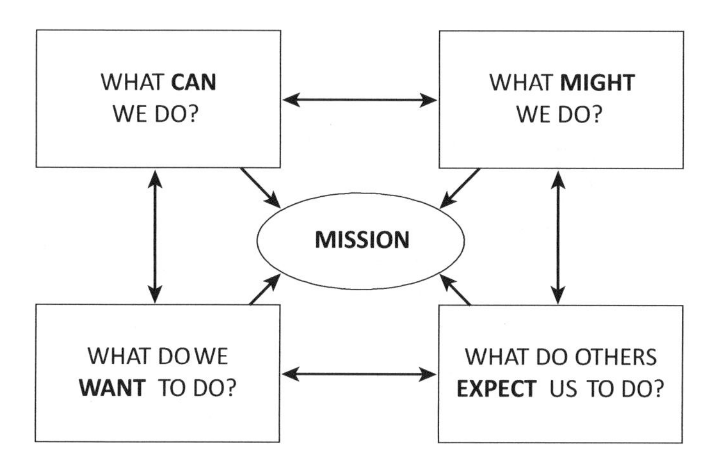

Mission statements will have some or all of the following characteristics:

- Usually a brief statement of no more than a page in length.
- A very general statement of entity culture.
- States the aims (or purposes) of the organisation.
- States the business areas in which the organisation intends to operate.
- Open ended (not stated in quantifiable terms).
- Does not include commercial terms, such as profit.
- Not time bound.
- Forms a basis of communication to the people inside the organisation and to people outside the organisation.
- Used to formulate goal statements, objectives and short-term targets.
- Guides the direction of the entity's strategy and as such is part of management information.

However, mission statements can create potential problems:

- They do not represent the actual values practised by the organisation.
- They can be too vague.
- They may be ignored.

1.8.1 The relevance of a mission for strategic planning

A statement of corporate mission is inextricably linked with the organisation's goals and objectives.

The organisational objectives comprise the specific targets of the company and the goals comprise its broad aims, the mission encapsulates the reason that the entity exists in terms of the service and utility provided to meet specific needs of society.

Before the preparation of a strategic plan the management should consider the mission of an organisation.

Many commentators have suggested that consideration and determination of the mission and its articulation into a statement of corporate mission constitutes the first stage in the strategic planning process and that, therefore, it is central to the whole planning process.

Johnson and Scholes have suggested that 'the mission of an organisation is the most generalised type of objective and can be thought of as an expression of its raison d'être'.

To enable an organisation to fulfil its mission, the mission must be translated into:

- Strategic plans and objectives
- Tactical plans and objectives
- Detailed operational plans and targets.

Each level should be consistent with the one above.

Learn

This process will involve moving from general broad aims to more specific objectives and ultimately to detail targets.

IE Illustrative example 1.5

'To be earth's most customer centric company; to build a place where people can come to find and discover anything they might want to buy online' is Amazon's mission statement. On the face of it this is very general, though buying online and being customer centric is useful to guide more detailed objectives.

Looking at more detailed possible parts of a company's (not Amazon's) mission and objectives:

Mission statement (extract)
The company will maximise the wealth and wellbeing of our shareholders...

Goal statements

1. We will provide our shareholders with a return on their investment which is commensurate with their expectations.
2. We will protect the security of our shareholders' investments.
3. We will endeavour to increase the capital value of our shareholders' investment.

Objectives
Goal 1: Shareholders' return on investment

- To realise a return on investment of 15% during the next 2 years.
- To achieve a growth in sales turnover of 10% in 3 years.
- To maintain net profit margins.
- That the return to shareholders should grow in line with the growth in net profit.

Goal 2: Security of shareholders' investments

- To maintain the quality of existing assets by investing not less than 12% of sales annually for the next 3 years, and to make new investment at rates of return applicable to the risk involved to meet the company's targeted return on capital employed.
- To ensure that loans should not exceed 35% of capital employed, unless required for exceptional circumstances of a short-term nature.

Goal 3: Growth in shareholders' investments

- To maintain a match between foreign currency assets and liabilities.
- To achieve a price earnings multiple of 12 by 2017.

1.8.2 Stakeholder analysis

Mission and objectives need to be developed with two sets of interests in mind:

- The interests of those who have to carry them out eg managers and staff
- The interests of those who focus on the outcome eg shareholders, customers, suppliers.

Together these groups are known as stakeholders – the individuals and groups who have an interest in the organisation and as such may wish to influence its mission, objectives and strategy.

Given the range of interests in organisations, it is not surprising to find that the mission may take several months of negotiation before it is finalised. The key aspect is that the organisation must take the stakeholders into account when formulating the mission and objectives of the company.

The problem is that stakeholder interests often conflict and so an order of priority is required, based upon relative power and interest. The different stakeholders need to be identified and potential for conflict needs to be ascertained in advance. The mission setting process can be a useful basis for getting the stakeholder groups to communicate their ideas and then be able to appreciate other viewpoints.

Stakeholder power analysis

This can be broken down into five steps:

1. Identify the key stakeholders.
2. Establish their interests and claims on the organisation, especially as new strategic initiatives are likely to be developed.
3. Determine the degree of power that each group holds, through its ability to force or influence change as new strategies are developed.
4. Consider how to divert trouble before it starts, possibly by negotiating with key groups in advance.
5. Develop mission, objectives and strategy, possibly prioritising to minimise power clashes. This may involve negotiation amongst the various groups of stakeholders.

Stakeholder groups and possible power sources

Managers

- Large or small company?
- Company performance against industry and economy – how well is it doing?
- Technical skills – are they in short supply?
- Non-executive directors – can they challenge?

Employees

- Unionised?
- Cultures?
- Skills base?

Government

- *Laissez-faire?* (how involved?)
- Shareholdings?
- Political involvement?

Lenders

- Loan conditions?
- Amount and terms of loan?
- Non-executive directors? Provided by lenders?

Shareholders

- Voting powers?
- Family influence?
- Number of shareholdings?
- Rate of change of holdings?
- Extent of staff and managers who own shares?

Customers and suppliers

- Power from grouping together?
- Volumes involved?

- Alternative suppliers?

Different groups will have different influence – each case will need to be treated in context.

Mendelow's Power Interest Matrix

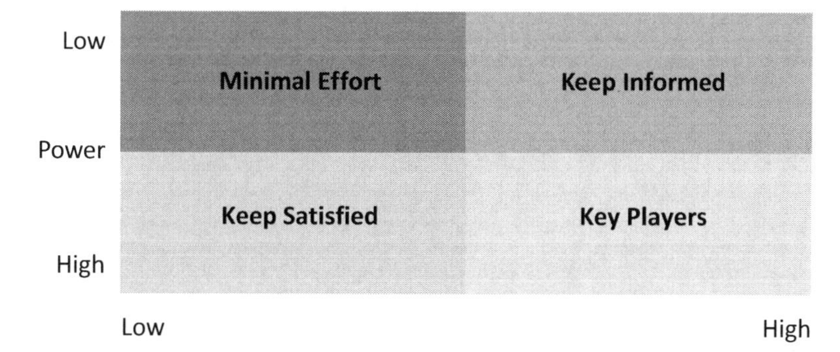

Key players will be the most significant. Look to see how many there are. The more there are, the greater the need for compromise and the larger the chance of conflict.

Keep satisfied will usually leave you alone, so long as you adhere to their conditions eg being socially responsible.

Remember things change and so the **keep informed** of today may be the **key player** of tomorrow.

Learn

Managing the relationship with stakeholder groups

Powerful stakeholder groups must have confidence in the management team of the organisation. The organisation should ensure therefore that adequate management systems are in place. Some suggestions:

- Frequent face-to-face meetings with the key player and keep satisfied groups
- Communication processes for the other two groups – possibly via public Q&A sessions
- Periodic formal reporting and the use of a website for 'frequently asked questions'

There will always be a conflict of interest between what different groups want. For example, giving employees better pay levels reduces the profit available for shareholders.

Stakeholders matter because objectives should be geared towards the needs of those with high power. Also any strategy followed will need to be acceptable to the key players.

In the P5 exam, you will usually have to consider the shareholders first. You might have to prepare information to show how your company is doing relative to others (this is known as benchmarking). The P5 Examiner might also give you information about possible future projects. If they are profitable they are likely to appeal to shareholders.

1.9 Exogenous variables

In addition to factors under their control, organisations are affected by a range of variables which do not originate from within the organisation itself and are not controllable by its management. These are known as exogenous variables.

Such variables may include long-term market trends, government policy in areas such as taxation, and technological development.

It may be possible to assess the impact over the immediate future for the purposes of short-term decision-making, but forecasting the long-term effects is much more difficult.

The existence of such variables means that long-term planning always involves an element of risk and uncertainty.

Changes in one of these variables could completely invalidate a strategy.

It is very difficult to quantify the impact of these variables.

Forecasting the long-term impact of exogenous variables is made more difficult because:

- The organisation's environment is complex.
- There are interrelationships between the environmental variables involved.
- Changes in these variables, such as political change, can be very rapid.
- There is limited data available to aid forecasting.

Certain trends in today's macro environment place greater pressures on companies. Foremost are:

- Rapid technological change. Pioneers of change will benefit; those who fail to keep up will fall by the wayside. Technology is expensive.
- Changing worker expectations. Quality of life at work is becoming an important issue and new working arrangements are constantly evolving thanks to information technology.
- Increasing environmental awareness and environmental pressure groups. Companies will have to conform to ever more exacting standards of environmental protection.
- Globalisation of industries and business. This increases the number of competitors in any one industry and intensifies competition.
- Deregulation of many industries and geographic zones removing protection from competitors.

The removal of non-tariff barriers will allow rivals more easily to compete across borders. This may present opportunities to some companies and threats to others,

especially if their traditional markets are being invaded. It is especially threatening to those companies which compete only domestically and do not have the competencies, resources or motivation to compete abroad themselves.

Definition

The term **industry** is defined as a group of firms whose products have so many of the same attributes that they compete for the same buyers.

The framework of industry and competitive analysis hangs on certain key questions:

- What are the chief economic characteristics of the industry?
- What are the drivers of change in the industry and what impact will they have?
- What competitive forces are at work in the industry and how strong are they?
- Which companies are in the strongest/weakest competitive positions?
- Who will likely make what competitive moves next?
- What key factors will determine competitive success or failure?
- How attractive is the industry in terms of its prospects for above-average profitability?

Some of the factors that describe the industry's dominant characteristics and their effect on competition are:

- Market size and market growth. Fast growth encourages entry; slow growth encourages rivalry and a shakeout of weak competitors.
- Numbers of buyers and their relative size. A small number of large buyers give the buyers a lot of power over competitors in the industry.
- Pace of technological change in product and process innovation. A fast pace raises the risk of obsolescence.
- Capacity surpluses/shortages. Surpluses push down margins; shortages pull them up.
- Commodity versus differentiated products/services. Commodity products enable buyers to switch easily between sellers, increasing buyer power.
- Capital requirements. Big requirements create barriers, but may also create exit barriers.
- Economies of scale. The necessity for economies of scale may increase intensity of rivalry for volume and market share.
- Industry profitability levels. High levels attract entrants; low levels may encourage exit.

Industries change because of driving forces. Some types of driving forces are as follows:

- Changes in long-term industry growth rate. Growth rates vary over the industry's evolution:

    (a) An embryonic industry – slow growth, industry has not yet taken off
    (b) A growth industry – demand taking off - eg wearable technology
    (c) A mature industry – replacement demand only - eg automobiles
    (d) A declining industry eg tobacco, coal

- Changes in who buys the product and how they use it eg increased consumer interest in mobile/smartphones provides a major new buyer segment to manufacturers.
- Product innovation eg the increasing use of social media has created a new industry.
- Technological change – can create changes in cost structures, new products, eg flexible manufacturing systems increasing variety of choice at lower costs.
- Marketing innovation eg Swatch watches sold in a variety of outlets instead of just jewellery stores.
- Entry/exit of major firms eg Japanese (Toyota Lexus) entry into high end car market intensified rivalry in this segment.
- Globalisation – usually associated with:

  (a) Industries based on natural resources, where supply is geographically scattered in concentrations eg oil;
  (b) Where low cost production is critical, so companies locate facilities in low cost countries
  (c) Where growth-oriented market-seeking companies are pushing hard to gain a significant competitive position in as many attractive country markets as they can eg Japanese in cars, electrical goods.
  (d) Changes in cost and efficiency, eg lower costs emerge because of economies of scale or technological process innovation; higher cost emerge because of sharply rising costs for a critical input, such as labour or raw materials or components or energy costs.
  (e) Emerging buyer preferences for a differentiated instead of a commodity product, or a standardised product instead of strongly differentiated ones (eg supermarket own brand labels on groceries instead of manufacturers' branded products).

Industry attractiveness is determined by five competitive forces, as described by Porter.

An organisation's environment is exceedingly complex, even the largest organisations may not have the time or resources to examine more than a fraction of the factors that might affect them. Not only is the organisation subjected to the effect of changes occurring in its immediate environment, such as its customers, trade unions or suppliers, it must also be aware of the more general influences which can affect the viability of the business. If an organisation is to be (or continue to be) successful it must at least attempt to ascertain the nature of the environment in which it operates and try to determine which elements of that environment represent *opportunities* and which represent *threats*. The analysis should also attempt to gain some insight into likely areas of change which may either adversely affect the organisation's operations or present it with new opportunities.

It is important to note here that the analysis of the external environment and the determination of the various opportunities offered by, and threats contained in that environment, may result in the need to modify the organisation's objectives.

A useful way of tackling the problem of environmental analysis is to follow the steps laid down by Johnson and Scholes. The process, presented below in a modified form, is sequential and moves from the consideration of general influences on the organisation's activities, through to the examination of specific forces which affect it.

The steps involved in this analysis of the environment are as follows:

1. Audit of general environmental influences: The organisation's attempts to identify which of the many and varied general environmental influences have affected its performance in the past, and which are likely to do so in the future.
2. Establish the nature of the general environment: The organisation establishes an initial view of the uncertainty (or otherwise) of its general environment.
3. Structural analysis: This involves a detailed examination of the organisation's immediate competitive environment, in order to establish key forces in the environment, competitive position and opportunities and threats.

A model depicting the environmental factors can be shown below.

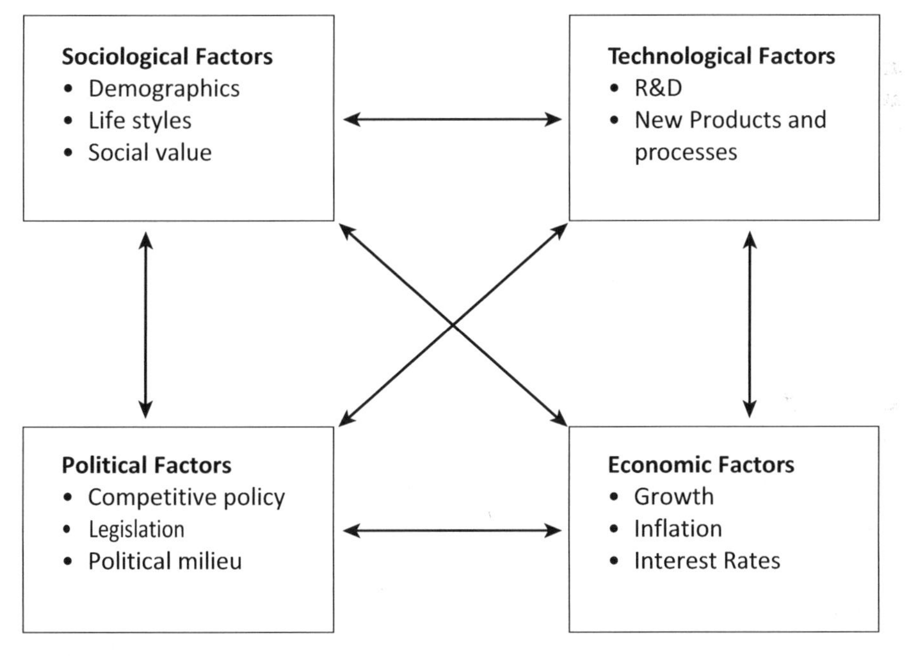

When it comes to the analysis of the business environment, Johnson and Scholes warn against a piecemeal approach (listing the environmental influences in a sort of statement of financial position) but it will suffice for purpose of illustration. They point out that listing the various environmental influences and attempting to gauge their respective impacts on the organisation is not a substitute for analysis. For one thing it ignores possible interrelationships between the variables. They recommend that the analysis should commence with "an initial view of the nature of the environment" in terms of its uncertainty. Because organisations are attempting to look ahead they are dealing with the future, which is inherently uncertain. The object of the exercise, then, is not to determine the future but to reduce this uncertainty.

The uncertainty of some elements in the environment is greater for some organisations than for others depending upon whether the conditions for the organisation are *static* and *simple*, or *dynamic* and *complex*. The more dynamic and complex they are, the more uncertainty the organisation faces and the more difficult the analysis.

The dynamism (or absence of it) of the environment is concerned with the rate and frequency of change, both of which are increasing. Rapid technological change creates problems eg obsolescence ... do we invest now and risk being out of date next year or do we wait for the better product which is surely just around the corner?

The complexity (or the simplicity) of the environment is the sheer diversity and possible interconnection of environmental influences (eg multinational companies have to deal with cultural problems, exchange problems – compare the activities of Coca-Cola with those of a local soft drinks producer, whose environment would be much less complex) or from the specialist knowledge required to deal with the environmental variables (eg handling the problems of a developing nuclear industry – problems of toxic waste disposal, loss of appropriately skilled people to the USA, technological advancement, etc.).

For example, how uncertainty exists where conditions are static and simple eg a local newspaper in a small town. There is little change (little serious competition, if any; relatively static market), and relatively few influences which could not be predicted. In these situations, say Johnson and Scholes, extrapolation techniques are useful for analysing the environment... the future can reasonably assumed to be a function of the past, with perhaps a few minor adjustments.

Compare this with the situation where conditions are increasingly dynamic and complex. Here, managers cannot rely on the past as a guide to the future and may employ 'inspirational' methods to help them interpret the changing conditions.

However, it does not seem reasonable to assume that major changes in the general environment would affect all organisations in the same industry (eg a change in interest rates) and that this particular 'first pass' at analysis would be more suited to the 'task' or immediate environment of the organisation in question.

Johnson and Scholes maintain that there is a much greater urgency or relevance in the analysis of the organisation's immediate competitive environment.

The implications for strategic planning

It is never possible to forecast the future with certainty. However there are a number of means by which organisations take account of the impact of exogenous variables in their strategic plans.

- Using structured methods such as scenario planning and sensitivity analysis, which can be used to quantify the impact of different factors on the long-term plan.
- Being sensitive to changes through constant scanning of the environment.
- Quantifying the probability and impact over a shorter timescale and taking a more general view of the long-term direction.
- Precise objectives are not specified for the longer term.

- Developing strategy incrementally in a more dynamic process which allows for flexibility in response to changes in the environment.
- Establishing wide ranging discussions inside and outside the organisation, in particular with operational staff who are closer to customers and may understand more about the environment than senior managers.
- Reviewing the accuracy of information on a continuous basis to improve forecasting ability.

1.10 Brand awareness, company profile and impact on business performance

Companies want to be successful and can take different strategic routes to achieve this. One of the most powerful ways of achieving this is to have a known brand. This means that there are many customers and potential customers that know the company.

EG Learning example 1.3

Think of a brand that you know and are loyal to. This could be your supermarket, the clothes you wear, the toothpaste you use, amongst many others. Think why you consistently use this brand and write your points down.

A brand:

1. Helps influence choice. It make it easier to choose the next product you buy, if you trust the brand.
2. Creates loyalty. You are likely to buy repeatedly once you are happy with the brand.
3. Influences prices. You are likely to be less price sensitive if you believe in the brand.
4. Differentiates. You believe you are getting something different to other products.

In terms of company performance having a respected brand helps:

- Charge higher prices
- Sustain revenue streams via product volumes
- The acceptability of new product launches.

On the other side there may be extra costs of:

1. Product development – to be able to stay ahead.
2. Marketing – to keep the brand name in people's minds.
3. After-sales service – so that customers trust the brand if there are any queries or complaints.

So long as the brand name is respected and customers are happy then the effect on performance of a good brand is likely to be beneficial. If a brand is tainted by bad news though, such as Andersens the accountants, which, despite being a big accountancy firm, was brought down by being involved in scandals like Enron.

Andersens was Enron's auditor and it missed some major problems with Enron. This meant its brand became tainted and it no longer exists.

1.11 The role of ethics

It is increasingly recognised that ethics, and – in particular – following appropriate ethical guidelines, are critical to the modern business organisation (corporate ethics or business ethics) and to the modern professional (professional ethics and personal ethics).

Ethical considerations should, as recognised by the P5 syllabus, be considered in business strategy, as well as in day-to-day business activities and transactions. A company's mission should include the recognition of ethical issues and managers responsible for strategic decision-making, therefore, are therefore obliged to apply ethical considerations to their decisions.

Some students confuse ethics and law: in fact these are related and sometimes overlapping, but separate concepts. Both ethics and law are essentially normative systems, ie systems that are concerned with minimum standards of behaviour in a social context. However, law is a mandatory system, whereas ethics represent an aspirational system: an example of where these two systems overlap is where human rights are enshrined in law.

Corporate ethics concern the interaction between corporate behaviour and ethics. Establishing and embedding corporate policies here might include, amongst other matters, consideration of:

- Bribery
- Environmental and sustainability considerations
- Equal opportunities
- Health and safety
- Political lobbying
- Safety issues particular to the sector(s)
- Support for the local community, cultural activities etc.
- The company might also be expected to establish policies relating to the ethical behaviour of individual employees, but some employees will also be bound by the ethical code(s) established by their profession.

Ensuring that the expected ethical standards are understood and disseminated, corporate ethical codes are often produced and distributed by companies. Such codes usually collate the various ethical policies developed by the company. Best practice in corporate ethics (and corporate ethical codes) includes:

- Ensuring that the documents are not written in a lengthy or overly-prescriptive manner: following the spirit, or principles, of ethical policies is more important than a legalistic approach to compliance
- Providing examples within these documents of relevant ethical dilemmas, and
- Ensuring that senior management in the company lead by example on ethical issues.

The potential reputational damage of unethical conduct or practices represents a significant risk for organisations. It should also be noted that businesses are concerned with profit-making, so there can be tensions between business practice and ethical considerations. That said, rejecting profitable but unethical business opportunities is what is demanded of the ethically-aware organisation. This emphasis on ethics does not necessarily pose a tension with profit-making: embedding ethics in an organisation's mission, business model, organisational strategy and decision-making processes is seen as allowing a more sustainable approach to business and assists in managing the reputation risk that unethical conduct poses: ie an ethical approach to business can help safeguard future profits.

1.11.1 Ethical threats and conflicts

Ethical threats apply to accountants whether they are working as an employee or are involved in providing professional services, such as audit or tax advice.

Ethical conflicts are situations where there may not be one clear course of action that is ethical, or morally, right. Sometimes such situations can be very difficult to solve. In some cases, such situations may be avoidable which solves the problem. For example, conflicts of interest may be avoidable by taking adequate precautions in advance.

1.11.2 Codes of ethics

A Code of Ethics has been developed by the International Federation of Accountants (IFAC) with the aim of promoting consistency and providing regional and national bodies with a starting point for developing their own codes.

ACCA's Code of Ethics

The *ACCA's Code of Ethics and Conduct* sets out five fundamental principles with which its members must comply. These are explained below.

Objectivity
Objectivity is a state of mind where the only matters considered when making a decision, or forming an opinion, are those matters relevant to the situation. Personal issues, conflicts, or the influence of others must be ignored, so that the final opinion given is fair, impartial, and justified.

For example, when deciding how to account for a business transaction, the only matters of relevance should be the facts of the situation and the relevant accounting standards. The effect on company profits is irrelevant to deciding on the correct accounting treatment.

Integrity
This principle requires members to act in a straightforward and honest manner in all their business and professional relationships. Someone with integrity inspires trust because they stick to their principles in all situations. What those principles are will depend on their personal ethical beliefs.

In a professional sense, someone with integrity would be expected to uphold the values of the profession, abide by relevant laws and guidance (but seek to change those laws and guidance where they are not consistent with the principles they believe in), and not look the other way when unethical practices are going on etc.

Due care and competence
Members have a duty to maintain their professional knowledge and skills. They should act in accordance with applicable technical and professional standards when providing professional services. Professionals should always carry out their work with professional care, and should only accept work that they believe they have the skills and experience to undertake properly.

Professional behaviour
All members of the ACCA should respect the laws and regulations of the profession. They should never act in a manner that would discredit their profession.

Confidentiality
Members should respect the confidentiality of their clients and not disclose any client information to third parties unless they have a legal or professional right or duty to disclose. Accountants will gain knowledge of client information that is private. Such information should not be disclosed to anyone else, unless:

- The law demands it (eg suspicion of money laundering, terrorism).
- The client allows it.
- It is in the public interest.

Corporate codes of ethics

Companies and groups often also develop their own codes of ethics which sets out the ethical values of the company for employees and other interested parties such as customers, suppliers, shareholders and the wider community. They are useful in that they set the standard of behaviour expected from employees and provide guidance in certain situations. The key factor in a company adopting a code of ethics is that it is seen to be adopted by directors and senior management, ie the tone is set from the top. If directors are seen to be acting ethically, then this sends a message that employees are also expected to behave ethically. Ethical behaviour then becomes part of the culture of the organisation.

1.12 The role of government policy

The ways in which government policies might influence future corporate strategy are difficult to forecast.

Government policies in a number of areas will be ingredients in the political environment facing enterprises.

The performance of many business operations is influenced very strongly by the statutory and regulatory environment – legislation, that affects business enterprises in domestic, national or international dimensions: local bylaws (for example, planning permission, construction of roads, licences), labour legislation (such as safety at work, employee protection, redundancy payments), trade union legislation,

consumer protection legislation, company legislation, taxation legislation, antitrust (monopolies) legislation and rulings, trade legislation (eg countries restricted for export), business legislation (eg contract and agency law), social legislation such as welfare benefits.

At a more general level, laws are passed that enable government to levy taxes which will have an impact both on demand and the organisation's profits.

There are special regulatory regimes for particular industries or sectors, such as nuclear energy, transport, broadcasting or food.

Principle

Impact of government regulations and policies on performance and measurement

Key Learning Points

- Understand the role of corporate planning in clarifying corporate objectives, making strategic decisions and checking progress towards objectives. (A1a, A1b)
- Be able to compare planning and control at the strategic and operational levels. (A1c)
- Know the ways in which stakeholder groups operate and be able to explain how they affect the organisation and its strategy formulation and implementation. (A5a)

What's the story?

Stop and think through the 'story' of this chapter and how it links with other chapters (use the Overview to help).

Learning example solutions

EG Solution 1.1

Maintain overall GP of 40%	GP% per month vs budget GP% by product per month vs budget
Increase customer satisfaction each year	Number/Value of repeat orders per customer
Be the most innovative company in the market	Number of products launched per month Number/value of new products as a percentage of sales Number of patents per month

EG Solution 1.2

Porter's model can be used to help clarify the overall business strategy. The model provides a framework to discuss areas where business techniques and systems can yield competitive advantage.

The advantages may be in defending the organisation against the forces or by attacking and influencing them in its favour. Management should use the model to determine which of the forces pose a threat to the future of the business.

By ranking these threats in terms of intensity and immediacy, the most critical can then be considered in terms of how information technology or systems can be used to gain advantage or avoid disadvantage.

EG Solution 1.3

Your solution will depend on what you chose but see if your answer includes any of the following:

- Convenience
- Advertising/image
- Reliability
- Performance
- The reaction of others (if a sports car, for example)
- Price

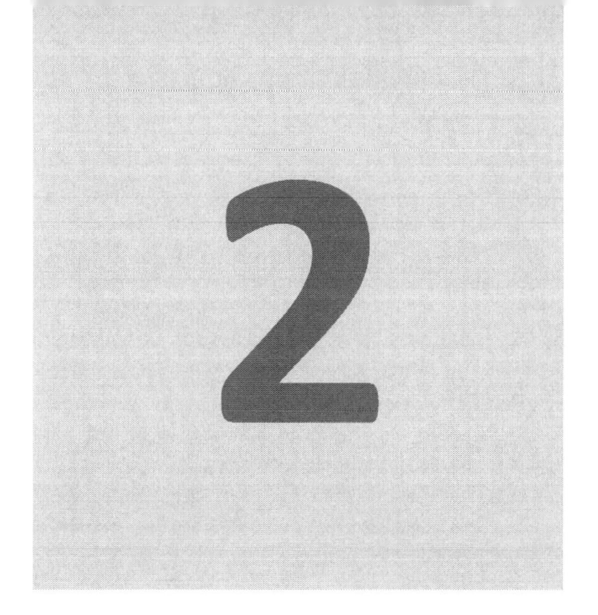

Performance Management and Control

Context

Performance management is central to this paper and we will look to understand that better. We are trying to achieve the best performance that we can for an organisation, so need to plan for this and monitor and control what happens.

3Q

1. Can you list the stages in the budgeting process?
2. What is 'beyond budgeting'?
3. What are the main features of not-for-profit organisations that should be kept in mind while preparing budgets for such organisations?

2.1 The problem with the traditional budgeting systems

The annual budget is one of the most fundamental performance measures used in companies. The starting point is to take last year's performance and then to try to improve. The annual budget is designed to:

- Turn business plans into figures
- Allow co-ordination between divisions
- Motivate managers
- Measure performance.

The budgeting process has a broad range of outcomes and will tend to reflect the complex nature of the modern organisation. The role of the budget and budgetary control include:

- Forecasting, planning and coordinating future activities
- Providing a motivational device
- Communicating the organisation's short-term goals to its members
- A system of authorisation
- A means of performance evaluation and control (efficiency and effectiveness).

Overall a budget is a quantitative model or summary of the expected consequences of the organisation's operating activities.

Any differences between actual results and the budget plan are called variances. Variances are part of a larger control system for monitoring results.

Budgeting brings together both planning and control as follows:

Planning	Identify organisational objectives and short-term goals
	Develop long-term strategy and short-term plans
	Develop a master budget
Control	Measure and assess performance using variances
	Re-evaluate objectives, goals, strategy and plans

The following are typical examples of the elements of a budgeting process.
The elements would be developed into a flow chart allowing managers to identify key relationships and information flows. Complex multi-divisional organisations are likely to prepare a range of consolidated budgets. (Atkinson et al 1996)

1. Organisation goals
2. Sales plan
3. Capital spending plan
4. Inventory policy
5. Production plan
6. Productive capacity planning
7. Materials purchasing plan
8. Labour hiring and training plan
9. Administrative and discretionary spending plan
10. Expected financial results
11. Statement of expected cash flows

The budgeting process will follow the organisational pattern of authority, responsibility and level of empowerment (top-down or bottom-up?). As previously identified, the organisational structure will tend to determine whether responsibility centres are treated as cost centres, revenue centres, profit centres or investments centres. The definition of the centres is likely to have a distinct impact on the application of the budget. Production budgets would, at the initial stage, be based on standard costing.

The design of the budget process is often identified a mechanical activity; however it is vital to recognises that is also a human activity. The degree of senior management control will be an important factor in the success of a budget. Authoritative budgeting, ie top-down, will tend to stretch targets. Participative budgeting, ie bottom-up, might lack direction and clarity. Consultative budgeting may in reality be pseudo participation. There is a great deal of conflicting research published on how participation influences performance.

It would be expected to find that participation in budget setting leads to:

- Improved attitude towards the budget system
- Standards becoming more relevant
- Improved communication
- Higher motivation
- Higher performance.

There has been a growth in research published into the adoption of participative budgeting.

2.1.1 Stages in the budgeting process

1. Communicating details of budget policy and guidelines to those people responsible for the preparation of budgets
2. Determining the factor that restricts output (limiting factors)
3. Preparation of the sales budget
4. Initial preparation of various budgets
5. Negotiation of budgets with superiors
6. Coordination and review of budgets
7. Final acceptance of budgets
8. Ongoing review of budgets.

Learn

Central to planning is the budgeting process. The budget is a financial plan of the organisational future. It typically comprises a budget profit and loss account, a budget statement of financial position and a budget cash flow statement for the organisation as a whole, as well as for its key sub-units, be they divisions, research laboratories, factories, sales organisations, etc. Organisations determine on a 'need-to-know' basis how far down in the organisational hierarchy they want to draw up complete budget profit and loss statements for organisational sub-units.

Sometimes a factory only budgets costs (especially when it is not involved in the process of selling and has little influence over revenues), and a sales office only budgets revenues and the costs of running the office. It would often not budget the costs of goods sold for the products that it sells, because those would be controlled by the factories that supply its products. In this case it would make sense for a larger entity, for example, a division that controls both the sales office and the supplying factories, to budget profits because this division is responsible for revenues and costs (and, by implication, profit and loss).

In the debate around strategic management accounting, budgeting has been criticised for being too administratively oriented, not producing enough commercially-relevant information, and being too time consuming.

In practice, budgeting processes that take up nine months prior to the financial year for which they are meant are not unusual. Typically, it takes a long time to collect cost and revenue estimates from numerous budget holders, co-ordinate them, and, finally, communicate a coherent plan.

2.1.2 Managerial use of budgets and potential biases

The management should attempt to distinguish between preparing and trying to achieve a budget target. Consider the potential causes for biases if budgets are used as forecasts. If the reward system of the company is based on performance relative to budget there is a clear risk of slack being introduced. The bias may be introduced by a subjective view that past history will continue eg sales will continue to grow at historic rates. During periods of insecurity of some managers, they may feel obliged to promise better future performance to protect themselves in the short-term.

The degree of difficulty introduced into the budget can impact on the actual performance of the budget. A budget level at or beyond the "optimal" will tend to be difficult to achieve and the increased level of difficulty could lead to a significant and growing adverse variance (Otley).

Potential causes for biases if budgets are used as targets are varied. Budgets will have no motivational effect unless the managers involved 'own' personal targets ie accept them. Demanding budgets are more relevant than the less difficult targets, but negative attitudes result if they are too difficult. Consideration needs to be given to the point where the budget target is no longer accepted. The more demanding the budget target the better the result achieved, up to a point.

For an effective system of budgetary control to exist the company must ensure that the management's authority is clear, that managers both accept the budgets and consider them to be attainable, and appropriate budgetary control information must be provided to and understood by managers.

Budgets have several roles, the most important being forecasting, planning and coordinating future activities. Therefore a budget is a control instrument.

IE Illustrative example 2.1

Trevethoe Logistics operates a fleet of transport vehicles. It estimates that it will carry packages for 40,000 miles at an average price of $1 per mile. However, past experience suggested that the total miles run would amount to 250% of the paid miles. At the beginning of April, Trevethoe Logistics employed ten drivers and decided that this number would be adequate for the month ahead.

The following cost estimates were available:

Employment costs of a driver	$1,000 per month
Fuel costs	$0.08 per mile run
Variable overhead costs	$0.05 per mile run
Fixed overhead costs	$9,000 per month

Revenue of $36,100 was generated by carrying packages for 38,000 miles. The total actual mileage was 105,000 miles. Other costs amounted to:

Employment costs of drivers	$9,600
Fuel costs	$8,820
Variable overhead costs	$5,040
Fixed overhead costs	$9,300

The saving in the cost of drivers was due to one driver leaving during the month; she was not to be replaced until early May.

Budgeted and actual profit and loss account for April

	Budget (B)	Actual (A)
	$	$
Sales	40,000	36,100
Less costs:		
Employment	10,000	9,600
(B: 10 $1,000)		
Fuel	8,000	8,820
(B: 40,000 2.5 8c)		
Variable overheads	5,000	5,040
(B: 40,000 2.5 5c)		
Fixed overheads	9,000	9,300
Profit	8,000	3,340
Actual profit	3,340	
Profit variance (adverse)	4,660	

Conclusion: We can see that the budget has not been met and the individual reasons for this. The managers of Trevethoe Logistics can use this information to try to control the issues and make changes to improve in the future.

The master budget aggregates all the information using the three major documents in accounting: statement of financial position, statement of profit or loss and cash flow statement.

Ideally, budgets should be closely adapted to the organisation structure, the management philosophy and the managers' information needs.

Since budgets "interact" with people, and employees' goals do not always coincide with those of the company, research has shown that managers need to be aware of behavioural aspects.

2.1.3 Maximising the benefits of budgeting

In order to get the most from the budget process, an organisation should do the following:

- Prepare budgets after the corporate strategy has been set.
- Conflicts between departments should be identified and resolved as soon as possible.
- Realistic short-term targets should be set.
- Managers should be committed to reaching targets.
- Managers should be responsible for expenditure.

- Any reports produced by the Management Information System (MIS) should be accurate and timely.

 **Learn**

2.2 Alternative types of budget systems

There are a number of alternatives to the annual budget that have been developed.

2.2.1 Zero-based Budgeting (ZBB)

A problem with the annual, incremental budget is that departments are given money each year because they have been given it in the past. Zero-based budgeting is designed to eliminate this wastage.

Definition

Zero-based budgeting is a method of budgeting that requires each cost element to be specifically justified, as though the activities to which the budget relates were being undertaken for the first time. Without approval, the budget allowance is zero.

It is important that managers involved in ZBB examine their current practices very carefully. Questions they should ask themselves include:

- Is the activity essential? What would happen if it ceased?
- Is the provision of the activity at the correct level?
- Are there other alternatives for achieving the same effect?

It is especially useful for:

- Service departments such as stores, maintenance, marketing, finance which pursue different projects each year
- Discretionary costs such as research and development (R&D)
- Public sector organisations such as local authorities
- A shakedown in an industry
- Possible mergers.

There are four distinct stages in the implementation of ZBB, which starts with the idea that each manager begins with a zero base of resources. The manager only receives resources if they can be justified.

1. Managers should specify for their responsibility centres those activities that can be individually evaluated.
2. Each of the individual activities is then described in a decision package. The decision package should state the costs and revenues expected from the given activity. It should be drawn up in such a way that the package can be evaluated and ranked against other packages.
3. Each decision package is evaluated and ranked usually using cost/benefit analysis.
4. The resources are then allocated to the various packages.

Strengths of ZBB

- Responds to changes in the environment, so that resources should be allocated efficiently and economically
- Should result in more efficient use of resources, as inefficient or obsolete operations can be identified and discontinued
- Managers are forced to consider alternative methods of achieving their objectives
- ZBB leads to increased staff involvement at all levels. This should lead to better communication and motivation
- Attention is focused on outputs in relation to value for money
- Knowledge and understanding of the cost behavior patterns of the organisation will be enhanced.

Weaknesses of ZBB

- Requires a lot of management time and cost involved in preparing the budget each year
- Involves participation by managers, so needs a suitable culture and managers and employees may feel threatened
- It may emphasise short-term benefits to the detriment of long-term benefits
- The rankings of packages may be subjective where the benefits are of a qualitative nature
- It is difficult to compare and rank completely different types of activity
- Incremental costs and benefits of alternative courses of action are difficult to quantify accurately
- The budgeting process may become too rigid and the company may not be able to react to unforeseen opportunities or threats.

2.2.2 Rolling budgets

A problem with the annual, incremental budget is that it can quickly become unrealistic. This leads to the targets becoming unreachable and managers becoming demotivated.

The rolling budget is regularly updated based on actual performance by adding another accounting period (eg month or quarter) when the earliest accounting period has expired.

This should lead to more realistic targets. The aim of such a budget is to keep tight control and always have an accurate budget for the next 12 months. This is suitable if accurate forecasts cannot be made, or for any area of business that needs tight control.

The major objection to rolling budgets is the time they take to update and that they are not particularly useful in a stable environment.

Also, they may lead to an increase in budgeting work which, in turn, leads to less control of the actual results. There is a danger that the budget may become the last budget 'plus or minus a bit'.

Strengths
- Useful in a dynamic environment
- Should be more realistic since includes actual events
- Should be better at motivating.

Weaknesses
- Requires time and effort to keep updating
- Managers may not see value in regular updating (if it diverts from the actual business).

2.2.3 Flexed budgets

A problem with the annual, incremental budget is that cost centres are given the same amount of money to spend regardless of activity.

Flexed budgets adjust the target to reflect the amount of work to be carried out and can identify if the company is likely to have any spare capacity.

The major objection to flexed budgets is that it is difficult to motivate managers to achieve a target if they do not know what the target is until the end of the period. Flexed budgets also assume that the standard cost per unit has been calculated correctly.

A further objection is that, if most costs are fixed then they are not particularly useful.

Strength
- Allows planning for potential spare capacity/idle time.

Weaknesses
- Limited usefulness if most costs are fixed
- Little benefit if the environment is not dynamic

2.2.4 Activity-based Budgeting (ABB)

Definition

Activity-based budgeting is defined as a method of budgeting based on an activity framework and utilising cost driver data in the budget setting and variance feedback processes and comes from the principles of activity-based costing.

The basic ideas are:

- The cost of an activity can be calculated accurately
- This can be compared with the value the activity adds to the customer.

If the cost of an activity is larger than its value added, then:

- The cost of the activity could be reduced
- The activity could be stopped/outsourced
- The price to the customer could be increased.

In addition, managers can identify if activities in one department are adding to costs in another (eg poor quality products needing to be replaced, leading to more distribution costs).

The idea behind activity based budgeting is that they focus on critical success factors and the activities which must be performed well in order to be successful.

This means that as a company's strategy changes the budget will also change.

Since ABB focuses on the whole activity there is more chance of getting it right first time (ie it links up with TQM).

Strengths

- Links budgets in with the overall strategy of the organisation
- Identifies critical success factors
- Concentrates on activities rather than individual cost centres, allowing for the "big picture" to be seen
- Can improve the commitment of managers.

Weaknesses

- Requires resources and time to prepare to establish an ABB system, for example to identify the key activities and their cost drivers
- ABB might not be appropriate for the organisation and its activities and cost structures
- A problem with ABB can be to identify clear individual responsibilities for activities
- It could be argued that, in the short term, many overhead costs are not controllable and do not vary directly with changes in the volume of activity for the cost driver. The only cost variances to report would be fixed overhead expenditure variances for each activity.

Principle

Alternative methods of budgeting, their need, underlying principles, strengths and weaknesses

2.3 Incremental budgeting

An incremental budget starts with the previous period's budget or actual results, and adds (or subtracts) an incremental amount to cover inflation and other known changes.

It is suitable for stable businesses, where costs are not expected to change significantly. There should be good cost control and limited discretionary costs.

Strengths

- Easy to prepare
- Assuming that the historic figures are acceptable, only the increment needs to be justified

Weaknesses

- Does not look for ways to improve – builds in previous problems and inefficiencies
- Is only suitable if current operations are efficient already
- Encourages slack in the budget setting process

It has also been argued that budgets:

- Add little value
- Are used excessively in measuring performance
- Are used as a method to communicate the values of the organisation rather than as a means of financial control
- Are too inwardly focussed
- Are a major barrier to change.

This has emerged because there is growing dissatisfaction among executives and business managers with the traditional approach to budgets.

The argument for abolishing budgets, referred to as 'beyond budgeting', was put forward by Hope and Fraser in 1997. The aim is to help companies to design and implement budget free performance management systems that are more useful in today's competitive conditions. In order to compete in the information age, companies (especially knowledge based companies) must go beyond budgeting as they have most of their value in intellectual assets, such as 'know-how'.

Maximising the value of these assets will do more for shareholder value than maximising the value of tangible assets.

Budgeting has also been criticised for inducing a culture of complacency with respect to performance targets. Managers whose departments perform well against budget may not be willing to push their subordinates to achieve better than budgeted results because, firstly, budgets tend to reward fulfilment of expectations, not over-fulfilment, and, secondly, over-fulfilment may lead to heightened expectations in subsequent budgeting rounds.

Managers may thus be tempted to initially hide the effects of process improvements and other cost savings and only use them to improve the financial results of their units gradually – as and when future budgets demand such improvements.

At the heart of the detection of organisational slack and similar problems lie the ways in which budgets are used and the kinds of expectations organisational members have of them.

A diverse group of organisations, that have come together in the Consortium for Advanced Manufacturing International, has formed a sub-committee, known as the Beyond Budgeting Round Table which is specifically concerned with improving the budgeting process.

The Round Table is exploring ways of using budgets more flexibly in ways that alleviate budgets' performance reducing effects, for example, by introducing 'stretch targets', and finding ways of overcoming the gaming and creation of slack that often occurs in the process of agreeing performance targets.

A commentary in the British newspaper, The Observer makes reference to the Beyond Budgeting Round Table.

They argue that using rolling budgets and non-financial performance indicators should:

- Create a culture based on beating the competition (since goals are related to external benchmarks) rather than simply gaining more internal resources
- Rewards can be team-based, increasing the amount of motivation
- It is easier to judge the performance of people lower down the organisation (who are closer to the customers)
- It empowers more junior managers, meaning they can respond more quickly to changes in the external environment

EG Learning example 2.1

An extensive literature on the behavioural aspects of budgeting discusses the propensity of managers to create budgetary slack.

You are required to explain three ways in which managers may attempt to create budgetary slack, and how senior managers can identify these attempts to distort the budgetary system.

2.4 The 'Beyond budgeting' model – Private sector

In the private sector, managers are forced to consider current and future opportunities and threats, particularly where rolling monthly forecasts of financial performance operate together with a focus on other non-financial 'value drivers'. In essence, the 'beyond budgeting' model entails devolved managerial responsibility where power and responsibility go hand in hand. The view held by proponents of the beyond budgeting model is that the following benefits will accrue as a result of its successful application by management:

- It creates and fosters a performance climate based on competitive success. Goals are agreed via reference to external benchmarks as opposed to internally-negotiated fixed targets. Managerial focus shifts from beating other managers for a slice of resources to beating the competition.
- It motivates people by giving challenges, responsibilities and clear values as guidelines. Rewards are team-based, in recognition of the fact that no single person can act alone to achieve goals.
- It devolves performance responsibilities to operational management who are closer to the 'action'. This uses the 'know-how' of individuals and teams interfacing with the customer, which in turn enables a far more rapid adaptation to changing market needs.

- It empowers operational managers to act by removing resource constraints. Key ratios are set rather than detailed line-by-line budgets. For example, gearing and liquidity ratios may be used to show there is enough cash in the bank to meet liabilities. Local access to resources is thus based on agreed parameters rather than line-by-line budget authorisations. This is aimed at speeding up the response to environmental threats and enabling quick exploitation of new opportunities.
- It establishes customer-orientated teams that are accountable for profitable customer outcomes. These teams agree resource and service-level requirements with service departments via the establishment of service-level agreements.
- It creates transparent and open information systems throughout the organisation, which should provide fast, open and distributed information to facilitate control at all levels. The IT system is crucial in flexing the key performance indicators as part of the rolling forecast process.

IE Illustrative example 2.2

At ALDI, retail success is achieved by a process of decentralisation and delegation, using 'cell divisions'. When a certain size is reached in a region (eg 50 or 60 stores), a division – in the form of a new company – is created. The new division has its own bookkeeping and includes all the functions that are present in the parent company. The constant quest to find alternative solutions to day-to-day issues has often reduced the overall costs of the individual ALDI divisions. It also helps faster decision-making and puts the company in a better position to interact with customers.

2.5 The public sector

The legal framework of public sector organisations would probably prevent such a system being introduced. As with all alternatives, the success of a particular process depends on the needs of the individual organisation. The alternative of the beyond budgeting model places considerable emphasis on the need for organisational, managerial and cultural changes in order that it may be successfully applied by organisations.

This will present considerable behavioural challenges and individual managers might become overwhelmed by the complexity of decision-making in such an unregulated decision-making environment.

In the public sector, the budget process inevitably has considerable influence on organisational processes, and represents the financial expression of policies resulting from politically motivated goals and objectives. Yet the reality of life for many public sector managers is an increased pressure to perform in a resource-constrained environment, while also being subjected to growing competition. In essence, a public sector budget:

- establishes the level of income and expenditure
- authorises that expenditure, once agreed, out of the planned income
- acts as a control on expenditure and income
- communicates policies and plans

- focuses attention on the future
- motivates managers and staff.

While these issues may be common with the private sector, a number of issues arise which are specific to the public sector. For example, UK local authorities are prevented by law from borrowing funds for revenue purposes or budgeting for a deficit. If the beyond budgeting model is to allow greater freedom for managers then it will take a considerable change of mind-set in the public sector to achieve the flexible agenda envisaged, especially where such flexibility would involve considerable and increased delegation to managers. One question is whether, from a behavioural perspective, such managers are capable of making this change, as it would entail the adoption of a radically different approach. Local authority financial regulations also tend to prevent the transfer of funds from one budget head to another without compliance with various rules and regulations. These rules (expressed in the financial regulations of public sector organisations) will be consistent with the policies of the organisation and are designed to prevent expenditure on items, such as permanent staff, where such costs would go beyond the budget year and represent a commitment of future resources.

Budgets in the public sector tend to concentrate on planning for one financial year ahead. Attempts are being made by UK central government, through the comprehensive spending review, to place an emphasis on the longer-term. However, considerable difficulties exist within the individual organisations that make up the public sector when creating a budget system that reflects longer-term objectives and goes beyond the annual cycle. It also remains to be seen how the relatively new system of resource accounting in central government will fit into the budgeting framework.

Traditional methods of budgeting in the public sector centre on the bid system and incremental budgeting. These approaches focus on changes at the margin and generally reflect acceptance of the budget base from the previous year. This is partly a reflection of the size and complexity of public sector organisations, but also the internal political power of large departments, which protect their positions through their relative strength. Bid systems also minimise conflict, as debate and power struggles are only concerned with the 'incremental' items. More advanced approaches are represented within financial planning systems, and include such concepts as zero-based budgeting and planned programme budgeting systems with a timeframe greater than one year. Whether the public sector can adapt to the concept of greater flexibility - which lies at the heart of beyond budgeting - remains a matter of ongoing debate. Such an adaptation would require a mind-set which not only moves away from control but also requires a reduction in the internal political power of large departments which has been at the heart of public sector budgeting for many years. The desire to generate improved performance - essentially considered the driver for the beyond budgeting model - is present in the public sector evidenced in initiatives such as key performance indicators and 'best value' plans. But this is not matched by a desire for the flexibility inherent in the model. In terms of beyond budgeting, managers in such organisations are likely to remain constrained by the inability of their organisation to change.

Conclusion

The beyond budgeting model has particular relevance for knowledge-based companies which are increasingly a feature of a developed economy. Other companies may see specific benefits in such a system, given the rapidly changing environment in which they also operate. These changes will not be introduced without conflict and difficulty due to the challenges faced in introducing change. Such challenges may be beyond the achievement of the public sector, due to the expression in the budget of politically-motivated policies and objectives developed within a complex legal and financial framework. For the successful application of the beyond budgeting model in both private and public sectors, then this must be underpinned by a considerable organisational, cultural and managerial change.

EG Learning example 2.2

What are the main differences between traditional budgeting and beyond budgeting?

2.6 Budgeting in not-for-profit (NFP) organisations

Not-for-profit organisations include schools and universities, social clubs, sports clubs, sports governing bodies, hospitals, museum/library/arts organisations, government organisations/local authorities and charities.

The main features of importance when preparing budgets in NFP organisations are:

- No profit motive, but they still need to control costs.
- Many of the benefits arising from expenditure by these bodies are non-quantifiable.

So how can measurable budgets be prepared which meet the organisation's objectives?

- Often revenue is not generated and there is a fixed budget for spending within which they have to keep (ie a capital rationing problem). 'Value for money' is often quoted as an objective here but it does not get round the problem of measuring 'value'.
- Multiple stakeholders give rise to multiple objectives, so there is a need to prioritise/compromise (eg hospital – patients, staff, government, taxpayers, local community, society at large, contractors, management, donors/contributors, etc.).
- Objectives may be difficult to define, may change as a result of the political process and may be achievable in different ways.

A budget in the public sector:

- Establishes income as well as expenditure
- Authorises expenditure
- Acts as a control on expenditure
- Communicates plans to staff.

Budgets tend to concentrate on planning for one year ahead. Attempts have been made to link expenditure in the longer term.

Incremental budgeting is traditionally used. This focuses on the change at the margin and reflects the size, complexity and internal power of public sector bodies in setting budget targets.

Other budgeting approaches such as ZBB and planned programme budgeting systems (PPBS) have been used.

PPBS breaks work down into programmes designed towards achieving various objectives.

Several departments may contribute towards a single programme and budget targets may spread over more than one year which means used to achieve programmes should be efficient and cost effective.

There are a number of issues that arise from budgeting in the public sector:

- Some organisations are legally prevented from borrowing money.
- It may be difficult or impossible to move funds from one part of an organisation's budget to another (making them inflexible).
- Most public sector budgets simply focus on the coming fiscal year rather than a longer timescale.
- Incremental budgeting (with all its inherent problems) is still widely used.

Learn

Key Learning Points

- Know the difference between budgeting in non-for-profit organisations and profit-seeking organisations. (A2b)
- Understand the various budgeting methods and be able to evaluate, discuss and assess them. (A2a)
- Appreciate why organisations have moved to a beyond budgeting philosophy. (A2c)

What's the story?

Stop and think through the 'story' of this chapter and how it links with other chapters (use the Overview to help).

Learning example solutions

EG Solution 2.1

Budgetary slack is the situation where managers set a budget that is easily achievable. Managers may attempt to create budgetary slack in the following ways:

Overestimating expenditure. Managers may overestimate expenditure so that actual expenditure is likely to appear favourable in comparison with budget. This is most common in areas where costs are not directly linked to production volumes, ie, discretionary expenditure, or where the use of absorption costing obscures the behaviour of fixed costs.

Underestimating sales. Managers may underestimate sales volumes so that actual volumes appear favourable in comparison with budget.

Disguising slack. Managers may try to disguise budgetary slack in previous periods, allowing slack to be built in to current and future budgets. In the case of expenditure this can be achieved by ensuring that expenditure levels reach the budgeted levels by unnecessary spending, particularly towards the period-end. This will not cause favourable variances against budget, but will make it unlikely that adverse variances will arise. It is more difficult to disguise an underestimation of sales volumes, but can be done, for instance, by delaying the despatch and invoicing of sales into future periods.

Senior management can identify attempts to build in budgetary slack by comparing the trend of actual results against budget over time, comparing budgets in similar divisions or cost centres with one another, and by analysing sales volumes and expenditure either side of the period-end for unusual increases in spending or decreases in sales volumes. Sales underestimation can also be investigated by analysing predicted market growth and market share.

EG Solution 2.2

	Traditional	**Beyond budgeting**
Target	Incremental targets Fixed incentives	Stretch goals Relative rewards
Plan	Fixed Variance controls	Continuous planning KPIs
Resources	Central coordination	On demand Dynamic coordination
Culture	Central control Management of the numbers	Value creation Front line authority
Rewards	Individual departments have their own targets and therefore are unwilling to share expertise, skills and information	Viewed as one team Break down barriers with emphasis on learning

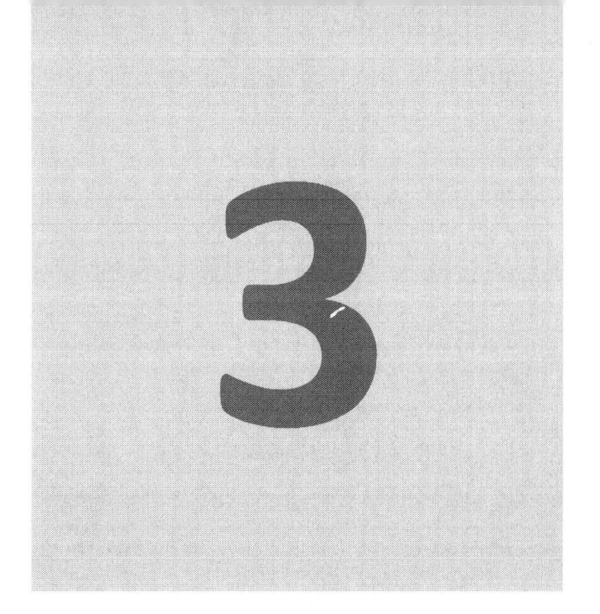

3

Organisational Structure and Business Integration

Context

The effect of the structure that an organisation adopts is important to decide how it will operate. The structure will be a response to a lot of external and internal factors, such as the locations it operates in and how complex its operations are.

Business integration relies on seeing the way that the people in an organisation are linked with the technology, operations and strategy. There are models that will help you see how they are integrated.

3Q

1. What is a virtual organisation?
2. Can you explain the concept of business integration?
3. What factors are likely to influence the methods and processes used to record and analyse information?

3.1 Organisational structures

The performance evaluation and management accounting system has to match closely the organisational structure that has been adopted.

	Functional	Divisional
Information needs	Tend to be centralised. Information on performance will be required at the top of the organisation for planning and control purposes. Data relating to a particular function is gathered together, passed up and only aggregated at the highest level. Feedback is given once the information has been aggregated.	These organisations tend to be more decentralised. There will be greater participation lower down the hierarchy in budgeting. Information needs to be available to those lower down the hierarchy.
Advantages for performance management	Easier to assess and control the performance of functions.	– Clearer responsibility for business units (divisions). Easier to assess divisional performance. – Depending on the degree of decentralisation, divisional managers can tailor performance systems to local needs.
Problems for performance management	Difficult to assess the performance of individual products or markets due to inability to ring fence costs and revenues. Makes this structure unsuitable for diversified organisations.	Allocation of head office costs. Impact of transfer pricing on divisional performance. Potential for a loss of goal congruence – the manager may improve divisional performance at the expense of company performance.

A diversified business with Strategic Business Units (SBUs) in very different business areas, with each SBU being a separate division, will have different performance management issues to a divisionalised multinational with different parts of the supply chain in different countries.

In the first case, as the SBUs are in unrelated markets, there is likely to be more devolved management, with the use of divisional performance measures and reliance on financial reporting measurement systems for control.

The divisionalised multinational needs a high level of interaction between business units, so senior management control is more important. The performance measurement system may be standardised, with detailed operational targets to aid communication between managers and provide a common 'language'.

Recent years have seen a move to 'flatten' organisation structures and a willingness to 'outsource' many functions which were traditionally carried on in-house.

Outsourcing and strategic alliances are examples of ways in which an organisation depends on relationships with other external organisations.

The virtual (or network) organisation is an extreme version of this. A virtual organisation consists of a group of companies, acting as one company, to fulfil a need in the marketplace. These companies collaborate, share skills, information, products, services, etc. in order to meet the goal of customer fulfilment.

IE Illustrative example 3.1

Many Internet companies operating as online retailers such as Amazon are virtual organisations – Amazon operates its website but relies on external book publishers, print on demand printers, book warehouses, couriers and credit card companies to deliver the rest of the customer experience in such a way that customer feels that they are dealing with one organisation, not many.

Amazon's partners are expected to provide information on, for example, stock availability, delivery times and promotional material.

Characteristics of a network organisation include:

- The decentralisation of control – control is normally exercised via shared goals and, in the case of inter-organisational collaborations, contractual arrangements
- The creation of more flexible patterns of working
- Greater empowerment of the workforce
- The displacement of hierarchy by team working
- The development of a greater sense of collective responsibility
- The creation of more collaborative relationships among co-workers
- Each party providing feedback as to how it is performing in relation to others.

3.2 Business Process Reengineering (BPR)

In today's competitive environment, organisations continually seek to improve their operations:

- Automation is the increasing use of machinery, the aim being to increase output through more mechanisation.
- Rationalisation is the reduction in labour in a process, the aim being to increase efficiency.

Definition

Business Process Reengineering (BPR) is the fundamental rethinking and radical redesign of business processes to achieve dramatic improvements in critical, contemporary measures of performance, such as cost, quality, service and speed. Improved customer satisfaction is often the primary aim.

Learn

BPR draws on the work of Porter's value chain, by viewing the organisation as a set of value adding processes rather than as a segmented structure of activities. The value chain is commonly used in BPR as a method to identify and analyse processes that are of strategic significance to the organisation.

The following are common features of the BPR process:

- Several jobs are combined into one.
- Workers make real decisions.
- Work is performed where it adds most value.
- Checks and controls are reduced.
- Reconciliation processes are reduced.
- Case managers provide points of contact.

A business process is a series of activities that are linked together in order to achieve given objectives. For example, credit control is a business process in which the separate activities are collecting customer information, storing this information, processing invoices, monitoring and updating customer accounts and issuing reminders.

Advantages of BPR

- BPR revolves around customer needs and helps to give an appropriate focus to the business.
- BPR provides cost advantages that assist the organisation's competitive position.
- BPR encourages a long-term strategic view of operational processes by asking radical questions about how things are done and how processes could be improved.
- BPR helps overcome the short sighted approaches that sometimes emerge from excessive concentration on functional boundaries. By focusing on entire processes the exercise can streamline activities throughout the organisation.
- BPR can help to reduce organisational complexity by eliminating unnecessary activities.

Criticisms of BPR

- BPR was sometimes seen (incorrectly) as a means of making small improvements in existing practices. In reality, it should be a more radical approach that questions whether existing practices make any sense in their present form.

- BPR was often perceived (incorrectly) as a single, once and for all, cost cutting exercise. In reality, it is not primarily concerned with cost cutting (though cost reductions often result) and should be regarded as ongoing rather than one-off. This misconception often creates hostility in the minds of staff who see the exercise as a threat to their security.
- BPR requires a far reaching and long-term commitment by management and staff. Securing this is not an easy task, and many organisations have rejected the whole idea as not worth the effort. In many cases business processes were not redesigned but merely automated.
- To make BPR work requires a focus on integrated processes (as discussed above) that often involves obliterating existing processes and creating new ones.
- Some companies became so focussed on improving internal processes that they failed to keep up with competitors' activities in the market.

Most companies are now more likely to talk about 'business process redesign' instead.

One of the principal accounting developments associated with BPR is activity-based costing (ABC).

BPR emphasises the importance of determining and reporting the costs of activities ie the emphasis is on the outputs of the operation rather than on the inputs.

Many organisations now use cost driver rates in order to measure efficiency. Elaborate ABC systems are needed to provide the depth and style of information that modern management operations need.

3.3 Business integration

The concept of business integration implies that all aspects and activities of the business operate in such a way as to ensure the most efficient and effective use of resources, in order to achieve organisational objectives. Therefore the business must be structured in a way which promotes goal congruence within and between business units and divisions.

Learn

When individual parts of the business (divisions or managers) pursue their own objectives, which may be in conflict with those of the organisation as a whole, this is referred to as sub-optimal behaviour and indicates that either the business structure or the performance management system, or both, need to be refined.

Porter's value chain, discussed earlier, is a key framework for understanding integrated processes and the relationships between them. An alternative framework for understanding integrated processes is the McKinsey 7S model, originally developed by Peters and Waterman. This model illustrates a business made up of 7 interrelated elements, each important in assuring achievement of organisational objectives, and all potentially influenced by changes in one or more of the other elements.

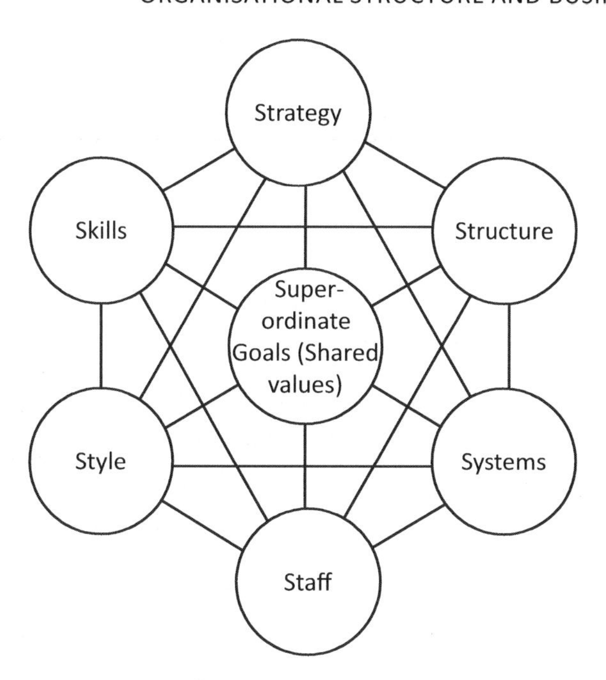

The hard elements are more easily identified and influenced by management:

- Strategy (the approach the company takes to achieving its objectives)
- Structure (the way in which the company is organised)
- Systems (the procedures put in place within the company)

The soft elements are less directly controllable by management and more open to subjective or unpredictable cultural influences:

- Style
- Staff
- Skills
- Super-ordinate goals/shared values

 **Learn**

3.4 Empowerment

Empowerment is the delegation of certain aspects of business decisions to those lower down in the hierarchy.

If staff are empowered to manage sectors or activities of a business, there will need to be a number of changes in the management accounting system which will enable the empowered individuals or teams to:

- make decisions
- receive feedback on their performance
- to have a budget for transparency and immediacy
- have targeted information to allow comparison across the organisation

- provide financial and non-financial information relevant to each empowered team of members of staff.

Thus the information that empowers the staff to manage sectors of the business has to be available when required and understandable. This is likely to rely on the use of IT networks to deliver the information to the staff. Hence the management accounting system needs to be built into these networks so that staff can gain access day to day.

3.5 Service industries and MIS

Service providers do not have a physical product so have always had to base competitive advantage on less tangible customer benefits, such as soundness of advice given, attitude of staff, ambience of premises, speed of service and flexibility/ responsiveness.

There are two key differences between the products of manufacturing companies and those of service businesses in terms of measuring and controlling performance which will affect the information needs of those organisations.

Intangibility: The output is the performance of a service rather than a tangible good

Heterogeneity: Heavy reliance on human input to meet the variability of customer requirements

3.6 Management accounting data: Instant access

Computer science and other IT developments continue to make it cheaper to store data and to make it accessible, and shareable, more quickly and easily. Data (information) can be in the form of, for example:

- Spreadsheets
- Word processing documents
- Emails
- Presentations
- Databases
- Graphics
- Audio files/voice mails

Data storage and data backup could variously be on-site, via the businesses' own hard drives and servers, or via a cloud computing solution. In terms of sharing information, both in-house and with clients – many businesses have moved beyond having their own intranet and extranets, and use Virtual Private Networks (VPNs) to allow staff to share information whilst on the move, or working from home, or they use cloud-based services or computer applications (apps) to achieve the same and to share information with clients.

Instant access to data allows businesses to monitor, benchmark and assess their performance more quickly and accurately than was traditionally possible. Rather than quarterly or monthly reviews, the performance of the business can be assessed in a much more granular and sophisticated fashion, with managers being able to assess performance in real time with accurate data.

This facility enables regular inputs to planning processes and decision-making and allows managers to react more quickly to prevent or correct problems. As businesses move closer to real-time management, the issue of how to represent, often complex, inter-linked and fast-changing data, becomes apparent. Traditional software packages and apps often provide a visual representation of data in the form of a 'dashboard': a single screen containing regularly updated infographics or charts summarising key performance indicators. Users, depending on their access to company data, can then 'click through' on the relevant chart or infographic to see more detailed data.

The Management Information Systems (MIS) can be described as a system for collecting and communicating information that will support decision-making and business activity. A significant amount of information will be management accounting information, although the MIS will also contain non-accounting information.

Advances in IT have allowed MIS to be more formally designed and supported, and some MIS, particularly in large companies, are now formally designed in such a way as to allow, and encourage, managers to consider information in much more detail than before. This is particularly the case in large, complex organisations that have a need for extensive and complex data and are able to justify devoting the resources to building and maintaining such a system.

EG Learning example 3.1

Braxton Hospital's Management Information System (MIS) provides information on the medical history of each patient. It includes detailed factual information on past illnesses and any recurring symptoms as well as the patient's name, address and other personal information.

Explain the characteristics of information being provided by the MIS system.

3.7 Inputting data

Data is only valuable if it is accurate as well as timely. Collecting or inputting the correct data in a timely fashion whilst ensuring its accuracy is, therefore, a challenge. Data collection can take a number of forms, for example:

- 'Traditional' on-site data inputting (ie post-transaction or carrying out a process, the separate, manual transcription of data in a report, spreadsheet, database etc.);
- Off-site data inputting (ie use of smartphones, tablet computers, laptop computers or other devices to manually transcribe data, such as customer orders, as and when required);

- Automatic transcription of data. Here, when transactions or processes are undertaken, the required data is automatically extracted and validated. This has the benefits of being more timely and reducing the risk of human error in data transcription;
- EPOS systems. The use of barcode or QR scanners not only allow timely transactions, but they allow the timely collection of detailed customer data. Some businesses have further leveraged such data by developing loyalty schemes: this allows for more detailed analysis and anticipation of customer demand and/or the sale of customer data to third parties (subject to relevant data protection best practice).

Output
The MIS must respond to the needs of the end users. As such, the best systems are flexible enough to produce high quality information, in a variety of formats (numerical vs non-numerical; tables vs graphics etc.). A good MIS will also be able to produce outputs of varying levels of detail and quality, in order to respond to specific needs of decision-makers.

3.8 The problem with traditional management information systems

The feedback loop

You may remember from your earlier studies that one of the main tasks of the management accountant is to control a business.

This means operating a feedback system like the one below:

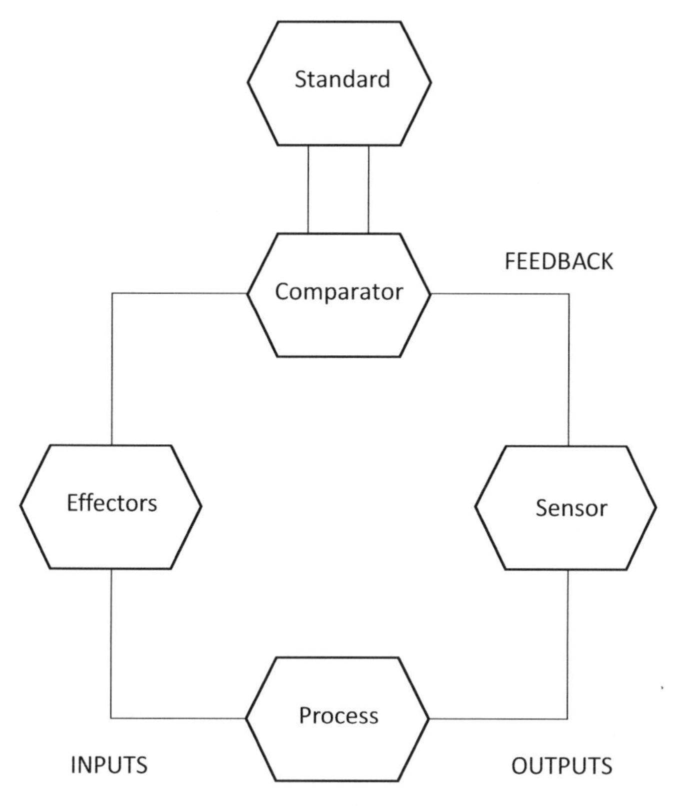

The key with the above diagram is to see that if something is not measured then no action can be taken to correct any problems (since no-one will know there is a problem).

- Imagine that a department has a monthly budget.
- The budget will be the standard.
- The costing system, which records actual costs, will be the sensor.
- The actual results for the period, collected by the costing system, will be the feedback.
- The performance report for the department, comparing actual with budget, will be the comparator.
- Managers, who in consultation with others, take action to minimise any future adverse variances and to exploit opportunities resulting from favourable variances, will be the effectors.

There are two kinds of possible action that can be taken:

- Reduce the spending next month to bring it back in line with the budget – this is known as single feedback.
- Adjust the budget – this is known as double feedback.

A feedback loop is useful for analysing what has happened and taking action to control events in the future (known as feedforward).

Such a feedback system is simplistic and does not reveal:

- what happens when there are delays at the sensor, feedback, comparator and effectors stages
- the impact of environment changes beyond the control of the organisation, such as raw materials price rises or increases in interest rates
- the accounting system may not be able to measure all the output of the department and therefore feedback will be incomplete.

MIS in the feedback process

A Management Information System (MIS) is used to assist with the feedback process. For example, if we are looking at monthly spending by a department the MIS will need to:

- Collect the relevant information
- Make sure all spending is recorded
- Measure performance based on spending for each department
- Compare performance with budget and prepare variance analysis
- Allow for action and send results to department managers.

The MIS providing these will be:

- Inward-focused
- Regular
- Standardised.

The main problem with this kind of report is that it is poor at dealing with strategic issues.

For the management accountant to be able to provide useful information, the following steps should be involved:

- Contact managers of responsibility centres to see what information they need, how and when it should be given to them.
- The accountant then designs a system to collect, process and distribute this information.

3.9 Management Information System (MIS)

As noted earlier, the traditional system is inward-focused, regular and standardised. This makes the system useful for controlling the actions of the business but makes it poor for the strategic management accounting issues that this course is about.

In order to carry out strategic management accounting, information will need to be collected about the external environment. Because of this the MIS will need to be:

- Externally focused (using exogenous variables)
- Carried out as needed
- Non-standardised

- Include non-financial performance indicators.

Learn

It is important to remember that the basic function of any MIS is the same. This is to provide information which is useful:

- At an appropriate time
- In an understandable format so that a decision can be made.

The types of MIS you will need to be familiar with are:

- Transaction processing systems
- Management information systems
- Enterprise resource planning systems
- Executive information systems.

The costs of a MIS will depend on:

- Reporting frequency
- Reporting level and quantity of detail
- Reporting accuracy and back-up
- Reporting system and style.

Motivation and MIS

- If managers have a poor attitude towards the information they receive then the information may prove to be less effective than expected.
- Management accounting reports may be viewed as unimportant by the users, creating a negative view of their use and worth.
- Managers may feel that the information reports are criticising the way they run their departments, which may motivate them to improve, though this is more likely to demotivate them.
- Managers may not understand the information they are being provided with, which will make them unhappy with the source of the information.
- Managers may focus on what they want to see. For example, if a manager believes that good customer service is important no matter the cost, then any adverse expenditure variances will simply be ignored rather than used as a motivation to improve.

Security and MIS

Business data will often consist of information which is confidential because it relates to individuals and may be governed by data protection legislation and/or be commercially sensitive.

Control can be exercised at three points:

- Input – passwords, range tests, format checks, check digits, specially constructed numbers, sequence checks, control totals
- Processing – initiated by authorised personnel only and passwords and software audit trails are important to track what processing was carried out

- Output – should be available to authorised personnel and authorised third parties only.

The external environment and MIS

- The more intense the competition, the more complex the management accounting system will tend to be
- The faster the environment changes the more frequently reports will be needed
- The larger the number of markets the organisation operates in, the more decentralised the system will be
- MISs can be affected by customers/suppliers etc who could insist on things being done in a particular way eg supplying a customer who operates a JIT system.

The cost of external data

- Direct search costs eg carrying out market research
- Indirect search costs eg wasted time trying to find information
- Management costs eg processing and distributing information
- Infrastructure costs eg necessary computer hardware.

Benefits of external data

- Better quality decisions
- Benchmarking
- Reduction in risks and uncertainty
- Improved ability to respond to changes in the outside world.

Limitations of external data

- Accuracy and validity
- Quality eg is the information complete
- Bias eg was the information used to show a particular point of view
- Motivation and the use of control information

EG Learning example 3.2

You are trying to establish a price for a new product that will be made available next year. This product, the Sensor PI, is controlled by voice activation and allows you to turn on lights, adjust heating settings and TV channels. As there is no similar product on the market at the moment, you are finding it quite difficult to find appropriate pricing information.

Identify the data sources and items that you could use to help set an appropriate price for the Sensor PI.

3.10 Recording and processing methods

The complexity and sophistication of the MIS and the actual methods used for recording and processing information will depend to a large extent on the nature and objectives of the organisation.

The following factors are likely to influence the methods and processes used to record and analyse information:

- The size of the business
- Its complexity and diversification
- The sector of the business (manufacturing, retail etc.)
- The extent to which different parts of the business interact with each other
- The availability of corporate databases containing useful information
- The engagement and ability of staff
- Developments in IT.

 **Learn**

3.10.1 Management reports

A high quality information system is more likely to produce high quality outputs. The MIS should be able to produce information:

- which is relevant to the decisions being made
- efficiently (ie cost-effectively)
- in a timely way.

The information produced should also:

- be presented clearly and appropriately
- be presented in such a way as to be comprehensible to the user
- be directly relevant to the decision being made and to the user of the information
- exclude any superfluous detail.

3.10.2 Strategic importance of performance management information systems

Management is reliant on information systems in order to get the information needed to make organisational decisions. The structure, characteristics and quality of the information systems therefore affect the information available for decision-making. A management information system will record and collate information from individual transactions and events in order to produce reports allowing managers to control the business.

The nature of the information system will depend partly on the size and structure of the organisation. A large business with a complex structure will need a sophisticated management information system, whereas a smaller simpler business would require a simpler, cheaper management information system.

Other characteristics of the business are also relevant, for example a high number of transactions between different business units, or a high level of integration between different business units, will introduce a requirement for a management information system which facilitates communication between different managers and analysis of the interdependencies of business units.

A larger, more complex or more diverse business is likely to have a greater number of strict financial targets in place, since otherwise it is too difficult to manage the large quantity of information and the diversity of business activities. The management information system will be required to enable managers to measure financial targets such as profitability, revenue growth, cost control etc. In large complex businesses, business units will be able to measure their performance independently of each other and so measures such as divisional return on investment or residual income may be used.

The development of the management information system over time will be influenced not only by the objectives and characteristics of the organisation but also by the system itself. A more flexible, expandable system will be better able to respond to changes in requirements.

In the exam, you may be required to discuss management information systems in the context of:

- evaluating whether the management information systems are appropriate for the business and assessing the value of the information that they provide.
- understanding how human factors may influence the design of a management accounting system.
- understanding how the structure of the business affects the information requirements of managers (cost centres vs profit centres vs investment centres; degree of centralisation, use of responsibility accounting etc.).

3.11 Controllability and information requirements

Controllability is very important in performance management as its principles refer not only to controlling costs but also to revenues and investments.

Controllability can depend on the time scale being considered:

- In the long term, most costs are controllable by someone in the organisation.
- In the short term some costs, such as rent, are uncontrollable even by senior managers, and certainly uncontrollable by managers lower down the organisational hierarchy.

There may be no clear cut distinction between controllable and non-controllable costs for a given manager, who may also be exercising control jointly with another manager.

The aim under a responsibility accounting system will be to assign and report on the cost to the person having primary responsibility. The most effective control is thereby achieved, since immediate action can be taken.

The information requirements for responsibility accounting need to be considered.

On the requirements, some would favour the idea that reports should include all costs caused by a department, whether controllable or uncontrollable by the departmental manager. The idea here is that, even if he has no direct control, he might influence the manager who does have control.

However, most agree that managers should only be judged on what they can control and the information that is gathered to assess managers should be based on this. For example, it would be unfair to judge a manager on the amount of fixed costs the finance department apportioned to their department. This will be particularly important when departments use each other's services or when costs are imposed from above (such as spending on a marketing campaign).

Methods to get around this include:

- Separating variances into planning and operational variances, so that changes in circumstances, particularly those outside the manager's control, as adjusted for
- Using flexible budgeting, to adjust for changes in activity
- Benchmarking against other parts of the business or similar organisations (if that information is available).

3.12 Capacity and development potential of a system

When considering a system, particularly a new one, it is informative to look at its potential. This helps give an idea of the money that might be earned from it. One example is that of the Internet. Initially there were many commentators that felt that this was an area where there were limitations to its potential. As time has moved on and the possibilities and capabilities have become apparent it can be seen that the possibilities are vast. They include:

- Control of devices from a distance
- 3D printing, manufacturing objects created remotely
- Large fundraising and political campaigns such as via JustGiving or Change.org
- Large virtual worlds, such as Minecraft
- Podcasts taking over from radio for people's listening time

amongst many thousands of other possibilities.

3.12.1 Business systems

The properties of a business system that help determine its capacity and development potential are:

1. How adaptive the system is
2. How scalable it is.

The Internet demonstrates both of these properties:

Definition

Adaptive – how quickly the system can change and develop.

IE Illustrative example 3.2

Facebook was founded in early 2004. This isn't a long time ago in relation to most businesses and, currently, it is one of the most well-known and valuable companies and the world. It has developed very rapidly. However there are many competitors that are already trying to develop companies to take away the market that Facebook has developed. Facebook as a system is less attractive to younger users of the Internet, particularly as their parents start to use it and hence these younger users of social media look for 'cooler' alternatives. The Internet can change rapidly but Facebook may not be able to and continue to grow at the same rate, or at all.

Definition

Scalability – how quickly the business can handle a growing amount of work in a capable manner or its ability to be enlarged to accommodate that growth

The Internet allows scalability throughout the world. Facebook can have users in almost every country without having to visit those countries, incur large marketing costs or set up physically in the countries.

EG Learning example 3.3

If you are considering setting up a publishing company, writing academic books, what could you do to ensure that you can develop your capacity and development potential?

3.13 IT developments influencing management accounting systems

There are increasing use in companies of information technology (IT). Over many years the labour component and cost of businesses has decreased and IT is another way that this is happening. On a basic level, the use of spreadsheets has helped companies perform calculations that would have taken employees of the company many days and weeks if performed on paper.

IT systems allows companies to create individual reports quickly and easily for management decision-making. Other capabilities of computerised accounting systems are the increased functionality, improved accuracy and faster processing.

Two examples of IT developments are unified databases and network technology.

Unified databases

One very powerful use of IT is the use of unified databases. This allows companies to gather information about their business and then use this to improve what they do. This can take many forms, for example sharing information from those databases with their partners or suppliers to show which of the company's products are being successful and which are not. This allows the partner or supplier to make changes to the inputs of the company and gives a chance to improve the final sales made.

IE Illustrative example 3.3

Amazon, the online retailer, can show the companies that sell via Amazon how successful they have been in absolute terms and relative to other companies. Amazon can share feedback from the users of Amazon's site with the companies so that they can monitor what customers are thinking of their product. This allows rapid changes to be made (in the product or service provided) to improve those sales.

Similarly supermarkets like Tesco have used their unified databases to see the shopping habits of the customers and the patterns and developments of those habits. In the UK they found that in the early evening there were a surprising number of customers buying both babies' nappies and beer. They found that many young fathers were coming back from work and buying these two products together. This data allowed them to consider offers to these customers and make it easier to do their shopping.

Given that management accounting systems are designed to help businesses get to the heart of how they are performing unified databases help extract this information rapidly in order to help the businesses run more successfully.

Network technology
Similarly network technology is also helpful in this respect. A network of computers allows a business to connect on various levels from the communications in the business to the sharing of information. This can be via cable or wirelessly.

This allows the information being used in the management accounting system to be much enhanced and connected, allowing more information to be taken into account in management decisions.

3.14 Performance management for different business models

Varying business models

As the world becomes more complex there are increasingly the need to have complex business models to deal with these complexities. Three of these are:

1. Strategic alliances
2. Joint ventures
3. Complex supply chain structures

Dealing with these in turn:

Strategic alliances

A strategic alliance is an agreement between two or more companies to pursue a set of objectives while remaining independent organisations. Examples of this include Starbucks, the coffee chain, who has partnered with book shops to supply coffee within those shops and with PepsiCo on bottling and selling one of their coffee drinks, the Frappacino.

A strategic alliance is likely to mean that the companies involved are separate but have a joint interest. This means that it can be easy to see what comes to each organisation but also mean that there is a lot of instability in the agreement. This makes it more difficult to measure performance on a longer term basis. When things are going well there are benefits to both parties. When things are not going so well, one of the parties is likely to pull out. Equally one of the parties may have other directions that it wants to go and will pull out anyway, even if things are progressing well.

Joint ventures

Joint ventures are a form of strategic alliance but with a more permanent foundation. An example is the car company, Jaguar Land Rover entering into a joint venture with a Chinese company called Chery Automobile in order to make cars in China. This joint venture uses the expertise of both parties to do something that they probably wouldn't be able to achieve otherwise.

The performance management issues with a joint venture are clearer than with a strategic alliance. The joint venture is likely to be set up as a company or at least under a legal agreement and the performance can be monitored similar to any other company, though without the uncertainties of a strategic alliance.

Complex supply chain structures

There are increasingly more complex supply chains as the global economy develops. This means that a company may be buying inputs from companies in other countries and selling to customers on yet different countries. There are threats within the supply chain and also externally as events may conspire to damage the chain eg bad weather, terrorist incident or anything else that stops the chain working.

Due to these threats the performance of a company becomes more difficult to judge. If the supply chain is working well then there are potentially great benefits to be had, with cheaper supplies and wider markets to sell them to. However if the supply chain gets disrupted this can cause difficulties in performance management both financially and also qualitatively, with effects on the brand(s) involved.

Key Learning Points

- Understand the techniques for coordinating resources within various business structures. (A3a, A3c)
- Appreciate how information technology allows greater capture of data. (A4b, A4c)
- Be able to explain the various information and system requirements to aid performance measurement. (A4d, A4e)

What's the story?

Stop and think through the 'story' of this chapter and how it links with other chapters (use the Overview to help).

Learning example solutions

EG Solution 3.1

The Management Information System (MIS) is the basic system for the hospital. Within it there are the records for each patient and, no doubt, the ability to produce reports either on statistical or individual bases. The MIS, in effect, has automated the record-keeping, and, instead of writing out patients' notes to be kept in a paper-based file, this information is input to the computer system to create an electronic file. Details of past illnesses and symptoms should therefore be accurate and give a true reflection of the medical history of a particular patient.

In the case of the MIS, this depends on inputs made to the system following the patient's visits. The doctor may input information during the consultation with the patient and would certainly need to record symptoms and any medication prescribed.

The MIS provides information quickly and response times of a few seconds would be typical for this type of application. The MIS would be record-based, within either a hierarchical or a relational database, and as such the patient's record will be able to be displayed quickly at the touch of a button.

MIS data will be reliable only if it has been input correctly. Even if the information is incomplete, the doctor can see from the screen where the gaps are and it should be possible to obtain a good indication of the patient's history. The MIS can therefore offer a degree of assurance that there is control over matching the patient to the information.

The records are processed in accordance with operating system controls and the information can be prevented from corruption by the database management system. Therefore control of data is good.

EG Solution 3.2

Customers
There are no customers yet. However, market research into the acceptability of the product along with indications of how much customers would be prepared to pay will help to provide an upper limit to the price to be charged.

Suppliers
The constituent parts of the product can be identified and the cost of manufacture determined. This will provide a lower limit on the price to be charged.

Rivals
No known rivals yet. However, the prices of substitute products, if there are any, may be useful to obtain as they provide a benchmark for the amount the customers are willing to pay.

Trade associations

Via trade associations you may get information on trends in technology, with details on innovative new products that become available. This will enable you to find out whether the Sensor PI has been anticipated as a new product. If it has and the trade associations are expecting this to be a useful product, then a premium may be available on the price to be charged.

Government

Details on demographics and disposable income will be useful. However, this information tends to be more useful where the product price is high.

Media

Details of trends and expected products may again be useful. A review of Discovery channel programmes such as Click or technical articles will again help to identify whether the Sensor PI has been anticipated in the market. Again, a product which is anticipated to be useful may command a premium price.

Research organisations

Research organisations may be able to indicate other uses for the product. A price premium may again be available for these specialist uses.

Finally, having determined the variable costs of production, the organisation must decide how much contribution is needed to cover fixed costs including R&D. If the contribution is less than the selling price estimated from the above sources, then the organisation should be able to make an acceptable profit. If the selling price is less than expected, then a review of costs or potential demand must be undertaken to check that the product should still be marketed.

EG Solution 3.3

To develop the capacity and development potential of a publishing company, using the concepts of adaptiveness and scalability:

Adaptiveness – Look at how your potential customers will consume your material now and in the future. For example, can they view the material on the Internet, via their smartphone, tablet device and so on. Publishers that are just able to publish as paper books are likely to miss out on sales over time. Also, can the books published include other valuable learning tools such as video or audio files?

Scalabilty – For the operations of the publishing company can they produce more books relatively quickly. For example, do they have a bank of talented freelancer writers that they can call upon as needed to produce new books? Can they employ new staff rapidly or do they have a relationship with an outsourcing company to produce the material, whether printed or electronic? If not they are unlikely to be able to grow as quickly as they would like.

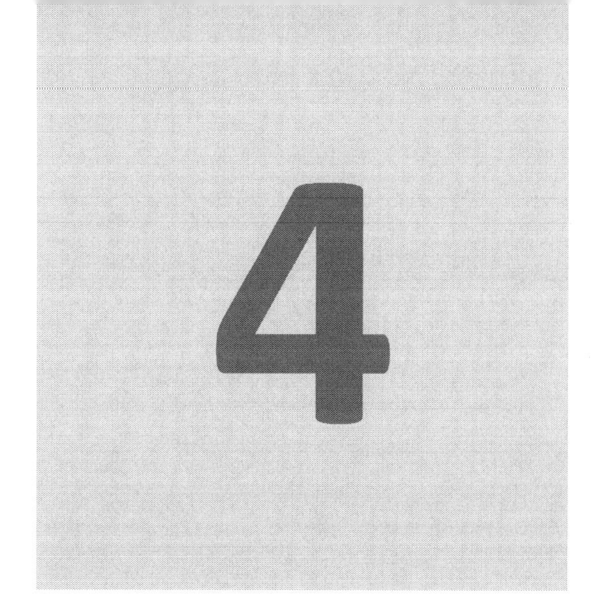

4

Risk and Uncertainty as Part of Strategic Planning

Context

We have seen business strategy and here we are looking at the risks and uncertainties involved. Business strategy looks to the future and the future is never guaranteed, even the best laid plans can be affected by new events happened that were difficult to predict. Risks and uncertainties are linked, with risks being capable of being quantified.

Once the risks and uncertainties have been identified then there are techniques that help us decide what the best approach is.

3Q

1. What is sensitivity analysis?
2. What is the difference between cost plus pricing and demand-based pricing?
3. What does the steady state on a learning curve represent?

4.1 Sensitivity analysis

Sensitivity analysis is a term used to describe how sensitive a result is to the change of one variable.

IE Illustrative example 4.1

For example, the budgeted profit for a company might be $100,000. However, since this is a budget, the chances are that the profit will not actually be $100,000. It may be more or it may be less.

Imagine that the company knows that it has to deliver profits of at least $80,000 to satisfy its shareholders. If things turn out as they are in the budget all will be fine, but what if something goes wrong?

Sensitivity analysis looks at one variable at a time. So, for example, if the number of items sold fell by 15% then the company would only make $80,000 profit. Alternatively if the volume of sales was the same but the variable cost rose by 6% then profits would only be $70,000.

The advantage of using sensitivity analysis is that it gives an indication of how risky something might be. For example, sensitivity analysis might show that costs can only rise by 1% before a company starts to make losses. In this case a company knows that there is a very large possibility that losses will be made.

Principle

The principle of sensitivity analysis

The examiner will often include sensitivity analysis along with calculating the budgeted profit on a project.

One of the factors when considering a project is the effect of changes to the primary variables caused by changes in sales volumes, sales price and operating costs; the capital expenditure; or the life of the project.

IE Illustrative example 4.2

The directors of Wing On Ltd. are considering the following investment project:

Capital investment (CI)	£1.25 million
Annual net cash flow (CF)	£ 0.45 million
Life of project	5 years

The directors are positive that the company's cost of capital is 12% but are concerned that in the past, forecasts have proved inaccurate.

By what % can each variable differ from the forecast before the project becomes undesirable, that is, when NPV is less than nil?

The NPV of the project based on the above forecast is −£1.25 m + (£0.45 × 3.605) = £0.372 m

Note: 3.605 is the cumulative discount factor at 12% over 5 years.

This NPV is positive so the amount of acceptable variation can be computed as follows:

Capital investment (CI)

Project remains acceptable provided that CI does not rise beyond

$-CI + (£0.45m \times 3.605) = 0$

This occurs when CI is a negative figure = £0.45m × 3.605 = £1.622m.

Amount of allowable upward variation or margin of error in capital investment is

$$\frac{1.622 - 1.25}{1.25} = 30\%$$

Annual net cash flow (CF)

Project remains acceptable provided that cash flow does not fall below the level where

$-£1.25m + (CF \times 3.605) = 0$

$$\text{This occurs when CF} = \frac{£1.25m}{3.605} = £0.347m$$

Therefore, the amount of acceptable downward variation in the annual cash flow is

$$\frac{1.622 - 1.25}{1.25} = 30\%$$

Life of project

The project remains acceptable provided that the Cumulative Discount factor (CDF) of 12% does not fall below the level where

$-£1.25\text{ m} + (0.45 \times CDF) = 0$

$$\text{This occurs when CDF} = \left(\frac{1.25}{0.45}\right) = 2.778$$

From the cumulative discount factor table, it can be found that the cumulative discount factor for 3 years at 12% is 2.402 and that for 4 years is 3.038.

$$\text{The shortest acceptable life is } 4 - \frac{3.038 - 2.778}{3.038 - 2.402} = 3.6 \text{ years}$$

The amount of acceptable downward variation in the life of the project is

$$\frac{5 - 3.6}{5} = 28\%$$

EG

Learning example 4.1

Amanda has decided to grow organic vegetables in a plot of land she is looking to buy and supply to two local supermarkets that have already shown an interest. She is concerned about several factors that could affect her business. Can you help her by making a list of these factors?

4.2 Expected values

Calculating expected values is a technique that can be used to give an approximation of what might happen when a project is undertaken.

It is usually used in a situation where there are a range of possible outcomes which might occur.

IE

Illustrative example 4.3

Revenue	Probability	Costs	Probability	Profit	Combined probability
100,000	0.2	80,000	0.5	20,000	0.10
100,000	0.2	50,000	0.3	50,000	0.06
100,000	0.2	30,000	0.2	70,000	0.04
50,000	0.7	80,000	0.5	−30,000	0.35
50,000	0.7	50,000	0.3	0	0.21
50,000	0.7	30,000	0.2	20,000	0.14
20,000	0.1	80,000	0.5	−60,000	0.05
20,000	0.1	50,000	0.3	−30,000	0.03
20,000	0.1	30,000	0.2	−10,000	0.02
					1.00

Now take each row and multiply the profit by the combined probability. Add these together to give the expected value.

In the above the expected value =

20,000 × 0.10 + 50,000 × 0.06 + 70,000 × 0.04 etc

This gives an expected value of −4,000

So the project may be unacceptable. One key thing to note is that a loss of 4,000 is not one of the actual possible outcomes.

There is still a chance that the project makes a profit. To calculate this probability, add together all the probabilities where the project shows a profit. In other words there is a 0.10 + 0.06 + 0.04 + 0.14 = 0.34 chance that a profit is made. Note the probabilities are added, since the profit could be 20,000 OR 50,000 OR 70,000 OR 20,000, we do not mind which.

There are a number of risk analysis techniques that can be used to help managers make decisions in the context of risk and uncertainly. It is not always possible to assign probability estimates to different outcomes in conditions of uncertainty. Maximin, maximax and minimax regret risk analysis techniques are used when the probability of different outcomes are not known. These techniques are best demonstrated through the use of an example.

Maximin, maximax and minimax regret risk analysis techniques

IE Illustrative example 4.4

Red Ltd has to choose between two different production processes, process X and process Y:

- **Process X** involves low fixed costs, but high unit variable costs, as a result this process is suited to low demand.
- **Process Y** involves high fixed costs, but low unit variable costs, as a result this process is suited to high demand.

Assume that there are only two demand levels: high demand and low demand. Red Ltd cannot estimate the probabilities of there being high demand or low demand. The estimated profits that will arise from using the different production processes will differ depending on customer demand for the product that Red Ltd is selling. The estimated profits according to the different demand levels and production processes can be seen in the table below.

	Low demand	High demand
Production process X	£120,000	£200,000
Production process Y	£20,000	£240,000

In this situation (where probabilities of different outcomes occurring are unknown) managers could use the following decision rules:

- **Maximin.** Here the manager will assume that the worst possible outcome will happen and thus the decision should be taken to maximise potential benefit given this outcome. Looking at the table above for Red Ltd the worst outcomes are £120,000 for process X and £20,000 for process Y. Therefore process X (with the highest payoff) should be selected. The manager is maximising the potential benefits assuming the worst will happen.
- **Maximax.** The maximax criterion is the opposite of maximin. Here the assumption is that the best payoffs will happen. Here the best potential outcomes are £200,000 for process X and £240,000 for process Y. Therefore, the Y process (with the highest payoff) would be chosen.
- **Minimax regret.** The aim here is to minimise the maximum potential regret. If a manager selected a course of action that does not end up being the course that generates the maximum potential benefit, they will regret it. Considering the Red Ltd example:
  - If process Y had been selected because the manager believed there would be high demand and there was high demand there would be no regret as the outcome with the highest outcome was selected. However, if they had selected process X then Red Ltd would lose £40,000 (£240,000 – £200,000). This £40,000 measures their regret.
  - Alternatively, if process X was selected because Red Ltd thought demand would be low and the low level of demand occurred, there would be no regret. But if they had selected Y and low demand occurred their regret would be £100,000. Using these figures it is possible to identify what the best course of action would be. It would be to select process X as it minimises the possible future regret £40,000 as oppose to £100,000.

The maximum possible regret for each production process is shown in the table below.

	Low demand	High demand
Production process X	£0	£40,000*
Production process Y	£100,000**	£0

* (£240,000 – £200,000)

** (£120,000 – £20,000)

4.3 How can prices be calculated?

In P5 the emphasis is more on why certain pricing strategies should be adopted and their impact on performance.

Selling price depends on:

- Costs – Selling price must cover variable costs and should be high enough to cover fixed costs at the sales volume achieved.
- Customers – What will customers be prepared to pay? How will they react to price changes (elasticity of demand)?
- Competition – What do competitors offer and at what price? How competitive is the market? Are there substitute products?
- Government – Some industries are subject to price controls. For example, many utility companies must have prices agreed by government regulators.

Pricing strategies have to be seen in the light of generic competitive strategies:

- **Cost leadership.** Here success depends on keeping costs very low. In a very competitive environment, where prices are determined by the market, this allows good margins to be earned when selling at the ordinary market price. Generally, large businesses will enjoy economies of scale and substantial production experience (learning) and will find cost leadership easier to achieve than small firms.
- **Differentiation.** Here products are made distinct (differentiated) from those of competitors. This means that they do not compete head on in the market and may allow the company to raise its prices. The company must judge what customers are prepared to pay for these differentiated products and what price will maximise profits.
- **Focus.** The company specialises in a small section of the market and gains a very good reputation there. Although the company could focus and be a cost leader, it would be more natural to focus and be a differentiator. Specialising in a small market segment should allow better products and services to be devised for that segment, and these should command premium prices.

If a company is going to carry out market development or market penetration the price chosen will be important.

There are several methods of setting prices:

Cost plus pricing

In cost plus pricing, a mark-up is added to the full cost per unit. There is no guarantee that the item will sell at the price arrived at. It is used mostly when investigating possible selling prices for a new product.

 **Learn**

With cost plus pricing the considerations are:

- Variable or full cost?
- How to absorb overheads?
- Should target costing be used?

Target pricing

The required profit for the organisation is estimated, from which selling prices are determined that should generate the profit calculated.

Demand-based pricing

MR (= MC – Profits) is maximised when marginal revenue = marginal cost. This is a theoretical approach that can be used only if the organisation has detailed knowledge about demand and cost curves. In practice a target profit is often used instead of 'maximising' profit.

The theoretical approach to pricing is MC = MR.

Marginal cost (MC) = the increase in total cost from making one more unit.

Marginal revenue (MR) = the increase in total revenue from selling one more unit.

MC is an increasing function.

MR is a decreasing function.

So, if:

MC > MR profit must be falling

MC < MR profit must be rising

MC = MR profit must be maximised

Steps to calculating the optimal price:

1. Establish price equation ($P = a - bQ$).
2. Establish MR equation ($MR = a - 2bQ$).
3. Find MC (usually just the variable cost per unit).
4. Make MC = MR to get the optimal quantity to sell.
5. Insert this quantity back into the price equation to get the optimal price.

Learn

The demand curve measures the relationship between selling price and sales volume. Usually this is an inverse relationship – as price increases demand falls and vice versa.

Finding the equation of a demand curve requires two selling prices and corresponding output levels.

A general equation of a demand curve is given by $P = a - bQ$.

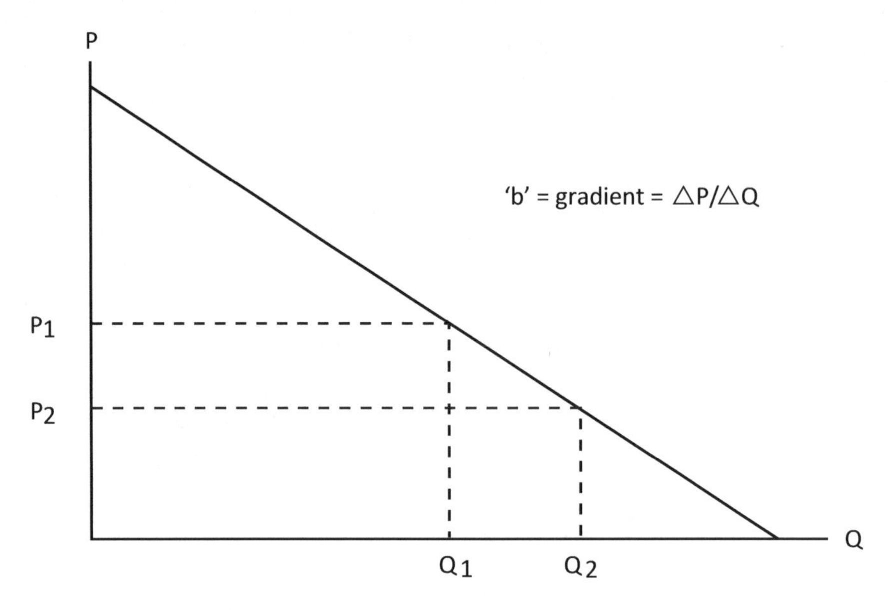

Marketing-based pricing

With marketing-based pricing, look at:

For a new product:

- Penetration pricing – how to price a product to get a market share (usually a lower price than competitors)
- Market skimming – charging a high price but attracting wealthier customers

For an existing product:

- Discount pricing – similar to penetration pricing but for a product already being sold
- Premium pricing – charging a high price to make the product seem more attractive
- Average rate pricing – going for the middle ground
- Price discrimination – different prices in different markets.

4.4 The learning curve

A learning curve relates to products that are labour intensive to manufacture. If the manufacturing method is repetitive, then the workers will learn how to manufacture the item more quickly. The production time per unit goes down as more items are manufactured.

At some point it will become impossible for the workers to improve their efficiency any further, this is known as reaching the steady state. After this point all units take the same length of time.

The learning curve formula is represented by $y = ax^b$

y = average time per unit for all units, x = total number of units

b = learning factor log (% learning)/log2

Learn

If output doubled, average time per unit falls by learning rate (constant %)

eg. learning rate 80% and time for first unit	= 4 hours	
Average time per unit for two units	= 0.8 × 4	= 3.2 hours
Average time per unit for four units	= 0.8 × 3.2	= 2.56 hours.

Learning curves typically vary between 70% and 90% (constant reductions of between 30% and 10%)

The use of learning curves is relevant for labour costs in budgets and planning cash flows. Its limitations include:

- Inaccuracy in estimating labour hours for first unit
- Inaccuracy of estimating length of time for learning effect
- Assumption of a uniform rate of learning
- Assumption that tasks are sufficiently repetitive
- Assumption that labour turnover will not affect rate of learning.

Where learning takes place with a regular pattern it is important to take account of the reduction in labour hours and costs per unit. This is important in production planning and work scheduling.

Experience curve describes the process of acquiring skills and abilities through working in a particular environment and dealing with new production technologies, this has relevance for strategic planning and Target Costing.

IE Illustrative example 4.5

B plc is currently preparing a budget forecast for the year to 30th June 2010 for product Omega.

Information gathered in relation to this budget is as follows:

(a) The production method is labour intensive and is estimated to be subject to an 85% learning effect. The budgeted labour cost for quarter two 2009 is £450.

(b) Only whole batches are produced and sold and a production capacity constraint limits the quarterly output to 45 batches.

(c) The product is perishable and no stockpiling to overcome production constraints is possible.

The spreadsheet extract of the budget calculations for product X provides production/demand estimates and calculations for budget labour cost for each quarter:

	QR2 2009	QR3 2009	QR4 2009	QR1 2010	QR2 2010
Product demand estimates (batches)	35	38	42	46	51
Production/Sales budget (batches)	35	38	42	45	45

Product Omega budgeted learning curve calculations for labour

Cumulative budget (batches)	35	73	115	?	?
Total labour cost (£)	6,843	12,013	17,012	?	?
Average labour cost (£)/batch	195.52	164.56	147.93	?	?
Total labour cost (£) per QR		5,170	4,999	?	?

Summary of key points

Quarterly output limited to 45 batches

Product perishable – no stockpiling

Budgeted demand QR1 2010 = 46 batches, QR2 2005 = 51 batches

Budgeted production/sales QR1 2010 = 45, QR2 2005 = 45

(a) Cumulative budget (batches)

QR1: 115 + 45 = 160

QR2: 160 + 45 = 205

(b) Average labour cost/batch (y)

Use the formula $y = ax^b$

$b = \log(0.85)/\log 2$

$b = -0.23446$

a = £450

QR1 $y = 450 \times 160^{-0.23446} = 136.91$

QR2 $y = 450 \times 205^{-0.23446} = 129.18$

(c) Total labour cost

QR1 160 × 136.91 =	£21,905
QR2 205 × 129.18 =	£26,481

Total labour cost per QR

QR1: £21,905 − £17,012 = £4,893

QR2: £26,481 − £21,905 = £4,576

EG Learning example 4.2

AB produces fresh executive lunch boxes which are a highly perishable commodity which can be sold on for $20 per box or for scrap as @ $1 per box at the end of the day to local farmers. The lunch box costs $10 per box and is only suitable for sale within 12 hours of preparation.

Orders must be placed in advance each day on AB's website.

AB has kept the following records of sales over the past 50 days:

Daily sales	Days sold
10	15
20	25
30	10

Required:

(a) Prepare a summary that shows the forecast net margin earned for each possible outcome.

(b) On the basis of maximising expected value, advise Amanda which quantity to prepare.

Key Learning Points

- Understand why risk and uncertainty have to be considered when looking at future decisions. (B1c)
- Appreciate why decision-making depends on exogenous variables. (B1c)
- Be able to apply different risk analysis techniques in assessing business performance. (B1d)

What's the story?

Stop and think through the 'story' of this chapter and how it links with other chapters (use the Overview to help).

Learning example solutions

EG Solution 4.1

- The effect of sudden changes in weather on her crop
- The effect of extreme climates – heat, rain and cold
- The impact of long-term and continuous use on her plot of land
- Economic climate and its effect on the disposable income of potential customers (the supermarkets) and consequently on her income

EG Solution 4.2

(a)

			Supply	
Demand	**Probability**	**10 boxes**	**20 boxes**	**30 boxes**
		$	**$**	**$**
10 boxes	0.3	100	10	(80)
20 boxes	0.5	100	200	110
30 boxes	0.2	100	200	300

(b)

Expected net margin	100	143	91

Therefore, if Amanda wishes to maximise EV she should order 20 cases per day.

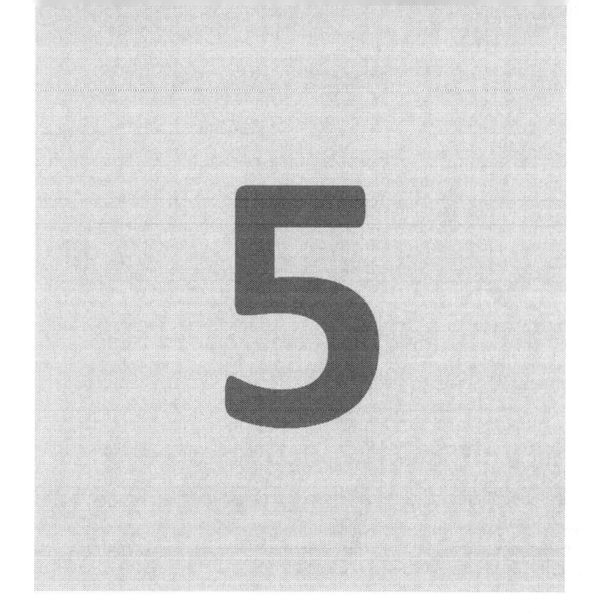

Financial Measures of Performance Evaluation

Context

As accountants we have a lot of financial information, whether via the management or financial accounts. We are likely to have other sources as well internally. Here we look at generating suitable measures of performance to assess the business strategy, the performance of the organisation including the operations.

Make sure that you know the measures to use as well as being able to discuss their results and their strengths and weaknesses.

3Q

1. What is the role of a decision-maker?
2. How will you calculate earnings per share?
3. What are the limitations of the net present value approach?

5.1 Relevant costing

You may remember from P3 that there are two different parts to choosing a strategic option or making a strategic decision.

Firstly a number of different options need to be generated (using a model such as Ansoff's matrix).

Then each option must be tested to see if it is

- Suitable
- Feasible
- Acceptable

A decision is a choice among various alternative courses of action for the purpose of achieving some defined goal or objective. Thus a prerequisite for a successful decision is the definition of the objective to be accomplished. In this topic we will discuss the criteria to be used in making operational or tactical decisions that have an impact in the short term.

The tactical decisions considered in this topic are usually non-recurring, in the sense that the specific decision taken is unique.

A fundamental requirement for good decision-making will be a careful examination of costs and revenue in order to include only those that are relevant to the analysis.

It is imperative to realise that decision-making should be a rational rather than an intuitive process. This means the selection of one of the potential courses of action should be conducted in a logical manner by identifying properly all factors pertinent to each decision alternative. If correct decisions are to be made a business should have in operation a dynamic decision model which continually evaluates the business's performance.

The role of the decision-maker is four-fold:

1. To recognise why a decision is necessary;
2. To identify the available courses of action;
3. To evaluate these potential courses of action;
4. To choose a course of action.

The choice of an alternative will be conducted by examining two sets of factors:

1. Quantitative factors which can be expressed in money terms;
2. Qualitative factors which either cannot be expressed in numerate terms, or their measurement is at best imprecise.

In practice the qualitative factors play a significant part in the decision-making process and there are four major areas where qualitative criteria may have to be considered:

1. Customer relations and public image;
2. Supplier relations;
3. Labour relations;
4. Environmental and ecological factors.

One of the major tests will therefore be – does the option improve profitability, contribution etc.

A common way to look at this in the exam is to use relevant costs.

The term relevant cost or revenue may be thought of as one which is affected or changed by a particular decision – if there is no effect, and then the item cannot be relevant to the decision. It will become necessary therefore to define in relation to each decision which items of cost or revenue will be changed as a result of taking the decision.

For a cost or revenue to be relevant it must satisfy certain criteria.

- Decisions relate to the future, so that only expected future cost or revenue implications can be relevant.
  Costs incurred in the past (sunk costs) and expenditure commitments taken will always be irrelevant and can have no direct bearing on a decision which by its nature relates to action for the future. Examples include obsolete stock and the book value of old equipment.

- Only cost and revenues which are specific to a decision can be relevant. Costs and revenues which will be identical for all alternatives are irrelevant. Thus apportionments and allocations of costs and revenue which are incurred in the general course of business operations cannot be relevant; that is, they are not differential (as they do not contain an element of difference between two or more alternatives).

- Relevant data may include opportunity costs and revenues. An opportunity cost measures the value of a benefit sacrificed when the choice of one action requires that an alternative is given up. An alternative way of describing opportunity cost/revenue is the maximum contribution foregone by using limited resources for a particular purpose.

The relevant value of an asset is identical in amount to the adverse value of the entire loss that the business might expect to suffer if it were deprived of the property. The definition of deprival value accords with the view that an asset should be valued at current value to the business. Whilst opportunity cost defines the cost of a proposed course of action in terms of the most beneficial alternative foregone, deprival values consider the value to the business now of an asset acquired as the result of an earlier decision.

There are three bases for asset valuation:

- Replacement Cost (RC) = current purchase price.
- Net Realisable Value (NRV) = proceeds of disposal at current value less disposal costs.
- Present Value (PV) = present value of future expected earnings from continued use of the asset.

The deprival value of an asset can be computed as:

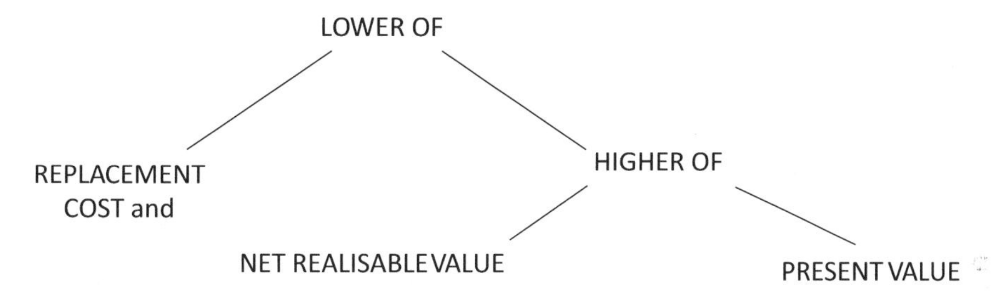

To ensure that you have understood the above analysis calculate the deprival values of the following assets and check your calculations with the answers below.

IE Illustrative example 5.1

Asset	Replacement cost	Present value	Net realisable value
	£	£	£
1	350	180	240
2	300	380	400
3	300	400	380

Answers:

Asset	**Deprival value**	
	£	
1	240	(NRV)
2	300	(RC)
3	300	(RC)

Asset 1 would not be replaced since replacement cost exceeds either of the two values that could be obtained from it. The deprival value is therefore the net realisable value. For both Assets 2 and 3, they would be replaced and so the deprival value must be the replacement cost in each case.

The deprival value may be a particularly useful concept in decision-making where prices are subject to inflation. We know that historic costs are irrelevant to any future decisions as they are sunk.

Decision-making is made more difficult under inflationary conditions because:

- Inflation increases the problem of accurately estimating costs and revenues for each alternative.
- Different factors may have different specific rates of inflation attached to them.

IE Illustrative example 5.2

As a simple example, consider the following choice between two projects both yielding the same returns.

	A	**B**
	£	**£**
Materials	24,000	12,000
Labour	2,000	12,000
Overheads	10,000	10,000
	£36,000	£34,000

Since B is cheaper we would select that option. However the anticipated inflation rates are:

Materials	2% per annum
Labour	30% per annum
Overheads	10% per annum

Our decision budget for next year, assuming for simplicity that the expenses are incurred and paid at the end of the year would be:

	A	B
	£	£
Materials (× 102%)	24,480	12,240
Labour (× 130%)	2,600	15,600
Overheads (× 110%)	11,000	11,000
	38,080	38,840

Project A now becomes the least cost alternative and so should be accepted as the project returns are the same.

In formulating decisions involving replacement we must therefore consider the impact of inflation on prices.

The simplest way to deal with this in the exam is to set up a table with a column for each option. Remember that one option might be to carry on doing things the way they are done at the moment.

In each column put in:

- Any costs that the option will have – these might include extra fixed costs or one-off costs
- Any savings that the option will give.

Then simply total each column and go with the best option (remember that if you just have costs then the lower cost option is best).

If the strategic option will last for more than one year then use the above in an NPV.

5.2 Other measures of performance valuation

5.2.1 Earnings per Share (EPS)

EPS is an investment ratio that can be used to measure performance. It is calculated by dividing the earnings (profit) generated, which is available to be distributed to the ordinary shareholder, by the number of ordinary shares in issues.

$$\text{Earnings per share} = \frac{\text{Earnings available to ordinary shareholders}}{\text{Number of ordinary shares in issue}}$$

Investment analysts see EPS as one of the major measures of share performance, allowing trends over time to be used to assess an organisation's investment potential. EPS figures should not be compared between organisations as different capital structures will make it difficult to make worthwhile comparisons.

5.2.2 Earnings before Interest, Tax, Depreciation and Amortisation (EBITDA)

EBITDA refers to an organisation's earnings before the deductions of interest, tax, depreciation and amortisation. It is a useful performance measure identifying how efficient and profitable an organisation is. It is a widely used measure in practice because by adding back on the two subjective costs of amortisation and depreciation, the resulting figure is closer to an organisation's true cash flow.

To calculate EBITDA the profit before interest and taxation figure is taken from the consolidated statement of profit or loss and the charges for net interest and amortisation are added back on to give the EBITDA figure.

5.2.3 Net Present Value (NPV)

If you were given the choice between receiving £100 today or £100 in one year's time, a logical, rational individual would choose to receive the £100 today. This is for a number of reasons. Firstly, you could invest that £100 and receive interest on it, so it would be worth more than £100 by the end of one year. Secondly, if inflation rose, the value of the £100 would be decreased over the one year period. Lastly, there is a risk attached to future. It is less risky to accept the money now.

The NPV is the sum of the discounted future cash flows arising from a project or an investment minus the initial capital outflow. Shareholder wealth will be maximised when projects with a positive NPV are accepted and those with a NPV of less than zero are rejected. One important assumption of the NPV technique is that money today is worth more than money in the future. For example, managers using NPV wish to know the value of money received in the future in today's values and this involves an understanding of the time value of money.

 **Learn**

5.2.4 The time value of money

Compounding

IE Illustrative example 5.3

Suppose that an organisation has £10,000 to invest, and wants to earn a return of 10% per year on its investments. This means that if the £10,000 could be invested at 10%, the value of the investment with interest would build up as follows:

- After 1 year £10,000 × (1.10) = £11,000
- After 2 years £10,000 × $(1.10)^2$ = £12,100
- After 3 years £10,000 × $(1.10)^3$ = £13,310

This is compounding.

The formula for the future value or terminal value of an investment plus accumulated interest after n time periods is:
$V = X(1 + r)^n$

where:

V is the future value or terminal value of the investment with interest

X is the initial or 'present' value of the investment

r is the compound rate of return per time period, expressed as a decimal

n is the number of time periods.

 **Learn**

Discounting

Discounting starts with the future value (a sum of money receivable or payable at a future date), and converts the future value to a present value, which is the cash equivalent now of the future value.

IE Illustrative example 5.4

If an organisation expects to earn a rate of return of 10% on its investments, how much would it need to invest now to have the following investments?

(a) £11,000 after 1 year

(b) £12,100 after 2 years

(c) £13,310 after 3 years

The answer is £10,000 in each case, and we can calculate it by discounting.

The discounting formula to calculate the present value of a future sum of money is

$X = V/(1 + r)^n$

(a) After 1 year, £11,000/1.10 = £10,000

(b) After 2 years, £12,100/$(1.10)^2$ = £10,000

(c) After 3 years, £13,310/$(1.10)^3$ = £10,000

The timing of cash flows is taken into account by discounting them. The effect of discounting is to give a bigger value per £1 for cash flows that occur earlier. £1 earned after one year will be worth more than £1 earned after two years, which in turn will be worth more than £1 earned after five years, and so on.

The discount rate (r) used when calculating the present value is the relevant cost of capital to the organisation in question.

 **Learn**

Discount factors

In the calculations above we were converting each cash flow into its present value by effectively multiplying by a discount factor. This discount factor is calculated as:

$1/(1 + r)^n$

The calculations could be presented as follows.

Multiply by 10% discount factor		**Present value £**
After 1 year £11,000	× 1/1.10	10,000
After 2 years £12,100	$\times 1/1.10)^2$	10,000
After 3 years £13,310	$\times 1/1.10)^3$	10,000

The discount factors can also be obtained from a present value table, which is at the end of this book and is also supplied in examinations. For example, to find the present value, instead of multiplying the future value by $1/(1 + r)^n$ the future value can be multiplied by one figure found in the present value tables.

When deciding whether or not an investment or project should be accepted the following NPV decision rules should be applied:

- Investments (or projects) should be accepted where NPV is positive.
- Where there are competing investments (or projects) the one with the highest NPV should be chosen.

Know when to accept an investment/project using NPV approach

IE Illustrative example 5.5

The table below gives information for an organisation called Micron. They are deciding whether or not to invest in a machine. The machine will cost Micron £200,000 to purchase. Once purchased the machine is expected to generate the following cash flows over its expected life of five years. Micron estimates that its cost of capital (discount factor) for undertaking the project is 10%.

Micron		**£000**	**Discount factor 10%**	**Present value £000**
Immediately	Cost of machine	-200	0	-200.00
1 year's time	Cash flow	40	0.909	36.36
2 years' time	Cash flow	80	0.826	66.08
3 years' time	Cash flow	120	0.751	90.12
4 years' time	Cash flow	120	0.683	81.96
5 years' time	Cash flow	40	0.621	24.84
5 years' time	Disposals proceeds from the machine	40	0.621	24.84
	Overall net present value			124.20

For Micron, they should invest in the new machine as the NPV for the investment is above zero. This shows that the cash flow returns are greater than the cost of capital to the company. By investing in the project they will be increasing shareholder wealth.

Limitations of the NPV approach

- The original cash flow figures could turn out to be incorrect.
- It is difficult to estimate the discount rate to be used.
- Non-financial managers may have difficulties understanding what the NPV figure represents.

Internal Rate of Return (IRR)

The IRR is a variation on the NPV method. With the NPV the discount rate has to be estimated. Estimating the correct discount rate is quite challenging as it depends on a number of factors such as interest rates, inflation and risk, which are constantly changing. With the IRR calculation the discount rate is not specified. The IRR is the discount rate which will make the sum of the discounted cash inflows equal to the discounted cash outflows.

IRR can be calculated as in the following example:

IE Illustrative example 5.6

The table below shows an investment opportunity. The original cost of the investment is £200 and it will generate the following cash flows over a five year period. To find the IRR of the investment, start with a low discount factor. Here 5% is used and the NPV is positive, showing that the IRR (the discount factor which will make the investment's NPV zero) is too low. NPV is then undertaken again using a higher discount rate. Here 20% is used, this make the NPV fall below zero showing that 20% is too high as a discount factor to be the IRR. The IRR must be between the two discount factors, it will be a number between 5% and 20%.

Year		Cash flow	5% Discount factor	Present value	Cash flow	20% Discount factor	Present value
0	Cost	-200	1	-200.00	-200	1	-200.00
1	Cash flow	40	0.952	38.08	40	0.833	33.32
2	Cash flow	40	0.907	36.28	40	0.694	27.76
3	Cash flow	100	0.864	86.40	100	0.579	57.90
4	Cash flow	100	0.823	82.30	100	0.482	48.20
5	Cash flow	20	0.784	15.68	20	0.402	8.04
5	Disposal value	10	0.784	7.84	10	0.402	4.02
			NPV	66.58		NPV	-20.76

The formula below can be used to determine the exact point between 5% and 20% at which the investment's NPV would be zero.

$$\text{IRR} = \text{SDF} + \left[\frac{\text{Positive NPV}}{\text{Positive NPV} - \text{Negative NPV}} \times (\text{HDF} - \text{SDF})\right]$$

Where:

SDF is small discount factor

HDF is high discount factor

$$\begin{aligned}\text{IRR} &= 5 + \frac{66.58}{66.58 - (-20.76)} \times (20 - 5) \\ &= 5 + \frac{66.58}{87.34} \times 15 \\ &= 16.43\%\end{aligned}$$

When deciding whether or not an investment or project should be accepted the following IRR decision rules should be applied.

- For an investment (or project) to be acceptable, it must meet a minimum IRR requirement which should be the opportunity cost of finance.
- If two *(or more)* competing investments or projects exceed the minimum IRR, the one with the higher IRR should be selected.

For the project above, 16.43% represents the yield of the investment. The IRR of 16.43% would be compared to the organisation's cost of capital and accepted if the IRR was greater.

Principle

Know when to accept an investment/project using IRR approach

Multiple IRRs

IRR calculations will produce a single percentage figure when an investment's cash flow follows a normal pattern of cash outflow followed by cash inflow. Where cash flow signs change over the life of the project it is likely that there will be multiple IRR solutions. In cases such as these, where two IRR solutions exist that are both equally valid, then NPV will be used to decide whether or not to undertake a project.

Comparison between the NPV and the IRR method

NPV	IRR
Money today is worth more than money tomorrow.	Takes time value of money into account.
It takes into account the size of an investment as the absolute change in wealth is measured.	Fails to take the size of the project into account. An IRR of 10% on £100 is quite different to a 10% return on £1,000,000.
Difficult for managers to understand as it is not a percentage figure.	Easier to communicate as it results in a percentage figure.
Results (NPVs) from a number of cash flows can be added together. This is known as additivity.	Additivity is not possible with IRR.
It can deal with unconventional cash flows.	Multiple solutions can arise with non-conventional cash flows.

Learn

EG Learning example 5.1

A company is considering which of two mutually exclusive projects it should undertake. The finance director thinks that the project with the higher NPV should be chosen whereas the managing director thinks that the one with the higher IRR should be undertaken especially as both projects have the same initial outlay and length of life. The company anticipates a cost of capital of 10% and the net after tax cash flows of the projects are as follows:

	Project X	Project Y
	$'000	$'000
Year 0	–200	–200
1	35	218
2	80	10
3	90	10
4	75	4
5	20	3

Calculate the NPV and IRR of each project and to recommend, with reasons, which project you would undertake (if either).

EG Learning example 5.2

Risk and NPV

Mentor Products plc are considering the purchase of a new computer controlled packing machine to replace the two machines which are currently used to pack product X. The new machine would result in reduced labour costs because of the more automated nature of the process, and, in addition, would permit production levels to be increased by creating greater capacity at the packing stage. With an anticipated rise in the demand for product X, it has been estimated that the new machine will lead to increased profits in each of the next three years. Due to uncertainty in demand however, the annual cash flows (including savings) resulting from purchase of the new machine cannot be fixed with certainty and have therefore been estimated probabilistically as follows:

Annual cash flows ($'000)					
Year 1	**Prob**	**Year 2**	**Prob**	**Year 3**	**Prob**
10	0.3	10	0.1	10	0.3
15	0.4	20	0.2	20	0.5
20	0.3	30	0.4	30	0.2
		40	0.3		

Because of the overall uncertainty in the sales of product X, it has been decided that only three years cash flows will be considered in deciding whether to purchase the new machine. After allowing for the scrap value of the existing machines, the net cost of the new machine will be $42,000.

The effects of taxation should be ignored.

Required

(a) Ignoring the time value of money, identify which combinations of annual cash flows will lead to an overall negative net cash flow, and determine the total probability of this occurring.

(b) On the basis of the average cash flow for each year, calculate the net present value of the new machine given that the company's cost of capital is 15%. Relevant discount factors are as follows:

Year	Discount factor
1	0.8696
2	0.7561
3	0.6575

Modified Internal Rate of Return (MIRR)

The internal rate of return calculation assumes that cash flows from a project are reinvested at the IRR. The modified IRR assumes that positive cash flows are reinvested at the organisation's cost of capital, and the initial outlays are financed at the firms financing cost. As a result of these modifications to the calculations, the MIRR more accurately reflects the cost and profitability of a project.

Key Learning Points

- Understand the main measures that a profit-making organisation would use. (D2a, D2c, D2e)
- Be able to apply these measures and discuss their appropriateness. (D2a, D2c, D2e)
- Be able to assess the performance of an organisation in relation to benchmarks. (D2g)

What's the story?

Stop and think through the 'story' of this chapter and how it links with other chapters (use the Overview to help).

Learning example solutions

EG Solution 5.1

Project: X

Year	CF	DF	PV	DF	PV
	$'000	10%	$'000	20%	$'000
0	–200	1	–200	1	–200
1	35	0.91	31.85	0.83	29.05
2	80	0.83	66.4	0.69	55.2
3	90	0.75	67.5	0.58	52.2
4	75	0.68	51	0.48	35
5	20	0.62	12.4	0.4	8
		NPV (10%)	29.15	NPV (20%)	–19.55

Project: Y

Year	CF	DF	PV	DF	PV
	$'000	10%	$'000	20%	$'000
0	–200	1	–200	1	–200
1	218	0.91	189.4	0.83	180.9
2	10	0.83	8.3	0.69	6.9
3	10	0.75	7.5	0.58	5.8
4	4	0.68	2.72	0.48	1.92
5	3	0.62	1.86	0.4	1.2
		NPV (10%)	18.76	NPV (20%)	–3.24

$$\text{IRR}(X) = 10 + \frac{29.15}{29.15 - (-19.55)}(20 - 10) = 16.0\%$$

$$\text{IRR}(Y) = 10 + \frac{18.76}{18.76 - (-3.24)}(20 - 10) = 18.5\%$$

NPV (X, 10%) = $29,150; NPV (Y, 10%) = $18,760

EG Solution 5.2

(a) The net cost of the machine is $42,000, so we are looking for combinations of annual cash inflows which total less than $42,000 for there to be an overall net cash outflow. It we assume that the cash flows for each year are independent (which seems unlikely in practice) we can then multiply the individual probabilities together to give an overall probability.

Year 1	Year 2	Year 3	Total inflow	Probability	$'000
10	10	10	30	0.3 × 0.1 × 0.3 =	0.009
10	10	20	40	0.3 × 0.1 × 0.5 =	0.015
10	20	10	40	0.3 × 0.2 × 0.3 =	0.018
15	10	10	35	0.4 × 0.1 × 0.3 =	0.012
20	10	10	40	0.3 × 0.1 × 0.3 =	0.009
					0.063

The total probability of an overall net cash outflow is 0.063.

(b)

Year	Expected average cash flow		$'000
1	(10 0.3) + (15 0.4) + (20 0.3)	=	15
2	(10 × 0.1) + (20 × 0.2) + (30 × 0.4) + (40 × 0.3)	=	29
3	(10 × 0.3) + (20 × 0.5) + (30 × 0.2)	=	19

We have a cash profile as follows:

Time	Cash flow	Discount factor at 15%	NPV
	$		$
0	(42,000)	1	(42,000)
1	15,000	0.8696	13,044
2	29,000	0.7561	21,927
3	19,000	0.6575	12,493
			5,464

The net present value of the new machine is $5,464.

6

Divisionalisation

Context

Divisionalisation is setting a business up to reflect its parts, whether internationally for a multinational company or for locations in a single country or for different types of activity. The external factors for a business will be important as will the complexity internally. We will need to look at measures to judge the divisions to see how much profit they are making relative to the investment in the division.

3Q

1. Can you list the possible reasons for a divisionalisation policy?
2. What are the advantages of the RI method over ROI?
3. What are the major problems with using financial indicators to look at the performance of a division?

6.1 Divisionalisation

Most companies today are large, often producing and selling a wide variety of products worldwide. It becomes difficult to manage such organisations from a functional structure. A divisionalised structure may be needed to manage such a company. Divisionalisation brings with it the need to devolve decision-making and this then gives rise to the need to monitor performance.

A divisionalised organisation is usually split up into discrete divisions in accordance with the products that are made. Each divisional manager will be responsible for all of the operations relating to their particular product. Each division will be classed as either a profit or investment centre. This will allow the managers to make pricing decisions, decide where to sell the products, how to make the product, the type of production system to use, what machinery to buy.

Learn

Possible reasons for a decentralisation/divisionalisation policy:

- Prevent size from becoming unwieldy
- Specialist nature work
- Motivation of managers can be improved
- Geographical, to be close to markets and sources of supply
- Fiscal, to report profits in low-tax areas
- Release top management to concentrate on strategic decisions.

Advantages of divisionalisation
- Improved quality of decisions
- Speedier decisions
- Increases managerial motivation
- More time devoted to strategic issues.

Disadvantages of divisionalisation
- Sub optimisation and may promote a lack of goal congruence.
- More costly to operate a divisionalised structure.
- Loss of control by top management.

Prerequisites for successful divisionalisation
- More appropriate for companies with diversified activities.
- Relations between divisions regulated so that no division, by seeking to increase its own profit, can reduce the profitability of the company as a whole.

The big issue for P5 is what indicators should be calculated to measure the performance of each division.
The first factor to be considered is that of whether it is the divisional performance that is being measured or the divisional manager's performance.

If the purpose is to evaluate the manager then the measures must be based on items over which the manager has control.

Determining which assets should be included in a division's asset base is also an important issue when using financial performance measures, as is the impact of inflation and depreciation.

There are a number of considerations when considering what measures to use:

- Senior management will base their decisions on these measures – if they do not accurately reflect what the division is doing then the wrong decisions will be made
- Measures should motivate division managers – if they do a better job then this will be good for the entire company and its shareholders, so motivate the manager of the investment centre, and the team, to achieve the goals of the group
- Provide the right incentive for the manager and the team to make decisions that are consistent with the goals of the group's management.

6.1.1 Measures to assess divisions in the short term

There are strong arguments for producing two measures of divisional profitability – one to evaluate managerial performance and the other to evaluate the economic performance of the division.

In the P5 exam, there are three key divisional ratios that the examiner frequently looks for:

- Return on investment
- Residual income
- Economic value added

6.2 Return on Investment (ROI)

Return on Investment (ROI) is calculated in exactly the same way as Return on Capital Employed (ROCE) and shows how much profit has been made compared to the investment. It is widely used because it links in with the figures on the statement of comprehensive income and the statement of financial position. In particular, it is one of only a few measures which can be used to ascertain divisional performance.

The main benefits of ROI are that:

- It is a relative measure and allows divisions of different sizes to be compared (since the answer is given as a percentage).
- The percentage calculated can be compared with the return required by investors.
- The performance of a division can be tracked over time (since a percentage is calculated).

Learn

	Division X	Division Y
Investment project available	£10 million	£10 million
Controllable contribution	£2 million	£1.3 million
Return on the proposed project	20%	13%
ROI of divisions at present	25%	9%

The overall cost of capital for the company is 15%.

The manager of X would be motivated **not** to invest and the manager of Y would be motivated to invest.

Problems with ROI

- It can highlight the different positions of shareholders and directors. The shareholders would prefer a higher return on less capital, whereas the directors would prefer a lower return on more capital. Shareholders' wealth will not be maximised if decisions are made on the basis of ROI.
- It can provide a disincentive to invest or force the sale of assets in order to better the return, even though they are not working efficiently for the organisation. This helps to create a short-term focus rather than a long-term focus.
- ROI may also motivate managers to make incorrect asset disposal decisions – as assets depreciate the ROI will improve, encouraging managers to keep older equipment rather than invest in new. It also encourages the use of leasing rather than buying.
- Comparison across divisions is difficult as a manufacturing division will have a greater level of fixed assets than a marketing division and thus a lower ROI.
- As a result of the above problems it can be seen that a manager may attempt to 'massage' the ROI to make their performance look better.

6.3 Residual Income (RI)

This is an alternative way of measuring the performance of an investment centre.

Residual income is calculated as:

Residual income = Profit less Imputed Interest (Investment × Required Return)

 **Learn**

The advantages of using this method over ROI are:

- RI will increase if new profitable investments are taken on and a cost of capital which is individual to each project may be used to give greater flexibility. This will allow for different risks by using different costs of capital when calculating imputed interest.
- This method is also more consistent with the overall objective of increasing shareholder wealth. The residual income is calculated by deducting an annual charge for financing assets from the profit.
- More useful in decision-making since more likely to give goal congruence.

- Empirical evidence indicates that RI is not widely used.

If RI is used it should be compared with budgeted/target levels which reflect the size of the divisional investment.

	Division X (£m)	Division Y (£m)
Proposed investment	10	10
Controllable profit	2	1.3
Cost of capital charge (15%)	1.5	1.5
Residual income	+0.5	−0.2

The manager of division X is motivated to invest and the manager of division Y is motivated **not** to invest.

There are a number of general problems which will exist whether ROI or RI is used as a measure, these include:

- Calculation of profit – There is always some scope for manipulating the profit figure used to conduct the calculation.
- Asset measurement – The treatment should be consistent and the number of leases should be monitored.
- Conflict with investment decisions – These should be made on the basis of DCF calculations which are designed to give a long-term view. It is possible to alter the effects of depreciation to make both ROI and RI more consistent with DCF.

IE Illustrative example 6.1

James Clark is presenting to divisional managers who have conflicting recommendations on what is the best performance measure for their division.

James starts by explaining that the measure should provide incentive to make decisions which are in the best interests of the overall company and that the measure should only include factors for which the managers can be held accountable for.

He goes on to say that the measures should recognise the long-term objectives as well as short-term objectives of the organisation and that the board is considering two measures – return on investment and residual income.

James explains that residual income will increase when investments earning above the cost of capital are undertaken and investments earning below the cost of capital are eliminated. It is more flexible since a different cost of capital can be applied to investments with different risk characteristics, whilst ROI is a very powerful and commonly used tool and thus arguably the most popular metric when comparing one investment to another.

Next James details the common problems associated with both methods:

- Identifying controllable profits and investment can be difficult.

- If used in a short-term way they can both over-emphasise short-term performance at the expense of long-term performance. Investment projects with positive net present value can show poor ROI and residual income figures in early years leading to rejection of projects by managers.
- If assets are valued at net book value, ROI and residual income figures generally improve as assets get older. This can encourage managers to retain outdated plant and machinery.
- Both measures require an estimate of the cost of capital, a figure which can be difficult to calculate.
- Both techniques attempt to measure divisional performance in a single figure. Given the complex nature of modern businesses, multi-faceted measures of performance are necessary.

Finally, he concludes that managers may use their decision-making freedom to make decisions that are not in the best interests of the overall company (so called dysfunctional decisions). To redress this problem, the board wants to introduce a performance measure to ensure, among other things, that the decisions made by the managers are in the best interests of the company as a whole. The managers are asked to go away and think carefully and convene the following week to suggest the best fit for the organisation.

EG **Learning example 6.1**

Residual income and return on investment are commonly used measures of performance. However, they are frequently criticised for placing too great an emphasis on the achievement of short-term results, possibly damaging longer term performance.

Discuss the issues involved in the long-term: short-term conflict referred to in the above statement.

6.4 Economic Value Added (EVA)

The concept of EVA was developed as an accounting measure by the consulting firm of Stern Stewart & Co. during the 1990's who refined RI and patented it as EVA™.

EVA™ is an estimate of the amount by which earnings exceed or fall short of the required minimum rate of return those shareholders and debtholders could get by investing in other securities of comparable risk. The formula is as follows:

EVA = Net operating profit after tax – WACC × Book value of capital employed

It is calculated in the following way:

	£'000
Operating profit after tax	300
Less: capital charge (weighted average cost of capital × net assets)	200
Economic Value Added	100

Another way of expressing this is

- EVA™ = Conventional divisional profit based on GAAP
  ± Accounting adjustments
  – Cost of capital charge on divisional assets
- Conventional divisional profit based on principles outlined for measuring divisional managerial and/or economic profits.
- Adjustments intended to convert historic accounting profit to an approximation of economic profit. Adjustments typically include capitalisation of discretionary expenses.

Learn

Value-based performance management is an approach which is based on the principle that an organisation's strategy should be measured on whether it adds value to shareholders, rather than looking at other objectives such as growth in turnover or market share.

The primary measure used is economic value added (EVA). Other measures which have been developed are market value added (MVA) and shareholder value added (SVA).

EVA has been proposed as a single top-level financial measure in order to avoid problems caused by having a number of conflicting objectives.

A number of advantages are put forward for the use of EVA:

- It is simple to translate into financial objectives.
- It reflects the performance of the organisation in monetary terms rather than as a ratio.
- It helps managers to link the statement of financial position to the statement of profit or loss.
- It takes into account the cost of capital in assessing whether an organisation is adding value for its shareholders.
- It is less easy to manipulate than accounting figures.
- EVA makes managers accountable not just for the results but also for the resources used in achieving those results and is more likely to lead organisations towards achieving a higher company value and hence a higher share price.
- If linked to incentives and divisional performance measures it will promote behaviours which add value to the organisation rather than destroy it – a positive EVA indicates value creation while a negative one indicates destruction. A series of negative EVAs could be a signal that a company needs to take corrective action, possibly involving restructuring.

EVA however has a number of disadvantages:

- Calculations can sometimes be complex and involve numerous adjustments to accounts.
- EVA is an absolute number – it will be bigger for larger divisions.

- EVA is usually computed on the basis of historical numbers: sometimes this produces distortions in incentives, and incorrect analysis.
- EVA measures can be difficult to understand, particularly for non-finance managers.
- As with other new approaches, for success EVA needs an implementation programme which includes raising awareness and educating staff.

EVA™ shows whether the management are adding or destroying value over a period of time. It is adaptable to measure performance at all levels, for example, it was originally used to assess the performance of companies quoted on the stock exchange but can also be used across all levels of management. It can also be used to aid in capital budgeting decisions in conjunction with NPV and payback.

Both RI and ROI have problems when being used to evaluate long-term decisions. This problem arises because of the way in which depreciation is calculated.

This is potentially a very big problem because most projects undertaken by managers are for the long-term and if managers are moved around inside the organisation regularly, the manager will only be interested in the impact of the decision on the division for the short-term whereas the company is interested in the long-term.

The way round this problem is to use a technique called **annuity depreciation** when the cash inflows are constant, so that in the short-term EVA™ will also be constant. In addition, the total present value of the EVA™ will be equal to the NPV calculation. In other words, decisions taken on the basis of the short-term measure will be consistent with decisions taken on the basis of the long-term measure or the NPV rule.

IE Illustrative example 6.2

A division has the opportunity to acquire a new machine for £100,000. The machine is expected to produce cash savings of £29,000 every year for five years. The cost of capital is 10%.

The net present value for the new machine is £9,939 and is calculated as follows:

	£
Investment cost	100,000
Present value of cash savings (29,000 × 3.791)	109,939
Net present value	9,939

The EVA™ for year 1 using the straight-line method of depreciation is:

	£	£
Annual cash inflow		29,000
Less Depreciation	20,000	
Interest on capital (10% of £100,000)	10,000	30,000
EVA™		(1,000)

There is a danger that this project will be rejected on the basis of the first year's EVA™ calculation if the straight-line method of depreciation is used. If we use the annuity method of depreciation, the annual depreciation will be equivalent to the capital element of an annuity required to redeem £100,000 borrowed at 10% over five years.

The capital element of an annuity can be derived from dividing the investment outlay (£100,000) by the annuity factor for 5 years at 10% (3.791).

A repayment of £26,380 per annum (£100,000/3.791) is therefore required to repay £100,000 borrowed for five years.

Year	**Annual Repayment**	**10% interest on Capital Outstanding**	**Capital Repayment**	**Capital Outstanding**
	(1)	**(2)**	**(3) = (1) – (2)**	**(4) = (4) – (3)**
	£	**£**	**£**	**£**
0				100,000
1	26,380	10,000	16,380	83,620
2	26,380	8,362	18,018	65,602
3	26,380	6,560	19,820	45,782
4	26,380	4,578	21,802	23,980
5	26,380	2,398	23,982	0

The £100,000 will be repaid with interest, and the capital repayment column represents the annual depreciation charge. The EVA™ calculation is

Year	Opening written down value	Cash inflow	Deprecia-tion	Interest on capital (10%)	EVA™
	(1)	(2)	(3)	(4)	(2) – [(3) + (4)]
	£	£	£	£	£
1	100,000	29,000	16,380	10,000	2,620
2	83,620	29,000	18,018	8,362	2,620
3	65,602	29,000	19,820	6,560	2,620
4	45,782	29,000	21,802	4,578	2,620
5	23,980	29,000	23,982	2,398	2,620

The annuity method of depreciation only produces a short-term measure that will lead to decisions consistent with the NPV rule when the net cash inflows are equal each year.

- Financial performance measures can encourage managers to become short-term oriented and seek to boost short-term profits at the expense of long-term profits.
- Approaches for reducing this short-term orientation:
  - Divisional performance evaluated on the basis of economic income (PV of future cash flows).
  - Adopt EVA™ incorporating many accounting adjustments.
  - Lengthen the measurement period.
  - Do not rely excessively on financial measures and incorporate non-financial measures that measure those factors that are critical to the long-term success of the organisation (ie adopt a Balanced Scorecard Approach).

EVA™ is believed to be the financial performance measure that comes closer than any other to capturing the true economic profit of an organisation, and is the performance measure most directly linked to the creation of shareholder wealth over time.

This view is supported by Peter Drucker who has suggested in a Harvard Business Review article, that 'until a business returns a profit that is greater than its cost of capital, it operates at a loss'. Drucker observes that such organisations return less to the economy than they consume in resources, and that instead of 'creating' they are in fact destroying wealth.

EVA™ explicitly recognises that when managers employ capital they must pay for it in the same way that they would pay other operating expenses.

6.5 Problems with using financial indicators

The major problems with using financial indicators to look at the performance of a division are:

- They are backwards looking.
- It is difficult to explain *why* the performance is improving or getting worse.
- Most staff will not be able to influence directly the financial performance.
- The division can lose sight of what the customers want.
- By the time a product is delivered it may be too late to control costs (many of which are built in at the design stage).
- It may be hard to directly compare company's financial performance, it may be easier to look at areas such as customer satisfaction.
- Managers may become obsessed with cutting costs and losing sight of the company's overall strategy.

Because of this, a number of writers have suggested performance measurement systems that include Non-financial Performance Indicators (NFPIs). Examples of these are customer satisfaction ratings, which can't be expressed in money terms but are obviously fundamental to the success of most businesses.

Learn

Advantages of using NFPIs

- Can be provided quickly
- Easy to calculate
- Easier for non-financial managers to understand
- Should focus managers on the longer-term
- More suitable in competitive environments.

Disadvantages of using NFPIs

- Financial aspects cannot be ignored
- Possible information overload
- May lead to managers focussing on their own small part of the business rather than the overall strategy.

EG Learning example 6.2

Think of three non-financial performance indicators for a university and why they are more meaningful for long-term success than financial performance indicators.

Key Learning Points

- Understand the differences among ROI, RI and EVA and be able to evaluate the performance of a division using suitable performance measures. (D3a)
- Appreciate the need for different metrics for measuring managerial and divisional performance. (D3b)
- Know the major problems with using financial indicators to look at the performance of a division. (D3a)

What's the story?

Stop and think through the 'story' of this chapter and how it links with other chapters (use the Overview to help).

Learning example solutions

EG Solution 6.1

The division managers in a company are responsible for, 'sales, cost of operation, working capital management, and acquisition and financing of divisional assets'. An important responsibility is therefore making investment decisions that relate to a long-term period, such as product and market development, the acquisition of space and facilities, development of management and staff, and so on. The measure used to appraise the performance of division managers should therefore have a long-term focus.

Profitability indices such as ROI and RI, although having the potential capability of measuring past long-term performance in the form of long-term trends, are not able to measure the effectiveness of recent decisions for which results are not yet known. These decisions are important and relate to the long-term, and need to be evaluated if the true performance of a manager is to be correctly appraised.

Some examples would help to illustrate this point:

A division manager commissions a strategic position audit which reveals that a dangerous product gap will begin to emerge in three years' time. Responding in a proactive manner the manager initiates a development project with a substantial budget and a duration of eighteen months. ROI and RI measures in the short term will be depressed. The division manager launches the new product into the market using a slow penetration pricing strategy. Market research findings have suggested that it would be in the best long-term interests of the product if it entered the market relatively slowly and took perhaps a year to reach critical mass. ROI and RI measures in the short term will be depressed.

The new product requires additional space and manufacturing equipment and facilities. The manager has a choice of either staging this investment, that is building the resources as and when the market demand grows, or investing as a 'one-off' by taking into account the maximum future capacity requirement. The manager evaluates the choices and decides that it is in the best interest of the company if he opts for the one-off investment, resulting in an over capacity in the early stages. When compared with the other decision choice the manager's short-term ROI and RI is depressed.

It is important to note that the decisions made by the manager may not be in the best interests of the company, in other words his decisions may not be effective. However the use of ROI and RI will not reveal whether these decisions set in the longer term are good or bad.

It could be suggested that ROI and RI be applied to longer-term profitability by using, for example, 3-to 6-year rolling or average profitability indexes. For example, a review of the ROIs for the two divisions in a company might indicate a growth in the returns for both divisions over a period of say five years. However the results for the early years might have resulted from decisions made by the predecessors of the present managers. Also, of course, business environments may have changed. Certainly both managers might have experienced a growth in the estimated overall industry sales of the sectors in which they are operating. Of what relevance therefore is the ROI trend?

Another short-term versus long-term decision problem relates to the basis by which assets are valued for the purpose of extracting data for measurement. Sufficient to say that if a manager is measured on the basis of net historic asset book value, it is in his best short-term interests to hold assets, even beyond their optimum economic potential, although this would adversely affect the long-term interests of the company. On the other hand, if assets are valued on the basis of replacement values, it might be in the best short-term interests of the manager to invest earlier than might be justified. In both cases there is a short-term focus, probably encouraged because of the use of ROI and/or RI measurements, which is detrimental to the long-term performance of the company.

If a company persists in placing an undue emphasis on these profitability indexes it can only expect adverse behaviour from its division managers. Worse, those managers who take a short-term view may be the ones selected for promotion and rewarded in other ways (although later the truth of their ineffectiveness may be revealed), and those who in the best interests of the company concentrate on long-term achievement, may become disillusioned and leave the organisation in the short-term, because of their lack of recognition and rewards. By the time their true merit is recognised it is too late!

EG Solution 6.2

Suitable non-financial performance indicators are:

- Student satisfaction ratings
- Exam grades
- Quality of jobs obtained afterwards
- Ratings externally
- Number of applicants for the university

The financial side of many universities is less interesting as often revenue is fixed by governments and costs are set, being property and people costs. So for long-term success the NPFIs above are better indicators for the future.

Transfer Pricing

Context

Transfer pricing happens between divisions of an organisation, whether the divisions are based in the same country or not. The usual requirement is for the transfer prices to be fair and to encourage the divisions to transfer between them when it makes sense to do so. However, other issues, such as taxation, can come into play, particularly if the transfers are happening between divisions in different countries.

3Q

1. What criteria should a good transfer pricing policy meet?
2. What is full cost transfer pricing?
3. What is the dual rate transfer pricing system and why is not widely used?

7.1 Transfer pricing

Managers in divisionalised organisations will be judged by the division's performance evaluated by ROI and RI. Both of these measures include a profit figure, so the manager of each division will try to:

- Maximise revenue
- Minimise costs

Since both divisions will be part of the organisation, the managers must be persuaded to make decisions that are good for the organisation as a whole, not just for their own division.

The idea behind transfer pricing is to promote goal congruence. In other words, both managers do what is good for the organisation as a whole because it is also good for their own division.

A transfer pricing policy is needed if goods or services are transferred between the divisions of an organisation. The transfer price adopted will affect the reported profit of each separate division and can therefore affect the level of motivation of each divisional manager.

7.2 Issues involved in transfer pricing

Two major questions to ask are:

- At what amount to set prices?
- Through what process?

A good transfer pricing policy should meet the following criteria:

- It should provide motivation for divisional managers
- It should allow divisional autonomy and independence to be maintained
- It should allow divisional performance to be assessed objectively
- It should ensure that divisional managers make decisions that are in the best interests of the divisions and also of the company as a whole (this is called goal congruence).

Learn

Its two overriding features should be:

- Simplicity in calculation and implementation
- Robustness (ie not requiring frequent adjustment).

Although different approaches will result in different figures, the limits within which the transfer price should fall can be summarised as follows:

- Minimum. The sum of the selling division's marginal cost and the opportunity cost of the resources used.

- Maximum. The lowest market price at which the buying division could acquire the goods or services externally, less any internal cost savings in packaging and delivery.
- The difference between the two limits represents the savings made by producing internally as opposed to buying in from outside.

There are three main types of transfer prices:

- Market-based prices
- Cost-based prices
- Negotiated prices

7.3 Simple market-based methods

Where an external competitive market exists for the product, both the producing and the receiving division will be happy with a transfer price set as the market price. This might be adjusted slightly downwards to reflect:

- Lower packaging and advertising costs
- Bulk volumes transferred
- Advantages of an exclusive supplier contract.

However, an external competitive market price might not exist.

Even where an intermediate market does exist, care must be taken where there is spare capacity (it not being a perfectly competitive market). Setting the transfer price at the outside market price may discourage managers from utilising spare capacity, which would in fact be a good thing for the company as a whole.

If a highly competitive market for the intermediate product exists then the market price is the proper transfer price.

Conditions:

- Producing division can sell as much of the product to outside customers.
- Purchasing division can acquire as much of the product from outside suppliers without affecting the price.

If the purchasing division cannot make a long-run profit at the outside market price, the division is better off not to produce the product and should instead go to the external market for its supply. If the purchasing division cannot make a long-run profit when it must acquire the product at the external price, the division should stop acquiring this product and should allow the producing division to sell all its output to the external market.

The organisation will usually benefit if a transaction occurs internally rather than having a producing division sell a certain amount externally while the Purchasing division is acquiring the same amount from outside suppliers.

Internal rather than external transfers are encouraged by means of a discount from the market price that reflects savings on selling and collection expenses, delivery, service or warranty terms associated with external sales.

Hidden costs can arise if the purchasing division makes unreasonable delivery demands on the producing division.

Sometimes the transaction must occur internally to maintain product quality or product confidentiality. The market price may be adjusted to reflect the extra cost required to meet a more stringent quality standard or special feature only available from the Purchasing division.

The challenge is to keep an accumulation of such special charges from driving the price for above the prices of comparable products available externally.

In reality the price-setting process and transfer price problem is complicated as the market is not perfectly competitive.

If market prices existed that allowed optional resource allocation and managerial evaluation decisions to be made within the organisation, little reason would exist to keep the different divisions within a single corporate entity – the divisions could function as independent market entities since no gain would arise from centralised control.

 **Principle**

The principle behind market-based methods of transfer pricing

7.4 Marginal cost transfer prices

Transfer price set is the short-term variable cost plus the opportunity cost of the capacity used to make the product. If the product has an outside market – transfer price will be the market price since the opportunity cost of using the product internally will be the profits foregone by not selling the product in the external market.

The opportunity cost will be either the contribution forgone by selling one unit internally rather than externally or the contribution forgone by not using the same facilities in the producing division for their next best alternative use.

The application of this general rule means that the transfer price equals:

- The standard variable cost of the producing division, if there is no outside market for the units manufactured and no alternative use for the facilities in that division;
- The market price, if there is an outside market for the units manufactured in the producing division and no alternative more profitable use for the facilities in that division.

The following general rule has been put forward for setting transfer prices.

Transfer price per unit = Standard variable cost in the producing division **plus** the opportunity cost to the company as a whole of supplying the unit internally

Or: TP = SVC + LCM

Transfer price = Standard variable cost + Lost contribution margin

LCM is the difference between the external market price and SVC.

 **Learn**

IE Illustrative example 7.1

Division A manufactures a product with a SVC of £5.

Division A can sell the product externally for £8 or it can sell the product to Division B which further processes the product at a SVC of £4 and sells the product externally for £14. CM/PU below is contribution margin per unit. See how the company total is the sum of Division A's plus Division B's. The transfer price cancels out when looking at the company as a whole.

Div A		**Div B**		**Company**	
£8	MP	£14	MP	£14	MP
(£5)	SVC	(£8)	TP	(£5)	SVC-A
		(£4)	SVC	(£4)	SVC-B
£3	CM/PU +	£2	CM/PU =	£5	CM/PU

But if the external MP for Division A is £11 the TP will be £11 also (£5 SVC + £6 LCM) which will if transferred to Division B lead to Division A negative contribution of £1. No transfer will occur – it is better for Division A to sell externally.

Suppose the cost saving to Division A of selling internally is £2 per unit because Division A avoids selling expenses, bad debts etc. If the TP is lowered by subtracting from SVC the amount of cost saved by selling internally, an adjusted MP is derived. CM/PU below is contribution margin per unit.

Div A		**Div B**		**Company**	
£9	Adjusted MP*	£14	MP	£14	MP
(£3)	SVC	(£9)*	TP	(£5)	SVC-A
		(£4)	SVC	£2	Cost saved from internal sales
				(£4)	SVC-B
£6	CM/PU +	£1	CM/PU	£7	CM/PU

This method is rarely used in practice. This is because often the selling division will incur a loss and the profits of the buying division will be overstated. This is not consistent with performance measurement.

7.5 Full cost transfer pricing

Recent surveys of transfer pricing practice indicate that the most popular method of determining transfer price in practice is a full cost pricing scheme using the traditional standard costing system to calculate manufacturing costs.

Problems arise when accountants estimate full cost using traditional accounting methods that assign capacity related costs to products in arbitrary ways – eg Capacity related costs ÷ number of units produced.

- Varying transfer price since cost per unit is constantly changing as capacity use varies.
- Short and long run components of cost are mixed and therefore difficult to ascertain how cost savings can be obtained by using capacity more efficiently.
- Formula approach that takes variable cost and adds an arbitrary mark-up to cover capacity related costs and a target profit margin is a cost recovery system that takes no account of underlying cost behaviour and may provide incorrect evidence.

The main problem with this system is that it is based on the traditional absorption costing system, which has numerous flaws.

 **Learn**

7.6 Negotiated transfer prices

The benefit of these exist where there is an imperfect external market and it allows managers to engage in a bargaining arrangement. Its advantages are that it is consistent with divisional autonomy and provides a forum to confront and resolve interdivisional conflicts.

It does have a number of disadvantages including:

- Can lead to sub-optimal decisions
- Can lead to inter-divisional conflict
- Divisional profits reflect divisional managers' negotiating ability (and ability to understand TP system) as well as competence in managing the business
- Time-consuming (an imposed solution may be quicker)
- Inappropriate in extreme situations, if either:
  - Perfect market exists (then unnecessary), or
  - No market at all (then S and R are not sufficiently independent to be separate divisions)

- Requires procedure in case of disagreement (arbitration by the centre?).

 **Learn**

IE Illustrative example 7.2

Oslo is the supplying division (No external market for the intermediate product).

Bergen is the receiving division (converts intermediate to final product).

Expected sales of the final product:

Net selling price (£)	Quantity sold Units
100	1,000
90	2,000
80	3,000
70	4,000
60	5,000
50	6,000

The costs of each division are:

	Oslo (£)	Bergen (£)
Variable cost per unit	11	7
Fixed costs attributable to the products	60,000	90,000

The transfer price of the intermediate product has been set at £35 based on a full cost plus mark-up.

Whole company profit computations

Output level (units)	Total revenues	Company variable costs	Company fixed costs	Company profit/(loss)
1,000	100,000	18,000	150,000	(68,000)
2,000	180,000	36,000	150,000	(6,000)
3,000	240,000	54,000	150,000	36,000
4,000	280,000	72,000	150,000	58,000
5,000*	300,000	90,000	150,000	60,000*
6,000	300,000	108,000	150,000	42,000

Oslo Division (Supplying division)

Output level (units)	Transfer price revenues	Variable costs	Fixed costs	Total profit/ (loss)
1,000	35,000	11,000	60,000	(36,000)
2,000	70,000	22,000	60,000	(12,000)
3,000	105,000	33,000	60,000	12,000
4,000	140,000	44,000	60,000	36,000
5,000	175,000	55,000	60,000	60,000
6,000*	210,000	66,000	60,000	84,000*

Bergen Division (Receiving division)

Output level (units)	Total revenues	Variable costs	Total cost of transfers	Fixed costs	Total profit/(loss)
1,000	100,000	7,000	35,000	90,000	(32000)
2,000	180,000	14,000	70,000	90,000	6,000
3,000*	240,000	21,000	105,000	90,000	24,000*
4,000	280,000	28,000	140,000	90,000	22,000
5,000	300,000	35,000	175,000	90,000	0
6,000	300,000	42,000	210,000	90,000	(42,000)

At £35, the transfer price (TP) does not motivate optimum output level for the company as a whole.

- To ensure overall company optimality the TP must be set at MC of the intermediate product (ie VC of £11 per unit or £11,000 per batch of 1,000 units).
- The receiving division will face the following net marginal revenue (NMR) schedule:

  Units net marginal revenue (£)

1000	93,000 (100,000 – 7,000)
2000	73,000 (80,000 – 7,000)
3000	53,000 (60,000 – 7,000)
4000	33,000 (40,000 – 7,000)
5000	13,000 (20,000 – 7,000)
6000	-7,000 (0 – 7,000)

At a TP of £11, the receiving division will choose to expand output to 5,000 units.

Consider a full cost TP without a mark-up (£23 if the denominator level to compute unit fixed costs is 5,000 units)

The receiving division manager will choose to produce 4,000 units.

- Negotiation:
  - No external market so supplying division manager has little bargaining power.
  - Could avoid £60,000 fixed costs, so would look for a TP of at least £23 per unit (assuming a denominator level of 5,000 units is used).

7.7 Resolving transfer pricing conflicts

Two approaches advocated:

1. Adopt a dual rate TP system.
2. Transfer at MC plus a lump sum fee.

7.7.1 Dual rate TP system

The dual rate TP system, as its name suggests, uses two transfer prices:

1. Supplying division may receive full cost plus a mark-up so that it makes a profit on inter-divisional transfers (eg Oslo TP > £23).
2. Receiving division charged at MC of transfers thus motivating managers to operate at the optimum output level for the company as a whole.
3. Profit on inter-group trading removed by an accounting adjustment.

It is, however, not widely used because:

1. Use of two TPs causes confusion
2. Seen as artificial
3. Divisions protected from competition
4. Reported inter-divisional profits can be misleading.

 **Learn**

7.7.2 Marginal cost plus a lump sum fee

- Intended to motivate receiving division to equate MC of transfers with its net marginal revenue to determine optimum company profit maximising output level.
- Enables supplying division to cover its fixed costs and earn a profit on inter-divisional transfers through the fixed fee charged for the period.
- Motivates receiving division to consider full cost of providing intermediate products/services (TP = £11 MC plus £60,000 lump sum plus a profit contribution in the example).

 **Learn**

7.7.3 TP conclusions/recommendations

- Competitive market for the intermediate product — Use market prices.
- No market for the intermediate product or an imperfect market — Transfer at MC plus a lump sum or negotiation may be appropriate in certain circumstances.
- Use standard costs for cost-based TPs.

7.8 Additional issues for multinational companies

For multinational companies, there are additional issues which arise in setting transfer prices.

Taxation

Different tax rules and differences in tax rates between countries mean that the location of taxable profits will affect the total amount of tax paid. For example, if the selling company is located in a low tax country while the buying company is located in a high tax country, the organisation may attempt to minimise the amount of tax paid by setting a higher transfer price. Whether this will be effective for tax planning purposes is another question and multinationals invest a significant amount of time and effort into ensuring that their transfer pricing system is tax efficient *and* robust enough to stand up to challenge by tax authorities.

Learn

EG Learning example 7.1

Innovate and Operate are two companies within the Alpha group. Innovate is located in Country A and Operate is located in Country B. Country A's tax rate is 10% and Country B's tax rate is 30%. In 2013, Innovate charged Operate €2m for the right to distribute branded products.

Show how this transaction generates a tax saving, assuming that it is effective for tax purposes.

Exchange rates

Fluctuating exchange rates add an element of transaction risk to intercompany transactions where the two companies use different functional currencies.

Often, a multinational group will specify a single exchange rate (for example, the US dollar or the euro) to be used in intra-group transactions.

Currency controls

The presence of currency controls in a particular country may influence the transfer pricing decision by motivating the group to limit the amount of profit located in a particular country. Put simply, to avoid currency restrictions, the group may aim to locate very little profit in a country where it will be difficult or expensive to repatriate profits.

EG Learning example 7.2

M has two divisions, X and Y. Division X is a chip manufacturer and Division Y assembles mobile phones. Division X currently manufactures many different types of chip, one of which is used in the manufacture of the mobile phones. Division X has no external market for the chips that are used in the mobile phones and currently sets the transfer price on the basis of total cost plus 20% mark-up.

The budgeted statement of profit or loss for Division Y for next year shows the following results:

Mobile phone range	**P**	**Q**	**R**
	$000	**$000**	**$000**
Sales	10,000	9,500	11,750
Less: Total costs	7,200	11,700	9,250
Profit/(loss)	2,800	(2,200)	2,500
Fixed costs	2,000	5,400	5,875

The total costs shown above include the cost of the chips.

Division Y uses a traditional absorption costing system based on labour hours.

M operates a performance measurement system based on divisional profits. In order to increase profit for the forthcoming year, Division Y has asked permission to buy chips from an external supplier.

The accountant of M has recently attended a course on activity-based costing (ABC) and has recommended that the divisions should implement an ABC system rather than continue to operate the traditional absorption costing system.

Discuss the current transfer pricing system and explain alternative systems that might be more appropriate for the forthcoming year.

Key Learning Points

- Understand the concept of transfer pricing and when it is used. (D3c)
- Be able to explain the various methods of transfer pricing. (D3d)
- Appreciate the issues that require consideration when setting a transfer price. (D3e)

What's the story?

Stop and think through the 'story' of this chapter and how it links with other chapters (use the Overview to help).

Learning example solutions

EG Solution 7.1

The group makes a net saving of €2m × (30% – 10%) = €0.4m.

Innovate's taxable profit is increased by €2m, and so its tax expense is increased by 10% × €2m = €0.2m.

Operate's taxable profit is reduced by €2m, and so its tax expense is reduced by 30% × €2m = €0.6m.

EG Solution 7.2

The current transfer pricing system in operation involves Division X setting the price at the total cost of the chips plus a 20% mark-up.

This price will allow Division X to generate some profit on internal sales to Division Y. It may also be a price that is acceptable to both selling and buying divisions. It may be seen as a 'fair' price.

However, the price is unlikely to encourage goal congruent behaviour from the divisional managers. The manager of Division Y has already asked permission to purchase the chips from an external supplier. This may or may not be in the best interest of M.

To bring about goal congruent behaviour, the transfer price should reflect the opportunity cost of the transfer. This relevant cost will depend upon the circumstances within the division. Cost plus 20% will not reflect the relevant cost.

The transfer price set by Division X should either be:

1. the marginal cost of the chip – if spare capacity is used to manufacture the chips; or
2. marginal cost plus contribution forgone from other products – if chips for Division Y are manufactured by producing and selling less of one of its existing products. Division X must be compensated for the loss in contribution from the other product. This opportunity cost is built into the transfer price.

If marginal cost, in particular, is used as the transfer price, the manager of Division X will be demotivated as no benefit (contribution) is received from internal sales.

If this proves to be the case, a dual pricing system may be implemented. This is where the selling division and buying division record different transfer prices.

Division X may record sales at cost plus 20%, but Division Y records purchases at marginal cost. This system will motivate the manager of X and encourage goal congruent decisions from the manager of Y.

An alternative to dual pricing would be a two-part tariff system. Under this method Division Y would pay a transfer price equal to the marginal cost per unit, but then a fixed fee would be paid to Division X each period to provide them with some benefit.

London
School of Business
& Finance
shaping success in business and finance

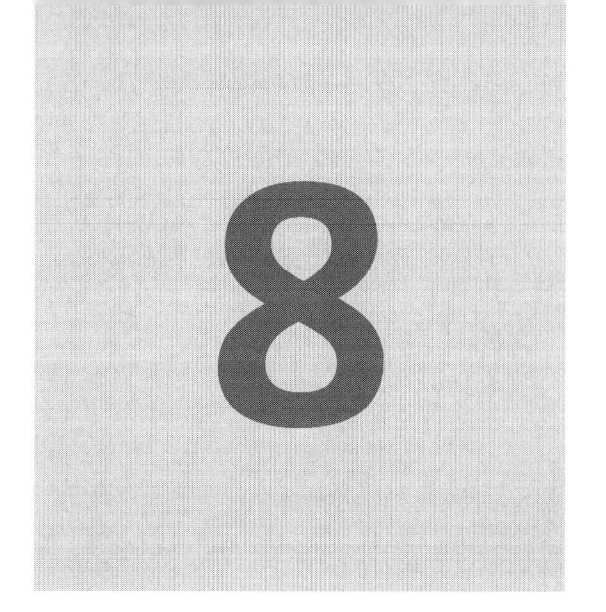

8

Non-financial Measures of Performance Evaluation

Context

Non-financial measures of performance can often be more useful and meaningful than financial measures. Often the financial measures are looking at the final effect of the performance of the organisation whilst non-financial measures, such as staff turnover, may reflect a major reason why an organisation isn't performing as well.

Similarly, customer satisfaction ratings are a non-financial effect that may demonstrate an underlying cause of why an organisation is doing well or badly financially.

3Q

1. Why is measuring performance in the public sector present difficulties?
2. What is quality control?
3. What is the six sigma level of performance?

8.1 Comparing profit and not-for-profit (NFP) organisations

If you are asked to benchmark a public sector organisation with a private sector one, there are some adjustments that might need to be made before a meaningful comparison can occur.

What would the public sector organisation's surplus/deficit be if:

- it had to borrow money and pay interest on it?
- it stopped providing services that are uneconomic (ie closed something)?
- it charged everyone for the service it provides?

8.2 Measuring performance in the public sector

This has often presented difficulties due to the following factors:

- There is often little, if any, competition for various public sector bodies.
- Different stakeholders have expectations of what the organisation should achieve (profit is obviously not one of them) – this may make it harder to run things as efficiently as they should be.
- It may be difficult to define performance measures and it may be hard to actually measure outcomes.

Many public sector organisations are measured on the three Es:

- Economy – the cost of treating a patient in a hospital
- Efficiency – the time taken to treat the patient
- Effectiveness – the success of the treatment.

There may be a trade-off between these three. Benchmarking can be used to examine performance versus other organisations.

There are a number of different ways of assessing performance in NFP organisations.

For example in a university: Have recruitment targets been achieved? Have attrition rates gone down? How many students graduated? Did the university manage to recruit the staff it needed? What was the average cost per student?

The best picture of the success of an organisation is obtained by using a number of approaches and by examining both financial and non-financial issues.

- The 'goal approach' looks at the ultimate objectives of the organisation, ie it looks at output measures.
- The 'systems resources approach' looks at how well the organisation has obtained the inputs it needs to function.
- The 'internal processes approach' looks at how well inputs have been used to achieve outputs – it is a measure of efficiency.
- The '3 Es' approach examines
  - Effectiveness – looks at the output
  - Efficiency –looks at the link between outputs and inputs
  - Economy – looks at the level of inputs.

8.2.1 Setting targets

Once suitable measures have been decided, the organisation will need to set targets to motivate the managers.

The most widely remembered approach is to aim for targets which are:

Specific – clear statement, easy to understand

Measurable – to enable control and communication down the organisation

Attainable – It is pointless setting unachievable objectives

Relevant – appropriate to the mission and stakeholders

Timed – have a time period for achievement.

8.2.2 Non-financial Performance Indicators (NFPIs)

Activity	Measurement	Non-financial Performance Indicators (NFPIs)
Input	Quality of purchased components	Zero defects
Work	Equipment productivity Maintenance effort Overtime Waste Throughput Production flexibility Product complexity	Actual vs standard Equipment failure (Downtime/ Total time) Time between overhauls Overtime/total hours % Defective items Return × Time available Set-up time Number of component parts
Product	Quantity of output Quality of output Safety Reliability Availability Obsolescence Commitment to quality	% Completion: Actual vs target Key product characteristics Safety records Warranty claims/costs % Stock-outs % Shrinkage % Conformance to quality

London School of Business & Finance
shaping success in business and finance

Market	Market share Leadership Growth Strengths Competition	Volume % New product innovation New clients/total clients Competitive value index Vulnerability index
Employee	Employee skills Employee morale Employee productivity	Educational attainment index Absenteeism/% Turnover $\text{Output efficiency} = \frac{\text{Output}}{\text{Payroll cost}}$
Customers	Customer awareness	% Repeat orders

Learn

Value for Money (VFM)

VFM is used to assess whether or not an organisation has obtained the maximum benefit from the goods and services it both acquires and provides, within the resources available to it.

It is appropriate for NFPs and public sector organisations as gaining the best value for the limited funds available is what stakeholders expect.

VFM is often described in terms of the 'three Es' and interpreted as providing a service in a way which is economical, efficient and effective.

VFM is:

- Largely subjective in nature – and a measure of judgement is required to determine whether VFM has been achieved or not
- Not only measures the cost of goods and services, but also takes account of the mix of quality, cost, resource use, fitness for purpose

VFM can be achieved through:

- Benchmarking an activity against similar activities in other organisations
- Using performance indicators
- Conducting VFM studies
- Seeking out and then adopting recognised good practice where this can be adapted to the institution's circumstances
- Internal audit work
- Retaining both documents that show how an activity has been planned to build in VFM, and evidence of the good practices adopted by examining the results or outcomes of an activity

8.3 Issues with interpreting results

Even if the correct measures are being used, they will need to be interpreted correctly by senior management in order to make strategic decisions.

There are a number of difficulties with comparing different companies/divisions.

Amongst the most common difficulties are:

- Public vs private sector company
- New vs established company
- Different industries
- One company may just be having an unusually bad/good year
- Companies in different locations
- Industries at different stages of the life cycle
- Differing objectives of companies
- Amount of capital spending (affects ROI/ROCE)

Another frequently asked question is:

What additional information would enable you to make a more valid comparison?

Look to see what the examiner has given you, one or two of the following will be missing so you can suggest they would help:

- Budgets
- More previous years
- Other organisations in a similar sector
- Non-financial performance indicators

Political influence in the public sector

In some cases, key stakeholders such as government can interfere in the decision-making process, either directly, by influencing decisions, or indirectly, by rewarding achievement of certain objectives.

In some cases, political interference means that long-term performance is sacrificed for short-term political achievements.

The managers of such organisations need to be skilled in dealing with conflicting stakeholder demands and often need to respond to changing objectives or objectives which are mutually exclusive.

8.4 Quality

The concept of quality in organisations is subjective and means different things to different people. Consumers will focus on the quality of the product and how it compares to other competitors (specification quality). Producers might measure conformance quality which looks at how well an item was produced. In general terms, quality can be defined as a product or service as being fit for purpose.

There are three interlinking approaches businesses use to ensure quality: quality control, quality assurance and quality management.

- **Quality control** is a process whereby organisations review the quality of all factors in the production process. It involves:
  - Establishing quality standards;
  - Designing processes to achieve the required quality;
  - Measuring the quality of the service or products;
  - Assessing the actual quality with planned quality;
  - Taking action where quality is substandard.
- **Quality assurance** in some ways is a more superior system then quality control as it aims to create quality rather than to control for it. Systems are set up so that quality failings are minimised and that products are right first time every time. Quality assurance is a systematic process where outputs are compared with standards, processes are monitored and feedback loops are established so that quality failings are prevented. Two of the major principles associated with quality assurance are the product or service should be fit for purpose and that it should be right first time, every time. Quality assurance must manage and account for the following:
  - The design of the product or service design;
  - Consistent quality of the materials;
  - Reliability of the production process;
  - High standard of operational procedures;
  - Adequate training so that human error is minimised;
  - Reliability of material supply.

- **Quality management.** Implementing quality control and quality assurance is part of quality management. Quality management is based on eight principles that can help organisations create a framework which should lead to improved performance.
  - **Principle 1 – Customer Focus**. Organisations are reliant on their customers and as a result, they should understand present and future customer needs and attempt to exceed their customers' expectations.
  - **Principle 2 – Leadership**. Leaders will direct organisational activities. They should create an internal environment that enables everyone to strive for continuous quality improvements.
  - **Principle 3 – Involvement of people.** Everyone at all levels should be involved with the quality process.
  - **Principle 4 – Process approach.** Results are achieved more effectively when activities and resources are managed properly.
  - **Principle 5 – Systems approach to management.** Good management of internal processes will lead to effective quality management.
  - **Principle 6 – Continual improvement.** Continual improvement should be a permanent organisational objective.
  - **Principle 7 – Factual approach to decision-making.** Decision on quality will be made based on the analysis of data and information.
  - **Principle 8 – Mutually beneficial supplier relationships.** The relationship between suppliers and organisations are mutually beneficial and a good relationship is key to ensuring high quality in the provision of goods and services.

Principle

Learn the three interlinking approaches businesses use to ensure quality

8.5 Quality compliance and certification

The International Organisation for Standardisation (ISO), among other bodies, produce quality standards suitable for application in a variety of settings and organisations.

ISO has a number of management system standards, each focusing on different issues affecting global businesses.

Example standards that are widely used include:

- ISO 50001 - Energy management
- ISO 14000 family - Environmental management
- ISO 9000 family - Quality management
- ISO 22000 - Food safety management
- ISO/IEC 27001 - Information security management
- ISO 20121 - Sustainable events management

The ISO 9000 series of standards provide a model for organisations to follow when setting up and operating a quality management system: the standards cover quality management system guidelines and requirements. Because the ISO standards are developed as a result of international, expert consensus, by implementing a management system standard based on ISO, organisations can benefit from global management experience and good practice.

ISO lists the benefits of an effective management system as:

- More efficient resource use
- Improved risk management, and
- Increased customer satisfaction as services and products consistently deliver what they promise.

ISO 9000 introduces users to the principles of quality management and develops a process approach to continual improvement.

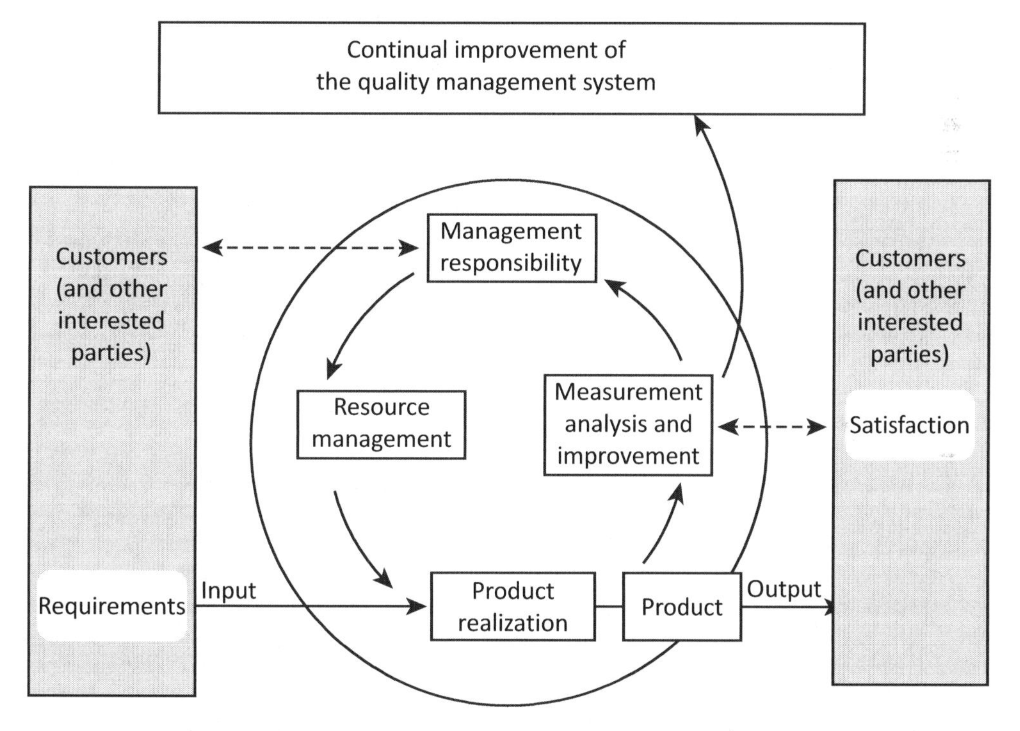

ISO 9001 contains the requirements for a quality management system: and the requirements can be certified by an external body. The following activities need to be considered when a system is implemented:

- Overall requirements for the quality management system and documentation
- Management responsibility, focus, policy, planning and objectives
- Resource management and allocation
- Product realisation and process management
- Measurement, monitoring, analysis and improvement

Source: http://www.iso.org/iso

Some organisations choose to be certified as compliant with ISO standards (and thus benefit from the assurance given by an expert third party), whereas some organisations will be compliant with ISO standards but will not seek certification.

8.6 Total quality management

Total Quality Management (TQM) is based on the following principles:

- Acceptance that customers are the most important thing
- Internal customers are just as important as external ones
- Preventing errors is better than detecting them through inspections
- Employees should be held responsible for quality in their areas
- The only acceptable level of quality is 100%
- All departments should aim to get things right first time
- The cost of poor quality should be measured and emphasised.

 **Learn**

TQM is a philosophy of quality management that originated in Japan in the 1950s and is a system which integrates the quality management efforts of all participants in an organisation.

The basic principle of TQM is that costs of prevention (getting things right first time) are less than the costs of correction and contrasts with the 'traditional' approach which takes the view that less than 100% quality is acceptable as the costs of achieving 100% outweigh the benefits. However, supporters of TQM argue that the impact of less than 100% quality in terms of lost potential for future sales also has to be taken into account. This pursuit of 100% quality or zero defects is the cornerstone of TQM.

A TQM philosophy aims to ensure that improving quality is the concern of every employee at every stage of producing a good or service. Each employee is empowered to be responsible for quality. JIT and TQM together lead to a multi-skilled workforce in which the factory layout may need to be simplified so that units of product can be efficiently pulled through the system without bottlenecks building up.

This requires supportive suppliers who must be prepared to deliver, at minimal lead times, defect free components as soon as required in the numbers required.

A system of Electronic Data Interchange (EDI) can mean a dedicated link between the purchasing department and each supplier's despatch department. Units required can therefore be ordered without the inefficiencies of having to raise paper based orders.

Companies benefit from TQM by having fewer goods returned (since they should all now be high quality) and by having a happier and more productive workforce (since they are genuinely empowered to be responsible for their outputs).

8.7 Just in time

Just In Time (JIT) is a manufacturing technique whose objective is to produce or procure products or components as they are required by a customer or for use, rather than for inventory. A JIT system is often described as a 'pull' system, which responds to demand, in contrast to a 'push' system, in which inventory at different stages of the manufacturing process acts as a buffer between the elements of the system, such as purchasing, production and sales.

Learn

JIT is a contrast to old-fashioned approaches to manufacturing is a stable environment where companies to operate their production line at a steady rate and thus build up inventory of a component, before moving on to another component. The inventory held of raw materials and finished products protected the company against problems arising from late deliveries from suppliers and defective goods. The company could simply run down the inventory while waiting for delivery of new units.

Although it originated with manufacturing systems, the JIT philosophy can also be applied to some service operations. For example, JIT in service operations will seek to eliminate internal or external queues of customers because queues are uneconomical – they waste the time of the customers in the queue, a queue needs space which uses up resources and money, but adds no value; and having to wait in a queue gives customers an adverse impression of the quality of the service.

EG Learning example 8.1

List the key features of a just-in-time manufacturing system and how those features affect management accounting.

EG Learning example 8.2

Suggest possible problems in applying just-in-time principles to a modern retailer.

8.8 Kaizen costing

Kaizen costing is a cost reduction system based on the principle of maintaining cost control for products currently in production. This philosophy implies that small, incremental and rapid improvements applied and sustained over a long period result in significant improvements to results. (The Japanese word 'kaizen' can be translated as 'continuous improvement'.)

Learn

Kaizen costing focuses on:

- identifying opportunities to eliminate non-value adding activities and waste using analytical techniques, such as value stream mapping in the targeted systems and processes of an organisation
- improving productivity and reducing costs to achieve sustained continual improvement
- involving workers from multiple functions and levels in the organisation in working together to address a problem or improve a particular process
- chosen improvements are rapidly implemented (often within 72 hours of initiating the Kaizen event)
- involving employees in finding ways to reduce costs and improve cycle times.

Kaizen costing (for products already in production) is thus consistent with the idea of target costing (for products still being developed).

8.9 Target costing

Target costing is used particularly where there is a lot of competition from similar products/services and is a product cost estimate derived by subtracting a desired profit margin from a competitive market price.

- Analyse the external environment to look at competitors/customers etc
- Set a realistic price
- Subtract the required return (probably using a target ROI from the investment in the project)
- This gives a maximum total cost
- Split this total cost into areas reflecting for example
- Variable manufacturing costs
- Variable distribution costs
- Overheads based on development
- Overheads based on marketing
- Come up with a target for each of these areas and design the product to meet these targets
- These targets become the standards to be used and in some settings, the firm's actual cost may be at or below the level required to achieve a target profit. However, for most firms, the task of driving the cost down to the level that ensures that the target margin is achieved creates many challenges. Meeting these challenges typically requires a combined organisational effort involving many different functioning areas (for example engineering, design, marketing and accounting).

Learn

A firm may employ the target costing philosophy in the following ways.

Price setting: It aims to undercut competitors and set a price that is most appropriate from the perspective of what customers are willing to pay. Because the price is driven by what customers are willing to pay, the company is adhering to the basic principles of target costing.

Design specification: It requires the design specification for each product and the production methods be examined for potential areas of cost reduction that will not compromise the quality of the products. For example:

- Can any materials be eliminated, eg cut down on packing materials?
- Can a cheaper material be substituted without affecting quality?
- Can part assembled components be bought in to save on assembly time?
- Can the incidence of the cost drivers be reduced?
- Is there some degree of overlap between the product-related fixed costs that could be eliminated by combining service departments or resources?

This cost reduction process is then carried out with the aim of providing a product which meets that target cost. The cost reduction process usually makes use of other techniques, including:

- Value analysis
- Value engineering
- JIT
- TQM
- Kaizen
- Activity-based costing (ABC) and management
- Cause–effect analysis ('fishbone' diagrams)

Historically, target costing has been developed and used in the manufacturing sector. However it may also be relevant for businesses in the service sectors because the principles of understanding the market and developing products and services which provide a satisfactory return at a given price are the same.

The cost analysis and management process can be applied to the design of the service offered and the delivery system; and target costing can provide a disciplined approach to the introduction of new services or extensions to existing ones.

As it can be difficult to estimate the costs of providing individual services where a range of services use one delivery system, a target costing system can consider the impact of new services on the whole system, to assess whether additional costs resulting from the service development, such as added complexity, are offset by the increased revenue.

There are a number of key features common to successful implementations of target costing systems and include:

- Customer focus
- Consideration of all costs
- Entire lifecycle considered
- Starts early on ie at the design stage
- Multi discipline ie involves all functions of the organisation
- Iterative – if a resultant estimated cost exceeds the target cost, the cost reduction process will be repeated to reduce the estimated cost further

- Cost targets – the final decision whether or not to introduce the product will be made once the cost estimate is on target or no further reductions can be made

8.10 The six sigma approach

The main theory of quality improvement in paper P5 is the six sigma concept. The idea is to try and reduce the chance of an item failing to be of a good enough quality. This does not mean having a single standard, there may be a range of values which are acceptable.

This range is known as the tolerance. For example, a hamburger chain may say that as long as a burger is not too hot or too cold it is acceptable. This would give a range of acceptable temperatures (the tolerance).

Six sigma is a performance measurement framework, first pioneered by Motorola in the 1980s, which has developed into a system for process improvement. The six sigma approach is about many gradual improvements to individual processes rather than occasional large ones and has been used by both manufacturing and service businesses to decrease wastage and improve products and services, leading to greater customer satisfaction and lower costs.

The stages that six sigma goes through are:

- Defining customer requirements
- Measuring existing performance
- Analysing the existing process
- Improving the process
- Controlling the new process.

Its aim is to achieve a reduction in variations and the number of 'faults' that go beyond an accepted tolerance limit. The ultimate aim of a six sigma is to reduce the variation in process output so that there are no more than 3.4 defects per million opportunities – the six sigma level of performance.

 **Learn**

Performance measures are based on customer requirements. While targets may appear very high at first, it should be remembered that just one defect can result in a lost customer.

The six sigma is a framework which makes use of a range of tools, such as:

- Fishbone diagrams
- Process mapping tools
- SWOT analysis
- Pareto analysis

IE Illustrative example 8.1

In the following example a clinic is using the Six Sigma process to improve patient waiting times. An investigation of the views of patients has revealed that:

- patients do not want to be called before their appointment time as they do not want to feel that they have to be at the clinic early to avoid missing an appointment
- the maximum length of time they are prepared to wait after the appointment time is 30 minutes

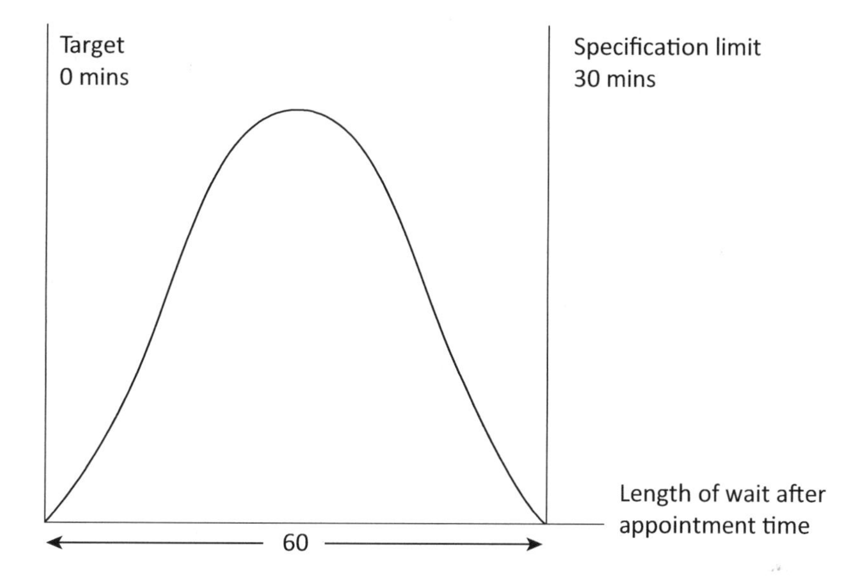

The clinic has therefore set 30 minutes as the specification limit for the wait, and the aim of the six sigma programme will be to ensure that no more than 3.4 waits in every million occurrences exceed 30 minutes.

There are a number of key requirements for the implementation of six sigma:

- Six sigma should be focused on the customer and based on the level of performance acceptable to the customer. Six sigma targets for a process should be related to the main drivers of performance.
- To maximise savings, six sigma needs to be part of a wider performance management programme which is linked to the strategy of the organisation. It should not be just about doing things better but about doing things differently.
- Senior managers within the organisation have a key role in driving the process.
- Training and education about the process throughout the organisation are essential for success.
- Six sigma sets a tight target, but accepts some failure – the target is not zero defects.

Some criticisms and limitations of six sigma include:

- Six sigma has been criticised for its focus on current processes and reliance on data. It is suggested that this could become too rigid and limit process innovation.
- Six sigma is based on the use of models which are by their nature simplifications of real life.
- Judgement needs to be used in applying the models in the context of business objectives.
- The approach can be very time consuming and expensive.
- Organisations need to be prepared to put time and effort into its implementation.
- The culture of the organisation must be supportive – not all organisations are ready for such a scientific process.
- The process is heavily data driven which can be a strength, but can become over bureaucratic.
- Six sigma can give all parts of the organisation a common language for process improvement, but it is important to ensure that this does not become jargon but is expressed in terms specific to the organisation and its business.
- There is an underlying assumption in Six Sigma that the existing business processes meet customers' expectations. It does not ask whether it is the right process.

The examiner may require you to calculate the cost to the company of poor quality. The main categories are:

- Prevention costs – money spent *before* products are made to prevent problems occurring. Examples include staff training, design and process engineering and machine maintenance.
- Appraisal costs – money spent *after* products are made to check quality is acceptable. Examples include inspection costs.
- Internal failure costs – money spent repairing a product *before* a customer receives a product that has been found to be faulty. Examples include rework costs.
- External failure costs – money spent repairing a product *after* the customer has received a faulty product. Examples include meeting warranty costs.

The above can be used in any situation. Often it is necessary for companies to appreciate the costs involved with not improving quality before they can accept the need to improve it.

In a TQM environment NFPIs should cover:

- Measuring quality of supplies
- Measuring quality of work done as it proceeds
- Measuring customer satisfaction.

8.11 The balanced scorecard approach

Kaplan and Norton devised a range of measures that assist managers to focus on what affects the performance of a division.

The four areas to look at are:

- **Financial perspective** – How does the division create value for the organisation?
- **Customer perspective** – What do new and existing customers value the division for?
- **Innovation and learning** – How can the division continue to deliver value?
- **Internal business** – What processes must the division excel at to meet the objectives of the organisation and the customers?

 **Learn**

8.11.1 Measurement of corporate performance through the balanced scorecard

In the present era of emerging intense global competition, organisations are facing increasingly knowledgeable and demanding customers and activist shareholders. This has changed the competitive environment from competition based on ability to invest in and manage physical assets to competition based on knowledge and the ability to exploit intangible and soft assets. In this changed business paradigm relying on only the financial measures, which are considered as the indicators of short-run performance, to measure the corporate performance is puzzling and often misleading. A balanced scorecard added three additional perspectives covering operating aspects of an organisation which exhibits not only the current position of the enterprise but also how it is progressing. But due to some practical difficulties in its development and implementation, the concept developed by Robert S. Kaplan and David P. Norton has not been widely accepted and its popularity has not yet peaked.

Performance is the final result of all activities. In evaluating performance the emphasis is on assessing the current behaviour of the organisation in respect to its efficiency and effectiveness. The appropriate performance measurement tool should be:

1. Relevant to the strategic goals of the organisation and accountable to the individuals concerned.
2. Focus on measurable outputs,
3. Verifiable.

8.11.2 Concept of balanced scorecard

The basic idea behind the introduction of the balanced scorecard was that the traditional financial measures (like ROI, EPS etc.) alone cannot provide a clear and comprehensive performance target or focus attention on all the critical areas of the business that bear significant impact on its long-term survival, growth and development. Rather, it requires a balanced presentation of financial as well as operational measures.

The balanced scorecard throws an insight into an organisation's performance by integrating financial measures with other key performance indicators around customer perspectives, internal business processes and organisational growth, learning and innovation, and enables organisations to track short-term financial and operating results while monitoring progress for future growth, development and success.

The balanced scorecard is an organisational framework for implementing and managing strategy at all levels of an enterprise by linking objectives, initiatives and measures to an organisation's strategy. The balanced scorecard is a strategic management system (not only a measurement system) that enables organisations to clarify their vision and strategy and translate them into action. When fully deployed, the balanced scorecard transforms strategic planning from an academic exercise into the nerve centre of an enterprise. The scorecard provides an enterprise view of an organisation's overall performance. The scorecard integrates financial measures like ROI, RI, Dividend yield, EPS etc. with other key performance indicators around customer perspectives, internal business processes and organisational growth, learning and innovation.

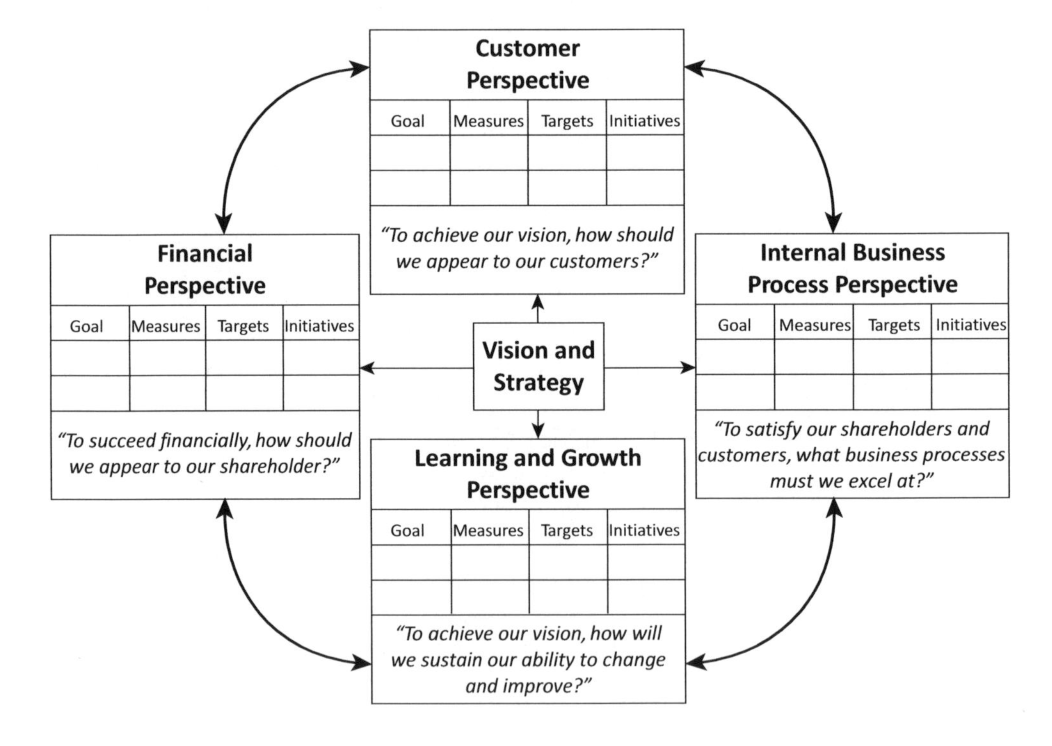

8.11.3 Balanced scorecard cause–effect hypothesis

1. Knowledge and skills of employees is the foundation of all innovation and improvements.
2. Skilled and empowered employees will improve the ways they work.
3. Improved work processes
4. Processes will lead to increased customer satisfaction.
5. Increased customer satisfaction will lead to better financial results.

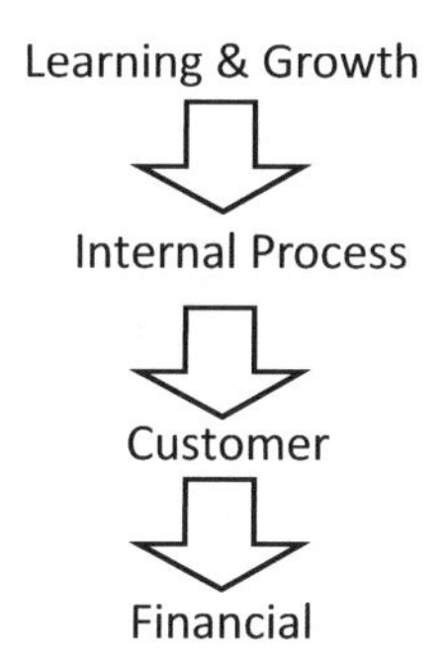

The above perspectives answer the following four basic questions:

1. How do customers see us?
2. What must we excel at?
3. Can we continue to improve and create value?
4. How do we look to shareholders?

To measure overall corporate performance, goals are set for each of these perspectives and then specific measures for achieving such goals are determined.

Each of these perspectives is critical and must be considered simultaneously to achieve overall efficiency and effectiveness and to succeed in the long-run. If any area is either overemphasised or underemphasised, performance evaluation will become 'unbalanced'. In this way, the aim of the concept is to establish a set of measures-both financial and non-financial through which a company can control its activities and 'balance' various measures to effectively track performance.

Thus, the balanced scorecard represents a fundamental change in the underlying assumption about performance measurement and strikes a balance between short-term and long-term objectives, between financial and non-financial measures, between outcome and process measures, between lagging and leading indicators and between internal and external perspectives.

8.11.4 Rationality behind the balanced scorecard

The traditional financial measures of corporate performance like ROI, EPS etc. are based exclusively on past performance and results have little predictive value to the management of an organisation. But an effective performance measurement system must encompass a blend of both results and process measures so that organisations can not only keep score but also can more reasonably predict what the score will look like. The lagging indicators of performance worked well for the industrial era but they have now become inadequate and often misleading in tracking complex management challenges posed by competitive and rapidly changing business arena.

Conventional financial performance measures focus on creation of shareholders value. But, placing too much importance on shareholder value for measurement of management's performance can jeopardise a company's long-term growth and success. The shareholders can reasonably expect maximum return on their risky investment. Before the commencement of taxation on dividends, this return on investment primarily consisted of dividends but after that commencement appreciation of share price assumed a greater role in providing return on investment because of the favourable tax treatment on capital gains. But the appreciation of share price as a criterion for measuring management performance has some major weakness. Firstly, stock price can rise or fall for reasons other than earnings such as competitive advantage, industry structure, stock market exuberance etc. Secondly, stock market is volatile and inconsistent in its judgement. Moreover, by focusing on shareholder value, the long-term potential and prospects of the business are sacrificed to short-term results. If the firm wants to maximise shareholder value in short-run it has to sacrifices its long-term prospect. In fact, most of the financial measures are rigid targets to be achieved, which discourage alternative action opportunities, no matter how promising they are.

Moreover, the conventional performance measurement systems generally don't communicate or explain the factors that drive performance. But once the drivers of performance can be identified performance achievement would be easier.

Again, traditional performance measurements systems measure the tangible and financial assets but an organisation has to measure and respond to intangible assets of value to the organisation because of their substantial effect on the bottom-line.

A serious shortcoming of the traditional management systems is their inability to link a firm's long-term strategy with its short-term actions. Most companies' operational and management control system are designed on the basis of financial measures and targets which have little relation to the companies' progress in achieving long-term strategic objectives.

The concept of Balanced Scorecard overcomes these drawbacks and inadequacies of the conventional financial measures and measures corporate performance both from financial and operational perspectives of an organisation.

8.11.5 Evaluation

The concept of balanced scorecard is new by its name but not by its origin. It has made only a development over a number of existing concepts and theories like activity-based management, management by objectives, total quality management, strategic management, behavioural theory of economics, delegation of authority, decentralisation of decision-making etc, but what is unique about balanced scorecard is that it brought and pooled together the fruits of such theories and concepts into a single integrated measure of corporate performance covering all aspects of an organisation.

The balanced scorecard was designed with the realisation that traditional financial measures were not adequate to measure and manage intangible assets. The scorecard added customers, internal business processes and learning and growth perspectives to evaluate the overall corporate performance and to correct that imbalance. This new dimension complemented the conventional financial measures and provided management with a broader perspective around both physical and intangible assets. The scorecard assists management to focus on long-term objectives rather than on the narrower, short-term, bottom-line financial outcomes. The scorecard's primary benefit is that it assists to focus everyone's attention towards the future. Firms achieve the greatest effect when they utilise the scorecard system to drive organisational change.

Moreover, utilising the scorecard, executives can see cause-and-effect relationships that clarify how every objective measurement they choose should be part of a chain of events that leads the corporate goal.

Beside performance measurement, the balanced scorecard provides the cornerstone for a new strategic management system. The scorecard enables organisation s to introduce new governance and renew process focusing on strategy. It does not rely on short-term financial measures as the sole indicators of performance but it does the following additional functions:

1. Translate strategy to action, making strategy everyone's job.
2. Manage the intangible assets eg customer loyalty, innovation, employee capabilities.
3. Leverage cross functionality without changing the structure of the business.
4. Measure what matters the critical few vs. the important many in real time, not just after the facts.
5. Create a daily management system for the day-to-day navigation of the business.

A balanced scorecard, however, suffers from some major drawbacks. The most important among these are:

1. The balanced scorecard decomposes the organisation's primary objectives (financial perspective) into customer, internal process and learning and growth objectives (operating perspectives) in a way that is reminiscent of the way that the Dupont formula decomposed the return on capital employed metric into front-line operational measures. But such a type of relationship does not necessarily hold between financial and operational measures and operational achievements do not guarantee the improved bottom-line measures; and in that case the management has to re-examine the basic assumptions of their strategy and mission to capitalise the operational achievements.
2. To make the scorecard useful, it should be prepared in conformity with the overall business strategies. Thus, companies may bias their scorecards to the dimensions that closely support their strategic direction. For instance, a company that seeks leadership through customer service would link, or bias, its

scorecard measures directly to customer satisfaction objectives and in that case the scorecard would become 'biased' rather than 'balanced'.

3. It is difficult to integrate a company's scorecard into its planning, budgeting and resource allocation process; especially when scorecard metrics are changed. One way to overcome this problem is that the measures on the scorecard should be the same measures around which planning and targets are set, budgets are developed and projects are prioritised; and in that case the scorecard becomes the agenda for the management process rather than an essential management tool.
4. In order to make the scorecard more useful and practical it is necessary to assign weights to different measures (both financial and non-financial) on the basis of their importance to the organisation for specifying trade-off between financial and non-financial measures. But it is a complicated task. Again, determining goals and corresponding measures under each perspective is also not easy. Thus, the development of balanced scorecard requires a lot of skill and expertise of the management, time and expenditure of money and for this reason still now it is the out of reach of most of the small and medium-sized organisations.
5. To make the scorecard more efficient and useful a large number of both financial and non-financial measures are to be included in it and these should be continually modified on the basis of measurement feedback. It may make the approach complicated and if implemented poorly, the scorecard will most likely contribute to the mass of data under which many organisations are straining to survive.
6. There are some organisations like investment companies to whom balanced scorecards have little value as they are interested in improving financial performance only.
7. The creditors, debenture holders and even shareholders of an organisation are interested in financial performance rather than operating performance which compels the management to give much emphasis on financial perspective of the organisation making the scorecard imbalanced.
8. A new doctrine of Corporate Social Responsibility (CSR) has become widely accepted in the business world. It is presented as the key to ensuring that business makes its full and due contribution to agreed social goals. An organisation, as a "corporate citizen", has to contribute for the welfare of the society and has to respond to society's expectations. In this lies the key to commercial success, since profits depend on reputation, which, in turn, depends on being seen to act in a socially responsible way. Thus, CSR will be good for enterprise-profitability and to pursue the goal of "sustainable growth and development". But this perspective of CSR is missing in Balanced Scorecard while stating the four perspectives.

In conclusion, in spite of theoretical superiority and comprehensiveness, the balanced scorecard approach for measuring corporate performance has some practical difficulties which are mainly associated with its development and implementation.

To make it more useful it is required to refine the concept and develop a better understanding of the key performance indicators for successful deployment. By becoming proficient in the approach, organisations can readily access their vision

and strategies by measuring performance against established goals. A strategic orientation driven by actual shareholders' needs and expectations, focused on the organisation's mission and supported by an integrated performance-measurement system like the balanced scorecard can greatly assist the management in steering their organisation in right direction and facing the competitive challenges of the new millennium. To make the scorecard more successful the following points should be considered:

- Reach cross-functional agreement on strategic direction.
- Translate the strategy into staff's everyday speak.
- Understand the cause and effect of linkages between strategy/process capability.
- Identify the measures of success, critical strategic initiatives and process drivers.
- Set up accountability contracts.
- Cascade the scorecard into the organisation.

The above additional actions help us to get:

- Alignment and focus of the organisation around a common purpose and strategic direction.
- Resource prioritisation and allocation.
- An on-going feedback mechanism to make real time, mid-course adjustments to priorities.
- A set of balances metrics.

The predicted future of the balanced scorecard is increased specialisation:

- Sector-based scorecard templates eg balanced scorecard for healthcare
- Department-level scorecard templates eg balanced scorecard for human resources.

Also there will be increased sophistication of the tools used:

- Linkage to executive information systems
- More rigorous economic analysis
- Performance simulation.

Last of all we can conclude that the balanced scorecard provides a framework needed for strategic alignment and organisational learning.

Note that the balanced scorecard is not a "flavour of the month" but an evolving management concept.

Main benefits of using the balanced scorecard include:

- Forcing managers to look at internal and external issues
- Focussing on key elements of a company's strategy
- Linking non-financial results with financial ones – for example highlighting the impact on customers if cheaper materials are used).

Major drawbacks of using the balanced scorecard include:

- Improving in some areas will probably lead to deterioration in others

- It may be hard to come up with measures in all areas
- It may lead to too many things being measured
- There may be too many measures to interpret easily.

8.11.6 Strategy mapping

Strategy mapping was developed by Kaplan and Norton as an extension to the balanced scorecard to make the implementation of the balanced scorecard more effective and successful.

This was because organisations have often found it difficult to translate the corporate vision into behaviour and actions which achieve the key corporate objectives.

In practice, many employees do not understand the organisation's strategy, and systems such as performance management and budgeting are not linked to the strategy.

A strategy map is a diagram which links the strategy to operational targets and objectives through the balanced scorecard.

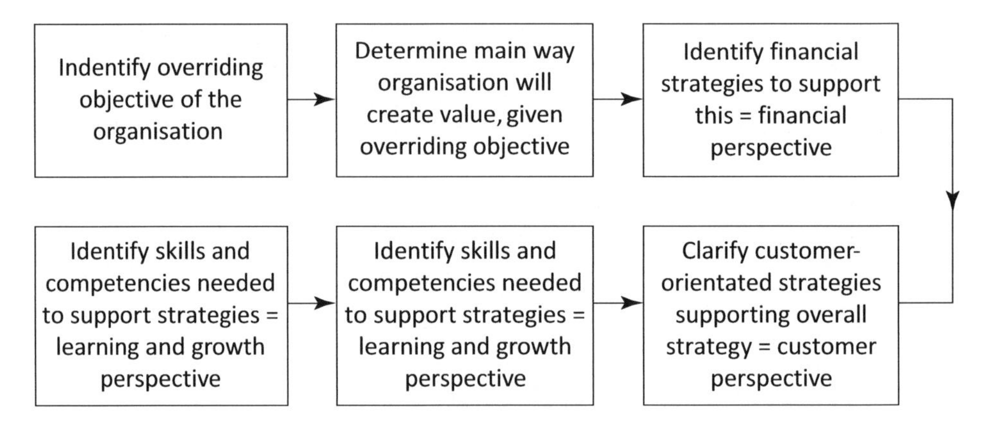

8.12 The performance pyramid approach

The idea behind this model is that the entire organisation needs to work together in order to achieve success. The approach is to try to link the overall strategy of the company with what is happening on a daily level.

The performance pyramid was developed by Lynch and Cross as a model to understand and define the links between objectives and performance measures at different levels in the organisation to ensure that the activities of every department, system and business unit support the overall vision of the organisation.

At the top of the pyramid is the vision through which the organisation describes how it will achieve long-term success and competitive advantage.

The second level, the business unit, includes the KPIs in terms of market related measures and financial measures.

The third level, the business operating systems, includes measures which relate to the internal systems and processes which are needed to meet the needs of

customers. For example, measures of flexibility which relate to how responsive the system is to customer demands.

The lowest level of the pyramid contains the daily operational measures.

The left hand side of the pyramid contains measures which have an external focus and which are predominantly non-financial.

Those on the right are focused on the internal efficiency of the organisation and are predominantly financial.

Objectives cascade down through the organisation, while measures and information flow from the bottom up.

The performance pyramid does tend to concentrate on two groups of stakeholders – shareholders and customers. It is necessary to ensure that measures are included which relate to other stakeholders as well.

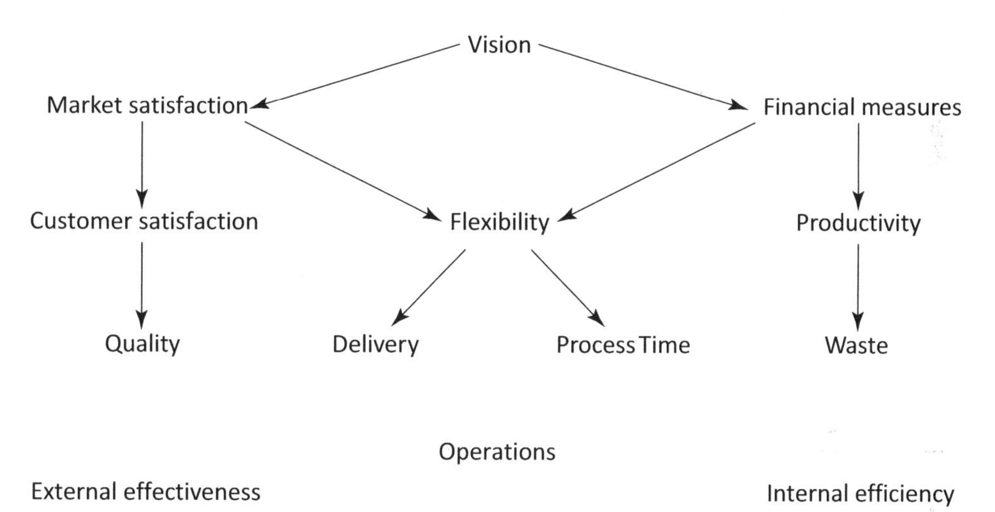

Learn

8.13 The building blocks approach

Fitzgerald and Moon designed a system of non-financial performance indicators specifically for service industries and developed an approach to performance measurement that is based on the three building blocks, defined below:

Definition

Dimensions are those aspects of performance that need to be measured.

These are determined by the key factors that determine the success of the organisation in achieving its objectives.

Definition

Standards are the benchmarks or targets for the measures identified for the different dimensions.

Definition

Rewards are the incentives given to managers who achieve the standards.

Learn

8.13.1 The dimensions of performance

In developing this model six generic dimensions of performance were identified and involved posing four basic questions:

- What has happened?
- Why has it happened?
- Is it going to continue?
- What are we going to do about it?

	6 Dimensions of performance	Types of measures
R	Competitiveness	Relative market share/position
E		Sales growth
S		Measures of the customer base
U		
L	Financial performance	Profitability
T		Liquidity
S		Capital structure
		Market ratios

D		
E	Quality of service	Reliability and responsiveness
T		Aesthetics/appearance
E		Cleanliness/tidiness
R		Comfort
M		Friendliness
I		Communication
N		Courtesy
A		Competence
N		Access
T		Availability
S		Security
	Flexibility	Volume flexibility
		Delivery speed flexibility
		Specification flexibility
	Resource utilisation	Productivity
		Efficiency
	Innovation	Performance of the innovation process
		Performance of individual innovations

Performance measurement is traditionally used to provide an answer to the first of these questions, but it can be developed to give insights that help answer the other three questions.

Measures can be developed to provide appropriate impressions for each of these 6 dimensions.

The first two are considered to relate to 'downstream results' – that is they describe what has actually been achieved in the past while not giving material insights into what might happen in the future.

The other four dimensions might be considered to relate to 'upstream determinants' in that they provide indicators for the ability to achieve results in the future.

The selection of performance measures to be used for a business, business sector or manager should be determined by the nature of the organisation and an identification of the key factors that determine the success of the organisation in achieving its objectives.

8.13.2 Standards

Consideration of standards involves:

- Ownership – managers who participate in the setting of standards are more likely to accept and be motivated by the standards than managers on whom standards are imposed.
- Achievability – an achievable standard is a better motivator than an unachievable one
- Equity – when setting standards across an organisation, care should be undertaken to ensure that all managers have equally challenging standards.

8.13.3 Rewards

Consideration of rewards involves:

- Clarity – goal clarity contributes to motivation, eg a standard of achieving X number of product innovations per year may be a more effective motivator
- Motivation – the actual means of motivation may involve performance related rewards
- Controllability – managers will be better motivated if they actually control the factors contributing to achievement of the measures and standards on which their rewards are based.

8.14 The performance prism

The performance prism was developed by the Centre for Business Performance at Cranfield School of Management and aims to look at organisational performance from the interests of all stakeholders, such as suppliers, employees, legislators, and local communities.

It takes a broader approach to stakeholder interests than many other performance management models which pay limited attention to stakeholders other than customers and shareholders.

The performance prism takes stakeholder requirements/satisfaction as the start point for the development of performance measures rather than the strategy of the organisation by asking – what do our key stakeholders want?

Strategies are based on the principle that the performance of an organisation depends on how effectively it meets the needs and requirements of all its stakeholders – what strategies do we follow to achieve the goals of the stakeholders?

It recognises the need to work with stakeholders to ensure that their needs are met and can be used to identify measures at all levels within the organisation by asking – what processes must we be good at to deliver these strategies; what capabilities will we need to be good at to carry out these processes and what do we need our stakeholders to contribute in order to deliver these capabilities?

Learn

IE **Illustrative example 8.2**

Example of application of the performance prism at Dell Computers

What do Dell's regular customers want and need?

- Delivery speed
- Confidence in Dell products
- Relationship with support services
- Information accessibility

What strategies will Dell adopt to ensure that these wants and needs are satisfied?

- Local contact
- Proactive availability of information
- Promote superiority of core service

What processes will Dell put in place to ensure that these strategies are delivered?

- Customer service strategy
- Product reliability
- Local support network
- Customer access tools

What capabilities does Dell require to ensure that these processes can be operated?

- Teamwork
- Technology
- Robust network
- Skills

What does Dell want from its stakeholders to allow the above to happen?

- Confidence in data
- Empowerment
- People based culture
- Customer feedback

8.15 Activity-based Management (ABM)

Activity-based Costing (ABC) is the practice of attributing overhead costs to products in a manner linked to the activities that give rise to the overhead costs and how far those activities relate to cost units at the product and batch level.

Activity-based Management (ABM) is the use of activity-based cost information for management purposes such as customer profitability analysis and value engineering.

ABM uses detailed economic analyses of important business activities to improve strategic and operational decisions.

It increases the accuracy of cost information by more precisely linking overhead and other indirect costs to products or customer segments.

To build a system that will support ABM, companies should:

- determine key activities performed
- determine cost drivers by activity
- group overhead and other indirect costs by activity using clearly identified cost drivers
- collect data on activity demands (by product and customer)
- assign costs to products and customers (based on activity usage).

Companies use ABM to:

- re-price products and optimise new product design
- reduce costs
- influence strategic and operational planning.

From a performance management perspective, two key features of ABM are cost visibility and the generation of activity cost profiles.

- Cost visibility: the activity based approach brings costs out into the open and helps management see what they get for the commitment of resources, eg it enables a much better understanding of margins.
- Activity cost profile.

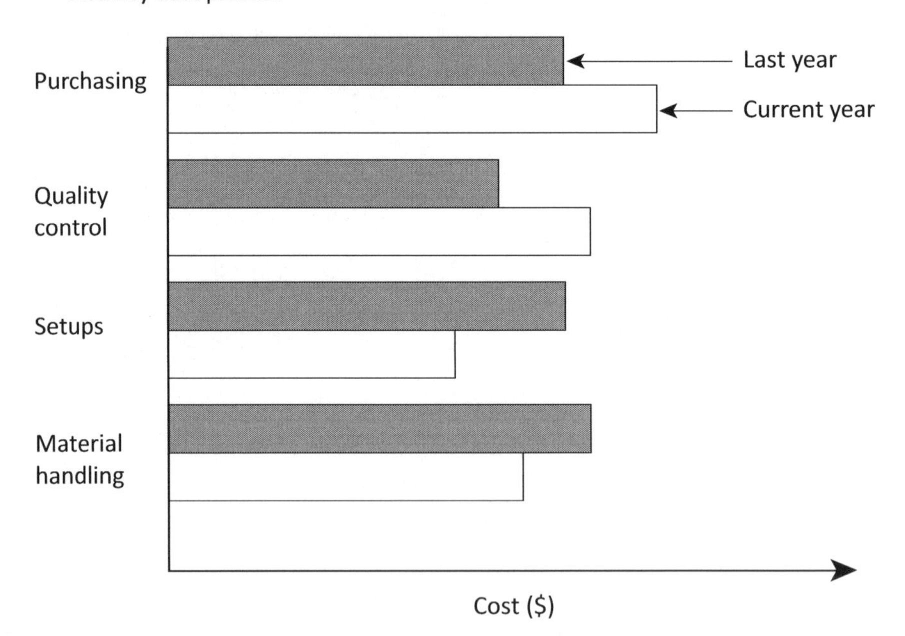

An activity cost profile compares costs in the current year with the previous year and from the cost profile an analysis can be performed such as:

- An increase in purchasing costs – This could be because of increased volume, diversity of products or change in mix of production runs.
- An increase in quality control costs – This may be offset by fewer external failures, fewer warranty claims and fewer recalls and may be due to the changing expectation of the customer, demanding a higher quality products.

8.16 Difficulties recording and processing qualitative data

Qualitative data is data that judges something that cannot be easily measured, such as the feelings of a business's customers. This is in contrast to quantitative data, which can be measured, such as sales, sales returns and costs.

To gather qualitative data there are various techniques that can be used:

- Observation, say of customers in a supermarket
- Interviews, where customers are asked directly about their views
- Focus groups, where groups of customers join in together to say what they think about a particular issue.

There are lots of types of questions that can be asked in interviews or focus groups, such as 'what are the three best/worst aspects of the delivery service we offer?' or gradings of customer experiences on different levels eg how happy they were with their shopping experience. Often the questions may be trying to create quantitative data, such as gradings.

This information needs to be recorded. This is difficult as there are many aspects to the data and being able to record one person's happiness against another's from the words that they say can be tricky, especially if the happiness is due to different aspects of the experience. For example, one person may be very happy with the parking arrangements at a supermarket whilst another may be indifferent to the parking but very happy with the customer service once inside the supermarket. Hence it is tricky to compare these.

There will be some information that is received verbally and some non-verbally eg a facial expression. It is difficult to record all of this information accurately, especially when there are be different levels that it is received on.

Similarly, processing the information can be testing. If a grading has been worked out for customers' happiness levels then that can help process the information. However, with various levels that the information is recorded on it may be better to analyse the meaning behind the data and try to get to an underlying understanding of this. From that understanding the recommendations for future actions can follow. A useful way of doing this processing is:

1. Organise the data.
2. Identify a framework the data can fit (such as 'quality of customer experience').
3. Sort the data into the framework.
4. Use the framework in a descriptive analysis to explain what the conclusions are from the process.
5. Write a report based around the processes and conclusions.

Key Learning Points

- Be familiar with non-financial indicators and their importance as companies seek to capture more rounded data on performance. (D4c, D4f, D5a–D5d)
- Understand various performance models and their application. (E1a–E1d)
- Understand activity-based management and its uses. (E1e)

What's the story?

Stop and think through the 'story' of this chapter and how it links with other chapters (use the Overview to help).

Learning example solutions

EG Solution 8.1

Since little or no inventory is stored, a company's performance would be improved by a JIT system because of a reduction in inventory holding costs.

It makes no difference whether FIFO, LIFO or Weighted Average Costs are used for inventory valuation as marginal or absorption costing is used for inventory valuation.

Costs can be reduced as large storage space becomes unnecessary when inventory is kept to a minimum.

Costs of production downtime (due to suppliers not delivering) will need to be identified so they can be recharged.

A close relationship with suppliers and customers must be developed as deliveries on-time and the supply of defect free goods at the right time will become key performance indicators.

Long-term contracts can be signed between supplier and customer so that marketing costs can be saved and the producer can concentrate on production.

Shorter production runs, small batch quantities and more products in the product range will require more time and money spent on preventative maintenance to ensure no holdups in production.

EG Solution 8.2

For a retailer operating in a dynamic, competitive environment it is not always easy to predict patterns of demand, especially not far in advance.

The concept of zero inventories and make to order is inapplicable in industries like retailing businesses which must obtain inventory in anticipation of future customer demand.

Guaranteed or reliable availability of product at short notice may be an essential part of the retailer's service proposition (especially for retailers operating convenience stores).

The organisation will be more vulnerable to disruptions in the supply chain since there will be no buffer. A delay in deliveries caused by supplier unreliability or other events such as weather will result in lost sales.

Geographically dispersed activities complicate the supply chain and introduce extra risk of disruption. (JIT was first introduced by Toyota when most of the company's manufacturing was carried out close to its corporate headquarters.

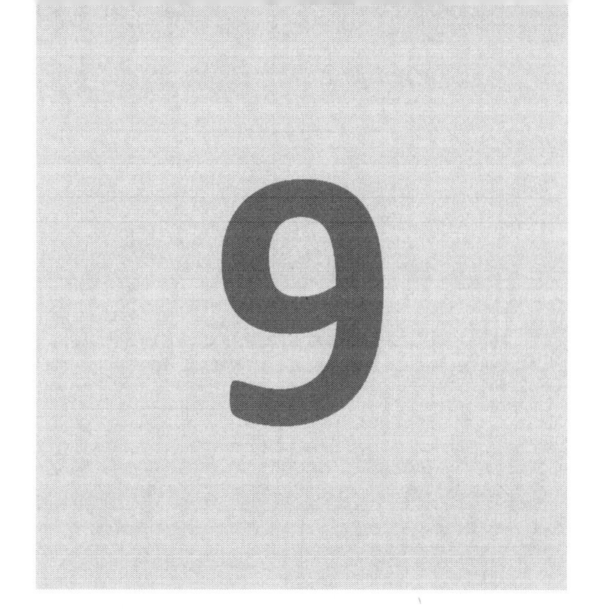

9 Performance System Issues

Context

Performance systems may take into account issues like the quality of the products the organisation makes and human resource factors such as performance appraisal and rewards systems.

3Q

1. How are performance measurement and performance management interlinked?
2. What are the benefits of linking reward schemes and performance?
3. What are the problems associated with performance measurement?

9.1 Human resource management

Increasingly, organisations are taking a coordinated approach to human resource management and this umbrella term is used to refer to all aspects of the interactions between an organisation and its staff.

Key HR activities include:

- Staff planning
- Job, role and person descriptions
- Advertising for staff
- Recruitment and selection
- Induction
- Training and staff development
- Appraisal
- Promotion
- Disciplinary procedures
- Termination.

9.1.1 Link between human resource management and strategic and operational success

The concept of operational success of the business involves combining both the business strategy and the employees to ensure the aims of the business are met.

Effective recruitment and selection is used an indicator as to how successful candidates could be. Employing the correct candidates could create an operational success, rather than a failure.

Effective management is essential for strategic and operational success. Even though many layers of the hierarchy (shown in a tall-structured business) could be a demotivating factor, if the correct management techniques are used this could help the business achieve operational success. Below are some management techniques which, if used correctly could enable strategic and operational success.

The motivation of employees is one of the most important factors for strategic and operational success. Herzberg's Theory of Motivation identified two groups of factors: hygiene factors and motivating factors, and only the second group was shown to have a positive impact on motivation. Motivating factors included primarily intrinsic factors such as interest in the job, recognition for good work and a sense of personal achievement

9.1.2 Assessment and appraisal

The concept of an appraisal allows both employee and employer to evaluate and judge work which has been carried out over a period of time against a performance indicator. McQuerrey suggests that there are six main indicators which should be considered. These together with the company's Key Performance Indicators (KPIs) should help employees set targets for improvements.

- Meeting goals

- Teamwork
- Job skills
- Communication
- Decision-making
- Work habits.

Source: McQuerrey, Houston Chronicle

Human resource management techniques show how appraisals and assessments can affect business performance. David Guest's model (1997) demonstrates a relationship between human resource management and the business strategy. This is shown below.

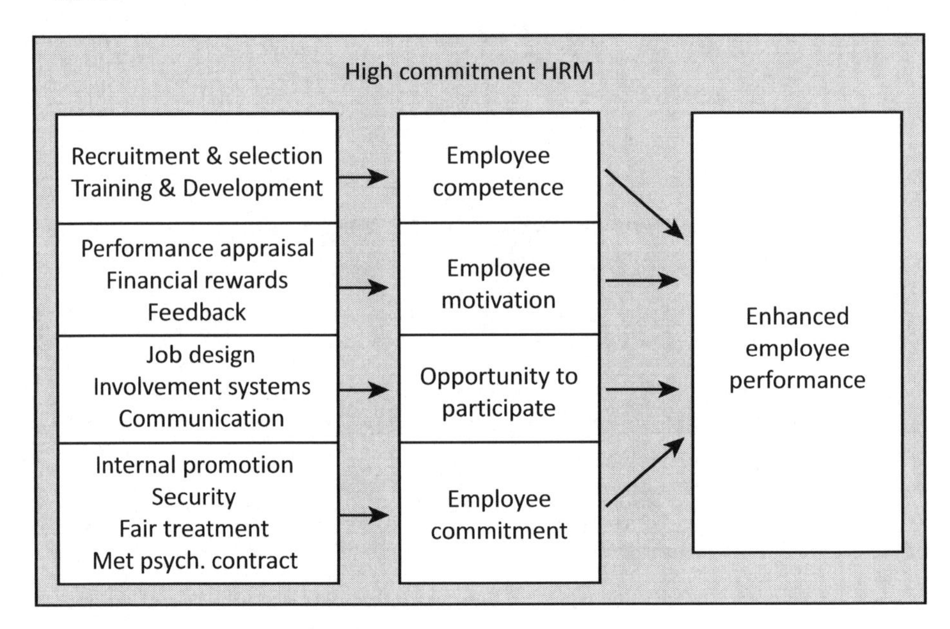

Source: David Guest, Strategic HCM, http://strategic-hcm.blogspot.co.uk/2009/11/david-guest-on-hr-measurement.html

EG Learning example 9.1

Explain the key issues that should be considered in the design and the implementation of an effective staff performance appraisal system for a Local Council.

9.2 Performance measurement and performance management

The terms performance management and performance measurement are interlinked. Performance management includes undertaking activities which will ensure objectives of both the company and employees are being met. Performance measurement is the process of collecting and analysing information which relates to either an individual or groups. It involves analysing processes to assess whether outputs of the company match with the budget. If performance measurement was not used alongside performance management, the company would not be able to measure the costs which relate to the objectives being met.

 **Learn**

Definition

Process redesign is the reconstruction of a business process in order to achieve a jump in performance measures.

 **Learn**

The key advantages and disadvantages are as follows:

Advantages

- Larger return on capital/investment.
- Aim of cost reductions.
- Improved quality of service.

Disadvantages

- Can be extremely costly as the process may involve laying off staff, relocation etc.
- It assumes the business activities are the main reason for failure, where it could be other areas in the business which need addressing.

Below are some of the implications of performance measurement to quality initiatives and process redesign:

- Performance measurement focuses on performance outputs and the costs involved, whereas process redesign concentrates on making larger returns of profit. One focuses on the outputs and the other focuses on inputs.
- Performance measurement issues (if costs are higher than budget) could be easily changed by using a different costing system. However this could be seen as a process problem, therefore a business may believe a complete process redesign needs to occur.

Performance measurement focuses on costs and therefore the quality of the products and process could be compromised by focusing too much on costs and returns.

9.2.1 Rewards for employees

Management will encourage employees to achieve the goals of a business by linking rewards to their success or failure in achieving desired levels of performance. It is critical that management establish an appropriate performance-rewards linkage. Management should consider a rewards package comprising both financial and non-financial rewards. Typical organisational rewards include salary increases, bonuses, promotion and recognition. Employees may also earn intrinsic rewards through a sense of achievement and perceived success. Management should also give serious consideration to the establishment of 'negative rewards' or 'punishments' which should be linked to failure to achieve desired levels of performance.

These may include failure to obtain potential rewards, demotions, and possibly the loss of employment.

9.2.2 Benefits for an organisation

There are benefits for an organisation that implements a reward scheme:

- Rewards and incentives can make a positive contribution to strategy implementation by shaping the behaviour of individuals and groups. A well-designed reward scheme will be consistent with organisational objectives and structure.
- There is evidence which suggests the existence of a reward scheme provides an incentive to achieve a good level of performance. Moreover, the existence of effective schemes helps not only to attract but also to retain employees who make positive contributions to the running of an organisation.
- Key values can be emphasised by incorporating key performance indicators in the performance-rewards mechanisms which underpin the scheme. This helps to create an 'understood environment' in which it is clear to all employees the performance aspects that contribute to organisational success.
- An effective reward scheme will create an environment in which all employees are focused on continuous improvement.
- Schemes that incorporate equity share ownership for managers and employees alike can encourage behaviour which, in the longer-term, focuses on actions aimed at increasing the market value of the organisation.

Things to consider by management include:

- Whether rewards should be in money or not. Money means different things to different people. In many instances people will prefer increased job security which results from improved organisational performance and adopt a longer-term perspective. For these employees share option schemes might appeal. Well-designed schemes will correlate the prosperity of the organisation with that of the individuals it employs.
- Whether performance targets should be set with regard to results or effort. It is more difficult to set targets for administrative and support staff since in many instances the results of their efforts are not easily quantifiable. For example, good sales administrators will improve levels of customer satisfaction but quantifying this is extremely difficult.
- Whether the reward promise should be implicit or explicit. Explicit reward promises are easy to understand but in many respects management will have their hands tied. Implicit reward promises such as the promise of promotion for good performance is also problematic since not all organisations are large enough to offer structured career progression. In situations where not everyone can be promoted, a range of alternative reward systems need to be in place to acknowledge good performance and encourage commitment from the workforce.
- The size and time span of the reward. This can be difficult to determine especially in businesses which are subject to seasonal variations. Activity levels may vary and there remains the potential problem of assessing performance when an organisation operates with surplus capacity.
- Whether the reward should be individual- or group-based.

- Whether the reward scheme should involve equity participation. Such schemes invariably appeal to directors and senior managers but should arguably be open to all individuals if 'perceptions of inequity' are to be avoided.
- Tax implications also need to be considered.

9.3 Benefits and problems with linking reward schemes and performance

Benefits

- There is evidence that linking pay with performance *does* encourage better performance.
- A good scheme attracts the best potential recruits and is better at retaining them.
- It can be made clear what the organisation must be good at to succeed.
- The focus becomes continuous improvement.
- Long-term decision-making can be encouraged through things such as share scheme.

Problems

- They may encourage dysfunctional decision-making.
- Measures to encourage long-term decisions may not motivate.
- It is difficult to design a set of performance measures to show exactly what an employee achieves.
- People may not cooperate with each other.
- Quality may suffer.
- They undervalue intrinsic rewards (such as job satisfaction) by focusing on extrinsic rewards (ie pay).

Learn

Factors that should be taken into account when designing the system

- Goal congruence should be encouraged
- Who should be offered equity in the business and its likely effect (being offered shares in a small private company may not motivate since there might be no market for them)
- Different rewards being offered for different staff
- When the reward scheme should be introduced and what time period should it relate to (monthly, annually etc.)
- The impact of tax (if an employee is likely to pay a high tax rate on any incentives then they may not be as motivational)
- The size of rewards relative to performance
- What forms rewards should take (including non-financial).

Additional considerations

When rewards are linked to quality initiative such as process redesign, it is important to ensure that the reward is influenced by a suitable measure. Improvements in quality control or redesigns of business processes are likely to increase local costs, at least in the short term, and the benefit from increased customer satisfaction or reduced failure costs may be less evident or make take longer to be realised. Therefore there should not be a negative incentive (such as a bonus based purely on short-term local cost control) that may discourage goal congruent behaviour.

9.4 Behavioural aspects of performance measurement

The most basic points are that:

- Managers will try and improve whatever is being measured.
- Making these improvements does not always assist with the organisation meeting its objectives. An example of this is price and usage variances.

It is important to appreciate that a control system is rarely 'neutral'. Most control systems contain within themselves a potential to distort the processes that they are meant to serve. In the present context, this may arise when they induce individual managers to do things that are not in the best interests of the business as a whole.

IE Illustrative example 9.1

The manager of a production line may get his costs within budget by cutting back on costs associated with quality with adverse consequences for the business as a whole when customers report consequent higher numbers of defective products.

Behavioural scientists refer to this phenomenon as 'dysfunctional behaviour'. A control system which is badly designed or which is applied in an insensitive manner may end up doing more harm than good as in the above example.

If performance measurement is used to motivate management a number of key issues need to be considered:

- Will the measures help the entire organisation achieve its objectives?
- Will the measures promote goal congruence?
- How do we recognise how much of the performance of a division can be attributed to its manager?

In very few organisations, performance management is viewed as a more comprehensive approach to leveraging human assets that includes identifying, measuring, and developing human performance. No matter what defined scope is involved, performance management in most settings is considered a "necessary evil," usually driven by the need to evaluate employees for retention, work assignments, promotion, and pay.

So why are employees so universally dissatisfied with performance management?

Many experts, including disciples of Deming, contend that performance management is actually harmful and should be eliminated. They consistently emphasise that performance management usually holds individuals accountable for outcomes beyond their control, that the potential benefits related to coaching and feedback can be achieved without appraisals, and that efforts focusing on managing performance should concentrate on operational systems and processes, since they account for almost all variances from ideal performance.

Other experts cite a range of human factors that undermine performance management, such as rampant sources of bias; conflicting purposes for appraisal; inconsistent, incomplete, and irrelevant assessment criteria; poor communication and execution of policies and practices; and lack of skills (and training) to support the process.

9.4.1 Major sources of dissatisfaction with performance management

The most frequent sources of dissatisfaction with performance management include:

1. Manager appraisal ratings linked to "administrative purposes" such as promotion, pay, and work assignments are generally an inaccurate assessment of performance (ie, mangers tend to "game the system" by being overly lenient).
2. Distortions are often known, tolerated, and even supported at the highest levels of organisations.
3. Performance ratings are often perceived as unfair because of problems related to the following dimensions:
   - **Outcome** (eg, evaluation consistent with expectations),
   - **Interpersonal** (eg, thorough, timely, honest feedback), and
   - **Procedural** (eg, a consistent process with criteria that are highly relevant to work).
4. Limited collaboration between the manager and employees around goal and standard setting, performance feedback, and final evaluation contributes to perceived unfairness and less reliable and valid ratings of performance.
5. Lack of clarity around expectations (eg, how to align individual and team behaviour and goals with organisation requirements) lead to sub-optimal employee satisfaction and performance.
6. Critical work priorities leave little or no time for ongoing feedback.
7. The process and administrative requirements for implementing performance management are too complicated.

9.5 Benefits and problems of a performance measurement system

Berry, Broadbent and Otley claim that performance measures can help an organisation:

- Clarify its objectives
- Give greater understanding of processes
- Make it easier to compare performance
- Make it easier to set targets
- Increase the accountability of the organisation to its stakeholders

Unfortunately there are also a number of problems associated with performance measurement identified by Berry, Broadbent and Otley leading to dysfunctional behaviour.

- Misrepresentation – 'creative' reporting to suggest that a result is acceptable

IE Illustrative example 9.2

EE Power Supply sends a client satisfaction survey to a carefully selected number of clients. The results were collated and the report showed that 90% of EE clients were satisfied with the service they received. However the satisfaction score is misleading as it wasn't sent to all of the company's clients.

- Gaming – deliberate distortion of a measure to secure some strategic advantage

IE Illustrative example 9.3

The local hospital trust has produced a report that has distorted its performance, making it appear better than it is. This can conceal potentially hazardous practice and endanger patients and staff, while providing the hospital an advantage against other hospitals in the area.

- Misinterpretation – failure to recognise the complexity of the environment in which the organisation operates
- Short-termism – leading to the neglect of longer term objectives

IE Illustrative example 9.4

AX Cars pay their staff commission on each car they sell, the more expensive the car more the commission. However over last year or so, this has led to cars being sold to clients who really didn't want that the larger, more expensive models they bought, but they were persuaded by the salesmen to do so, while other customers walked out in disgust.

- Measure fixation – measures behaviour in order to achieve specific performance indicators which may not be effective
- Tunnel vision – undue focus on stated performance measures to the detriment of other areas

IE Illustrative example 9.5

AJ solicitor's practice uses a staff utilisation ratio in terms of its chargeable hours as a proportion of total hours. However this could lead to an insufficient amount of time on staff development and training and could lead to the wrong advice being given to clients.

- Sub-optimisation – focus on some objectives so that others are not achieved

IE Illustrative example 9.6

LX College focuses too much on winning new students and the fees that this would bring. However, they have just realised they lack the resources to be able to deal with the quantity of students and how this would affect the quality of service in all areas.

- Ossification – an unwillingness to change the performance measure scheme once it has been set up

EG Learning example 9.2

Explain the potential behavioural issues that may arise in the application of performance monitoring.

 **Learn**

9.6 Process principles to help performance management

Human behaviour represents a large source of error and variation in implementing plans and processes. The types of issues are the misalignment of individual actions with purpose, strategy, and goals; low motivation; poor fit to roles; and skill deficits are always major contributors to performance problems. These issues must be addressed in some systematic fashion to create and sustain a high performance enterprise.

The primary solution to performance management problems is to adopt a quality process approach. Defining and continuously improving, operational processes have become a fundamental requirement for business success; comparable rigour has not been applied to people management and development processes.

Successful performance management systems

These systems:

- Ensure alignment between criteria applied throughout the process to business values and goals and customer outcomes (eg, specific clear "inputs" and "outputs" for the process).
- Define performance criteria individuals can impact significantly that are:
  - Relevant to the job
  - Encompass both goals and behaviours
  - Represent excellent standards that can be monitored and measured over time.
- Clearly define the boundaries of the process (ie, where does it start, end, and restart; what activities are included and what activities, such as pay decisions and promotion, are not).
- Specify the roles and responsibilities for all participants in the process.
- Define the workflow and rules for the process clearly (eg, specific steps, decisions, and actions for managers, employees, and teams).
- Define the relationship(s) between performance management and other human resource processes (eg, succession planning, assessment, and development, etc.), including key interdependencies, synergies, and conflicts.
- Determine fair, consistent methods for gathering "measurement" data (eg, sources—such as self, manager, peers, customers, etc.).

- Decide on guidelines for "measuring" success (eg, scales, weighting, criteria) that can be tracked consistently.
- Clearly communicate expectations and train those involved in the process methods to:
  - Rate in an unbiased manner
  - Provide behavioural feedback
  - Identify and determine root causes of performance problems (including situational constraints)
  - Hold everyone involved in the process accountable for process excellence and continuous improvement
  - Apply technologies, whenever possible, to simplify, manage, support, and distribute workflow, and capture process data to apply for improvements.

9.7 Accountability within the organisation

There are a number of steps an organisation must go through to ensure that its performance measurement system will help.

- Choose and publicise accepted performance measures
- Identify the benefits of the measures
- Identify and understand problems in their use
- Consider how to counter perceived problems.

In addition, the organisation must ensure that it has a system of accountability set up. This covers:

Hard accountability
- Converting activities into numbers
- Explaining why an outcome occurred
- Being held accountable for the results.

Soft accountability
- The human impact on the system and its role in deciding what to measure and how high targets should be set

Key Learning Points

- Be able to advise on the relationship of performance management to performance measurement. (D7a–D7c)
- Learn about linking reward schemes to performance measurement. (D8a–D8c)
- Understand the ways in which performance measurement systems may result in undesirable consequences. (D8e, D9b)

What's the story?

Stop and think through the 'story' of this chapter and how it links with other chapters (use the Overview to help).

Learning example solutions

EG Solution 9.1

Performance appraisal systems can have many objectives including assessing employees' performance, potential and development needs and linking performance with pay. It is thus important that the primary purpose of the system be determined and communicated. For a Local Council the system should focus on performance, though in the longer term it could be developed to link performance to rewards.

The purpose of the appraisal must be clearly expressed and understood by both appraisers and the appraisees. Particularly within a Local Council there is a danger that it is seen as yet another bureaucratic form filling activity. Greater effectiveness will result if all stakeholders (staff, managers, etc) are clear about what the system is for and how it integrates with other organisational activities. Ideally, any performance measures should link to the key strategic objectives of a Local Council.

To ensure widespread commitment to the new system it would be worth including staff from different backgrounds in the Local Council to contribute to the design of the system. The greater the extent of appraisee participation in the development of the system, the greater the chance of ownership.

It is important that measures used to assess performance are seen to be relevant, fair and objective, rather than subjective. This is to reduce the potential for biased managers or personality differences to distort assessments. Furthermore, there should be a consistent approach across the different areas of the Local Council with criteria standardised where possible.

Both those undertaking appraisals and those being appraised will need to be trained in areas such as interviewing and assessment techniques. In particular, feedback should be communicated in a balanced way to avoid compounding current poor morale.

The developmental aspect of appraisal systems must be followed through to avoid cynicism. Action plans need to be agreed by both the appraiser and appraisee and monitored to make sure that they do take place. For example if training needs are identified, and the member of staff does not actually receive the training, this failure to follow up may lead to the system losing credibility.

Appraisals should be frequent and sufficient time given so both parties can make a constructive contribution. However they should be viewed as part of a continuous process of performance management, and not just as an annual event.

EG Solution 9.2

There is a general acceptance of the idea that an organisation that monitors performance and rewards individuals for 'good performance' is more likely to encourage behaviour that is consistent with the objectives of the organisation.

This involves the organisation 'transmitting signals' to its people as to what it deems desirable activities and outcomes in the workplace. This approach has resulted in such terms and activities as, performance monitoring, performance related pay, payment by results, bonus systems – the reward for the achievement of desired outcomes could be money, promotion, job security, preferred work activities, alternative work environments.

Unfortunately this is a very complex task and problems are likely to arise in a number of areas:

- It is very difficult in many work environments to measure individual performance – and if you resort to team performance, it is difficult to gauge the contribution from individual members.
- It is difficult to ensure that individual targets are not inconsistent with other individuals or corporate objectives.
- Current measured performance may discourage consideration of longer term issues that may have adverse repercussions.
- Can a performance monitoring system comprehensively measure the key variables eg the desire to achieve greater volume/activity may be at the cost of quality that is more difficult to identify and appraise.
- Measure fixation – concentrating on the measurement process and not on what needs to be achieved.
- Misrepresentation – 'creative' responses that give a favourable view of activities.
- Myopia – short sighted viewpoint with limited consideration to long-term issues.

The problems highlighted above can be managed if the following points are considered:

- Do not underestimate the scale of the task in designing a performance monitoring system.
- Consider the expectations and likely responses of all the parties concerned – take a broad view.
- Ensure that the people designing and operating the system have a comprehensive understanding of the organisation's activities and the interrelationship between all of the stakeholders.
- Ensure that all parties involved believe that they will be beneficiaries of the system.
- Be prepared to reappraise and modify – it is unrealistic to believe that it can be perfected at the first attempt.

10 Corporate Failure

Context

Corporate failure is an example of an extreme problem with performance systems! It is a common assumption that businesses will continue in the long term but in practice a business has a life cycle and then will face challenges, such as alternative products offering better features that mean that the company will drop in its performance and potentially fail.

We will see measures to judge the likelihood of corporate failure and the issues with these measures. As always there are likely to be non-financial aspects to the failure, such as falling market shares.

3Q

1. When does a company become insolvent?
2. How can a company avoid failure?
3. What are the phases in a turnaround strategy?

10.1 Reasons for corporate failure

Corporate failure occurs when a business is unable to make sufficient profits to provide adequate returns to its investors and to meet its obligations to lenders. Ultimately, when a company becomes unable to pay its debts as they fall due, it is insolvent. While many insolvent companies have negative net assets, a business which is unable to continue trading profitably, and generating positive net cash flows, is at high risk of failure.

Many high profile failures of recent years illustrate a situation where the company's traditional business model is no longer profitable because of changes in the environment in which it operates or where the business model was unable to cope with a change in market conditions. There are also situations where the activities of the business are fundamentally unprofitable and unsustainable and/or the managers of the business are incompetent or dishonest.

Sometimes a profitable business becomes unprofitable and fails because it does not adapt to changes in its environment. One possible explanation for this failure to adapt is that the directors may be conservative, or even complacent, and thus reluctant to change. However, often, business failures are analysed after the event and so it is possible to see with greater clarity that changes should have been made. Similarly, directors will sometimes adopt a risk averse approach to decision-making. With the benefit of hindsight it is possible to suggest the changes should have been made, although at the time it may be impossible to predict the success or failure of any particular course of action.

Other possible reasons for failing to change may include:

- difficulty in identifying new opportunities (new products or markets)
- difficulty in raising finance to support investment for change
- limited opportunities for diversification
- lack of experience on the part of directors
- loss of strategic focus
- inability to deal with a dynamic market environment
- cultural reluctance to change.

Learn

EG **Learning example 10.1**

Think of a business, or find one by searching on the Internet, that has failed. For example, a chain of shops that has closed down. Look to discover why it did and use the suggestions above to help think why it happened.

10.1.1 Possible causes of strategic failure and business decline

Possible reasons for a decline in business performance include changes in the external environment and internal problems, specific to the products or services of the organisation or its business model.

Common causes include:

- poor management in general
- poor marketing or sales
- poor financial controls
- poor decision-making (for example, inappropriate financing, entry into unprofitable markets)
- over-extending the business (for example, large, risky investment projects or unsuitable business combinations)
- low sales volumes
- inappropriate pricing (for example, prices set too low to generate profit)
- high costs.

Learn

On the UK insolvency website there are 65 reasons for failure listed! However it has been suggested by Brian Tracy, 'Leadership is the most important single factor in determining business success or failure in our competitive, turbulent, fast-moving economy.' Alternatively from a study by the US Bank, the main reasons why businesses fail are:

- poor business planning
- poor financial planning
- poor marketing
- poor management.

We can see that in reality there are lots of potential reasons, so make sure you can suggest some in the exam. Using models like Porter's value chain or 5 forces will help you generate ideas quickly.

IE Illustrative example 10.1

HMV, the British entertainment retail company, went into administration in 2013, unable to sustain itself in the face of intense competition from online music sales, supermarkets and illegal downloads.

10.2 Predicting corporate failure

It is possible to try to rely on a single financial ratio (such as cash/debt, which often deteriorates towards the end of a failing company's life)) as a way of predicting corporate failure. However, as we have seen above, there are a lot of potential factors that can mean a company fails. Relying on one financial ratio may mean that a failure is missed. So qualitative and quantitative models exist to predict corporate failure. Quantitative models focus on particular values and ratios which are said to be indicative of future financial health, whereas quantitative models identify particular risk factors and, often, assign scores and weightings to these risk factors.

10.2.1 A quantitative model: The Altman Z score

The Altman Z score formula, first published in 1968, is used to predict debt defaults by companies within a 2-year period and is based on financial ratios that are key to measuring the overall level of financial distress of a company. The model's attraction is that a number of financial ratios our combined, using weightings, to produce a single score. The score can then be interpreted as a prediction of the likelihood of insolvency.

The calculation is as follows:

Z = (1.2 × T1) + (1.4 × T2) + (3.3 × T3) + (0.6 × T4) + (0.999 × T5)

where

T1 = Net current assets/Total assets

T2 = Retained earnings/Total assets

T3 = Earnings before interest and taxes/Total assets

T4 = Market value of equity/Total liabilities

T5 = Sales revenue/Total assets

A Z score of 3 or above indicates a safe company, a score of 1.8 or below indicates a company in significant danger of insolvency.

Principle

Identify when a company is in danger of insolvency, using the Altman Z score formula

The limitations of quantitative models such as the Altman Z score include:

- They can be over simplistic, trying to capture the complexity of an entire business in a single number.
- The values of individual variables are open to manipulation such as window dressing.
- They focus on short-term performance.

Similarly, other models have been developed by people such as Taffler and Tishaw, who devised an alternative Z score and claimed a 99% successful rate based on the companies from which the model was derived. However, this was less successful on further testing, though still valuable as an indicator. The Z scores have all been developed over time.

For example, Ezzamel, Brodie and Mar-Molinero reviewed the earlier research and reported their UK-based study of financial ratios. These ratios showed five broad patterns:

- Capital intensiveness
- Profitability expressed as earnings, or cash flows as related to assets or funds

- Working capital position
- Liquidity position
- Asset turnover.

They saw that the patterns were unstable during the period of their study, even when considering the same group of companies. However, their conclusions were that it was possible to identify clear financial patterns. These could be used to reduce the number of ratios being used, but that the overall variability of the patterns made using them in different parts of the world or time periods tricky.

10.2.2 A qualitative model: The Argenti A score

This model is based on the assertion that failing companies tend to follow a similar sequence of events, broadly defined.

- Firstly, defects such as weaknesses in management and poor financial control arise.
- Secondly, as a result of the defects above, mistakes will occur, for example, over-trading, high gearing, poor decision-making.
- Thirdly, only after some time (possibly years), there will be visible signs (symptoms) of failure, for example, deteriorating financial ratios.

Firstly, defects can be divided into management weaknesses and accounting deficiencies. The management weaknesses include issues like a passive board of directors, an autocratic chief executive, lack of enough management depth or a lack of some crucial skills. Accounting deficiencies include not budgeting or having weak cashflow management.

Each weakness/deficiency is given a mark or zero if there isn't that particular problem. The total mark for defects is 45, and Argenti suggests that a mark of 10 or less shows a company is not at risk.

If management is weak, Argenti says that it will make mistakes which may not become apparent in the symptoms for some time. This may be several years, possibly five or more. The three main mistakes likely (each scoring 15 marks) are:

1. high gearing – a company allows gearing to rise to such a level that one unfortunate event can have disastrous consequences.
2. overtrading – this occurs when a company expands faster than its financing is capable of supporting. The capital base can become too small and unbalanced.
3. a big project – any external/internal project, the failure of which would bring the company down.

The suggested pass mark for mistakes is a maximum of 15.

The last part occurs when the symptoms of failure become visible. Here Argenti uses the categories:

1. Financial signs
2. Creative accounting
3. Non-financial signs eg falling market share, rising staff turnover
4. Terminal signs, these are very obvious ones.

Again, a score is obtained to judge a company's position. The A score therefore attempts to quantify the causes and symptoms associated with failure. As such it is a powerful model as it looks qualitatively first and then quantitatively to give a score, looking at causes and then trying to assess their effect.

10.3 Avoiding failure

Ross and Kami (1973) proposed a series of imperatives for avoiding business failure, commonly referred to as the 'Ten Commandments':

1. You must have a strategy.
2. You must have controls.
3. The Board must participate.
4. You must avoid one-man rule.
5. There must be management in depth.
6. Keep informed of, and react to, change.
7. The customer is king.
8. Do not misuse computers.
9. Do not manipulate your accounts.
10. Organise to meet employees' needs.

Source: The Liquidation/Merger Alternative; Peel, Michael J. ISBN: 9781587981579

 **Learn**

10.4 Improvement strategies

Improvement strategies need to address the root cause of the business failure and as such should focus on the specific factors which have been identified as contributing to the problem. For example, if the business is endangered by poor financial controls then the solution is to improve financial controls, perhaps with the help of a new financial director or an interim manager.

A business which is operationally sound but inappropriately financed may be able to solve the problems by refinancing. However if the problem is a high cost structure or poor marketing, then simple changing the capital structure of the company will not help.

Most turnaround strategies involve distinct phases:

1. Stabilise the business to exit the crisis:
   - Reduce short-term costs, particularly direct costs and seek operating efficiencies,
   - Increase revenues.
2. Install new senior managers.
3. Manage communication with key stakeholders.
4. Develop strategies that address the root cause of the business decline and that are able to achieve business objectives.
5. Prioritise actions and resources to achieve those objectives.

 **Learn**

IE Illustrative example 10.2

Jessops is a British photographic retail company. The company started facing financial difficulties in 2007, leading to a refinancing with HSBC in 2009. This led to the group's trade being transferred to a new holding company, Snap Equity Limited, whilst Jessops plc was placed in liquidation and the group's final salary pension scheme transferred to the Pension Protection Fund. Snap Equity was formed as a private company with 48% owned by HSBC, 33% by pension trustees and 20% by an employee trust.

Jessops Group Limited went into administration on 9 January 2013. All its stores were to close and 1,370 employees were to lose their jobs.

However, entrepreneur Peter Jones purchased the Jessops brand and various assets associated with it and formed Jessops Europe Limited. The retailer re-launched the high street brand with retail stores coming up again. The supermarket retailer Morrisons was reported to have agreed to purchase seven of Jessops' larger store sites from the administrators for an undisclosed price, to be converted to Morrisons convenience store format M Local.

EG Learning example 10.2

Altman's Z score can be used to assess the likelihood of a company's failing. This method is a combination of statement of financial position ratios, to measure financial risk, and a score of 1.8 or less, according to Altman, is a good indication of future problems. About 23% of big British companies have Z scores below 1.81. An example is BAE systems.

(a) Briefly explain the meaning of corporate failure.

(b) List the main symptoms of failure.

Key Learning Points

- Be able to identify situations where there is a risk of corporate failure. (E3a, E3d)
- Be able to recommend performance improvement strategies to avoid corporate failure. (E3c, E3e)
- Learn the difference between quantitative and qualitative corporate failure prediction models. (E3b)

What's the story?

Stop and think through the 'story' of this chapter and how it links with other chapters (use the Overview to help).

Learning example solutions

EG Solution 10.1

There are no shortages of businesses that have ceased to exist. Searching on the Internet for 'business that has failed' will bring up many examples. Using the business planning model from P3 will generate you lots of ideas why – the external environment, internal problems, poor strategy – but also bad luck can play a part, or bad timing.

EG Solution 10.2

(a) Corporate failure occurs when a company cannot achieve a satisfactory return on capital over the longer term. If unchecked, the situation is likely to lead to an inability of the company to pay its obligations as they become due. The company may still have excess assets over liabilities, but if it is unable to convert those assets into cash it will be insolvent.

For not-for-profit organisations, the issue is usually one of funding, and failure is indicated by the inability to raise sufficient funds to carry out activities effectively.

Although stated in financial terms, the reasons behind such failure are rarely financial, but seem to have more to do with a firm's ability to adapt to changes in its environment.

To assess the risk of corporate failure will thus involve an analysis of both financial and non-financial factors.

(b) Many lists of symptoms of failure exist:

- Failure to control cash by carrying too much inventory, paying suppliers too promptly, and allowing customers too long to pay.
- Failure to focus on a specific market because of poor research.
- Failure to control costs ruthlessly.
- Failure to adapt your product to meet customer needs.
- Failure to carry out decent market research.
- Failure to build a team that is compatible and has the skills to finance, produce, sell and market.
- Failure to pay taxes (insurances and VAT).
- Failure of businesses' need to grow. Merely attempting stability or having even less ambitious objectives, businesses which did not try to grow didn't survive.
- Failure to gain new markets.
- Under-capitalisation.

- Cash flow problems.
- Tougher market conditions.
- Poor management.
- Companies diversifying into new, unknown areas without a clue about costs.
- Company directors spending too much money on frivolous purposes thus using up all available capital.

London
School of Business
& Finance
shaping success in business and finance

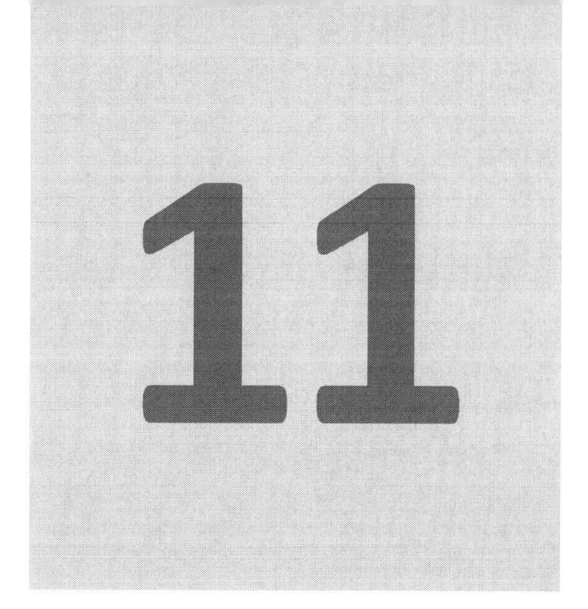

11 Current Developments and Emerging Issues in Performance Management

Context

Current developments in performance management encompass new techniques to be able to judge performance, new areas such as the environment and how an organisation should respond successfully to that challenge and other areas such as integrated reporting.

Emerging issues in performance management looks at the changing role of the management accountant and what they will do as well as how organisations will change in response to new techniques.

We end with looking at why the performance system matters and Key Performance Indicators (KPIs).

3Q

1. What is enterprise resource planning?
2. What are acquisition costs, operational costs and end life costs?
3. What is an integrated report and what is its purpose?

11.1 Modern developments in management accounting

Management accounting is changing as the needs of modern management change. Some of the ideas in this course are relatively recent (eg the rise of non-financial performance indicators).

In the past management accountants were deliberately kept separate from the operational side of the business (so they could report on management without being biased).

The role of management accounting has recently refocused its attention on performance management as the techniques and systems used today are very different from those of 50 years ago and there are current developments which are likely to lead to further changes:

- Emerging new technology
  Technological improvements have a significant impact on performance management as it is possible to measure more and more different indicators of performance and produce this information much more quickly and in real time. Because more indicators of performance can now be measured, the challenge is to ensure that the aspects being measured and managed are the right ones.
  - The production of performance reports is no longer the responsibility of a small number of specialists – rather their role is to design the overall system to ensure that it provides the information required by managers which can be interpreted to ensure that it is useful.
  - Performance management is about more than the information produced – what is important is how it is used and how the organisation acts in response to it.
- Significant growth in the use of non-financial measures of performance
  - There is a growing recognition that the performance of organisations depends on more than purely financial performance and techniques have been developed to enable measurement of performance in a number of different dimensions. Examples are the balanced scorecard and the performance prism.
  - Historically the focus of performance management has been on outputs of the organisation's activities. Organisations are now beginning to focus on outcomes, or achievements, and then using output measures to achieve those outcomes.
- Issues relating to governance
  - There is a recognition that not only does everyone in the organisation need to be involved in performance management but that there is also a need to extend involvement outside the organisation to the entire supply chain, as organisations recognise that others have an influence on their performance.
  - Over recent years, the issue of corporate governance has become a major area for concern in many countries. Organisations are now under increased pressure to demonstrate that they are effectively managed. This has led to:

- o pressure to demonstrate improvements in performance
- o more demands for accountability from external agencies
- o legislation and regulation relating to performance
- o looking for ways to measure and report on improvements in governance

In summary, there are a number of reasons why management accounting has changed:

- Information needs (on competition, customers etc.) are becoming more important.
- Change of all kinds inside organisations is regarded as helpful.
- Technology has allowed more information to be processed in more complex and flexible ways.
- Responsibilities in many organisations have been pushed down to junior managers resulting in more people having responsibilities, but each being involved in narrower areas of the business.
- Realisation that focusing solely on the bottom line (ie financial accounting) is not particularly helpful.

 **Learn**

Modern developments include:

- Total quality management
- Manufacturing resource planning
- Enterprise resource planning
- Optimised production technologies
- Just in time
- Kaizen costing
- Life cycle costing.

We have discussed some of these developments (total quality management, just in time and kaizen) earlier. Let us now look at the rest:

Manufacturing Resource Planning

Manufacturing Resource Planning (MRP) is a system for managing resources (primarily inventory of raw materials, work in progress and finished goods) which delivers efficiency savings and cost benefits such as reduced inventory holding costs, better and more efficient sales and distribution and more streamlined relationships with suppliers and customers.

Enterprise Resource Planning

Enterprise Resource Planning (ERP), sometimes referred to as MRP II, is an extension of the principles of MRP to external processes and processes outside of the context of manufacturing. ERP is therefore best described as a resource management system which aims to deliver efficiency savings in all areas of management, including manufacturing, but also business planning, labour management, finance etc.

Optimised Production Technologies

Optimised Production Technologies (OPT) is built on the theory of constraints and refers to improvements made to production methods by eliminating bottlenecks (for example, particular tasks within the production process) that limit the total throughput of production and/or create inefficiencies.

11.2 Life Cycle Costing

Life Cycle Costing (LCC), also called Whole Life Costing, is a technique to establish the total cost of ownership. It is a structured approach that addresses all the elements of this cost and can be used to produce a spend profile of the product or service over its anticipated life span. The results of an LCC analysis can be used to assist management in the decision-making process where there is a choice of options. The accuracy of LCC analysis diminishes as it projects further into the future, so it is most valuable as a comparative tool when long-term assumptions apply to all the options and consequently have the same impact.

11.2.1 Why is it important?

The visible costs of any purchase represent only a small proportion of the total cost of ownership. In many departments, the responsibility for acquisition cost and subsequent support funding are held by different areas and, consequently, there is little or no incentive to apply the principles of LCC to purchasing policy. Therefore, the application of LCC does have a management implication because purchasing units are unlikely to apply the rigours of LCC analysis unless they see the benefit resulting from their efforts.

There are four major benefits of LCC analysis:

- Evaluation of competing options in purchasing
  LCC techniques allow evaluation of competing proposals on the basis of through life costs. LCC analysis is relevant to most service contracts and equipment purchasing decisions.

- Improved awareness of total costs
  Application of LCC techniques provides management with an improved awareness of the factors that drive cost and the resources required by the purchase. It is important that the cost drivers are identified so that most management effort is applied to the most cost effective areas of the purchase. Additionally, awareness of the cost drivers will also highlight areas in existing items which would benefit from management involvement.

- More accurate forecasting of cost profiles
  The application of LCC techniques allows the full cost associated with a procurement to be estimated more accurately. It leads to improved decision-making at all levels, for example major investment decisions, or the establishment of cost effective support policies. Additionally, LCC analysis allows more accurate forecasting of future expenditure to be applied to long-term costing assessments.

- Performance trade-off against cost
  In purchasing decisions cost is not the only factor to be considered when assessing the options. There are other factors such as the overall fit against the requirement and the quality of the goods and the levels of service to be provided. LCC analysis allows for a cost trade-off to be made against the varying attributes of the purchasing options.

11.2.2 Who is involved?

The investment decision-maker (typically the management board) is accountable for any decisions relating to the cost of a project or programme and should be responsible for ensuring that estimates are based on whole life costs

11.2.3 Principles of LCC

The cost of ownership of an asset or service is incurred throughout its whole life and does not all occur at the point of acquisition.

The diagram below gives an example of a spend profile showing how the costs vary with time. In some instances the disposal cost will be negative because the item will have a resale value whilst for other procurements the disposal, termination or replacement cost is extremely high and must be taken into account at the planning stage.

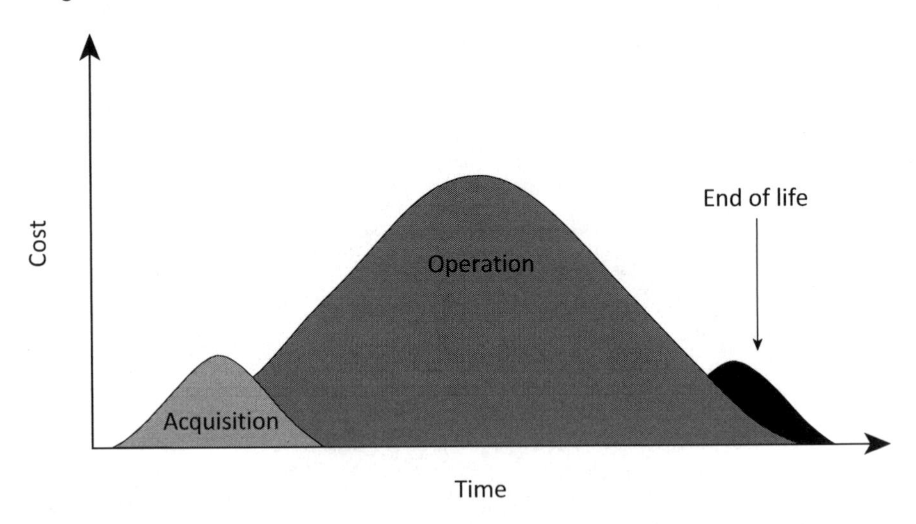

Definition

Acquisition costs are those incurred between the decision to proceed with the procurement and the entry of the goods or services to operational use.

Definition

Operational costs are those incurred during the operational life of the asset or service.

Definition

End life costs are those associated with the disposal, termination or replacement of the asset or service.

In the case of assets, disposal cost can be negative because the asset has a resale value.

Learn

A purchasing decision normally commits the user to over 95 per cent of the through-life costs. There is very little scope to change the cost of ownership after the item has been delivered.

The principles of LCC can be applied to both complex and simple projects though a more developed approach would be taken for say a large PFI project than a straight-forward equipment purchase.

LCC involves identifying the individual costs relating to the procurement of the product or service. These can be either "one-off" or "recurring" costs. It is important to appreciate the difference between these cost groupings because one-off costs are sunk once the acquisition is made whereas recurring costs are time dependent and continue to be incurred throughout the life of the product or service. Furthermore, recurring costs can increase with time for example through increased maintenance costs as equipment ages. The types of costs incurred will vary according to the goods or services being acquired, some examples are given below.

Examples of one-off costs include:

- procurement
- implementation and acceptance
- initial training
- documentation
- facilities
- transition from incumbent supplier(s)
- changes to business processes
- withdrawal from service and disposal.

Examples of recurring costs include:

- retraining
- operating costs
- service charges
- contract and supplier management costs
- changing volumes
- cost of changes
- downtime/non-availability
- maintenance and repair
- transportation and handling.

11.2.4 The methodology of LCC

LCC is based on the premise that to arrive at meaningful purchasing decisions full account must be taken of each available option. All significant expenditure of resources which is likely to arise as a result of any decision must be addressed. Explicit consideration must be given to all relevant costs for each of the options from initial consideration through to disposal.

The degree sophistication of LCC will vary according to the complexity of the gods or services to be procured. The cost of collecting necessary data can be considerable, and where the same items are procured frequently a cost database can be developed.

The following fundamental concepts are common to all applications of LCC:

- Cost breakdown structure
- Cost estimating
- Discounting
- Inflation.

Cost Breakdown Structure (CBS)

CBS is central to LCC analysis. It will vary in complexity depending on the purchasing decision. Its aim is to identify all the relevant cost elements and it must have well defined boundaries to avoid omission or duplication. Whatever the complexity any CBS should have the following basic characteristics:

- It must include all cost elements that are relevant to the option under consideration including internal costs.
- Each cost element must be well defined so that all involved have a clear understanding of what is to be included in that element.
- Each cost element should be identifiable with a significant level of activity or major item of equipment or software.
- The cost breakdown should be structured in such a way as to allow analysis of specific areas. For example, the purchaser might need to compare spares costs for each option; these costs should therefore be identified within the structure.
- The CBS should be compatible, through cross indexing, with the management accounting procedures used in collecting costs. This will allow costs to be fed directly to the LCC analysis.
- For programmes with subcontractors, these costs should have separate cost categories to allow close control and monitoring.
- The CBS should be designed to allow different levels of data within various cost categories. For example, the analyst may wish to examine in considerable detail the operator manpower cost whilst only roughly estimating the maintenance manpower contribution. The CBS should be sufficiently flexible to allow cost allocation both horizontally and vertically.

Cost estimating

Having produced a CBS, it is necessary to calculate the costs of each category. These are determined by one of the following methods:

- Known factors or rates are inputs to the LCC analysis which have a known accuracy. For example, if the Unit Production Cost and quantity are known, then the Procurement Cost can be calculated. Equally, if costs of different grades of staff and the numbers employed delivering the service are known, the staff cost of service delivery can be calculated.
- Cost Estimating Relationships (CERs) are derived from historical or empirical data. For example, if experience had shown that for similar items the cost of Initial Spares was 20 per cent of the UPC, this could be used as a CER for the new purchase. CERs can become very complex but, in general, the simpler the relationship the more effective the CER. The results produced by CERs must be treated with caution as incorrect relationships can lead to large LCC errors. Sources can include experience of similar procurements in-house and in other organisations. Care should be taken with historical data, particularly in rapidly changing industries such as IT where can soon become out of date.
- Expert opinion: Although open to debate, it is often the only method available when real data is unobtainable. When expert opinion is used in an LCC analysis it should include the assumptions and rationale that support the opinion.

Discounting

Discounting is a technique used to compare costs and benefits that occur in different time periods. It is a separate concept from inflation, and is based on the principle that, generally, people prefer to receive goods and services now rather than later. This is known as 'time preference'.

When comparing two or more options, a common base is necessary to ensure fair evaluation. As the present is the most suitable time reference, all future costs must be adjusted to their present value. Discounting refers to the application of a selected discount rate such that each future cost is adjusted to present time, ie the time when the decision is made. Discounting reduces the impact of downstream savings and as such acts as a disincentive to improving the reliability of the product.

Inflation

It is important not to confuse discounting and inflation: the discount rate is not the inflation rate but is the investment "premium" over and above inflation. Provided inflation for all costs is approximately equal, it is normal practice to exclude inflation effects when undertaking LCC analysis.

However, if the analysis is estimating the costs of two very different commodities with differing inflation rates, for example oil price and man-hour rates, then inflation would have to be considered. However, one should be extremely careful to avoid double counting of the effects of inflation. For example, a vendor's proposal may already include a provision for inflation and, unless this is noted, there is a strong possibility that an additional estimate for inflation might be included.

Risk assessment

Cost estimates are made up of the base estimate (the estimated cost without any risk allowance built in) and a risk allowance (the estimated consequential cost if the key risks materialise). The risk allowance should be steadily reduced over time as the risks or their consequences are minimised through good risk management.

Sensitivity

The sensitivity of cost estimates to factors such as changes in volumes, usage etc needs to be considered.

Optimism bias

Optimism bias is the demonstrated systematic tendency to be over-optimistic about key project parameters. In can arise in relation to:

- Capital costs
- Works duration
- Operating costs
- Under-delivery of benefits.

Optimism bias needs to be assessed with care, because experience has shown that undue optimism about benefits that can be achieved in relation to risk will have a significant impact on costs. A recommended approach is to consider best and worst case scenarios, where optimism and pessimism can be balanced out. The probability of these scenarios actually happening is assessed and the expected expenditure adjusted accordingly.

11.3 Environmental Management Accounting (EMA)

Environmental management accounting looks at the costs to the environment of decisions. For example, changing the material that is used to package a product might result in cost savings for the company, but produce more waste for governments to clean up.

The idea is to make managers aware of the environmental costs associated with their decisions. This is becoming increasingly important due to the higher profile that environmental issues have gained over the last few years.

11.3.1 The importance of environmental management accounting

- All organisations are beginning to recognise that environmental awareness and management are not optional, but are important for long-term survival and profitability.
- All organisations are faced with increasing legal and regulatory requirements relating to environmental management.
- All organisations need to meet customers' needs and concerns relating to the environment.
- All organisations need to demonstrate effective environmental management to maintain a good public image.

- All organisations need to manage the risk and potential impact of environmental disasters.
- All organisations can make cost savings by improved use of resources such as water and fuel.
- All organisations are recognising the importance of sustainable development, which is the meeting of current needs without compromising the ability of future generations to meet their needs.

 **Learn**

11.3.2 The contribution of environmental management accounting

Environmental Management Accounting (EMA) focuses on the optimisation of production and products by tracking all environmental costs back to their sources.

In the early stages of its development, EMA focused on finding the 'hidden' costs related to the treatment of generated pollutants. However, it now focuses even more on the other costs of pollution that are 'hidden' in production costs, such as those associated with the costs of raw materials, energy that goes wasted and the value that is added from the process but which does not enter into the final product.

Experience with EMA has shown that, on average, these hidden production-related costs can be ten to twelve times higher than waste and emissions treatment costs, such as the operational and investment costs associated with pollution treatment equipment and the transport of waste and its disposal at a dumping site.

Environmental management strategies have traditionally overlooked these system costs when assessing pollution costs. EMA is filling this gap today by providing a diagnostic tool to maximise the profitability of the entire process responsible for creating a particular product. The same process of analysis can be applied to identify costs buried in the life cycle of a product.

IE Illustrative example 11.1

The costs associated with the disposal of packaging discarded by distributors or customers, or, the additional costs borne by customers when they use products that produce pollution or waste energy are also the costs that customers pay (directly or indirectly) when they dispose of the products: the disposal cost itself and the shadow cost related to the value of the materials in the product that could be reused but are not.

However a standalone EMA initiative is less than optimal when it is not fully incorporated into the management system and culture of an organisation: the data it generates are not automatically considered in all aspects of an enterprise's decision-making.

An EMA can generate data that can be used for more than just assigning total costs to particular products; the data can also be used for the optimisation of the production process, products and/or product-service systems.

Without this integration, an EMA can be difficult to maintain, as their full potential and value to the company is not realised.

EMA is concerned with the accounting information needs of managers in relation to corporate activities that affect the environment as well as environment related impacts on the corporation. This includes:

- Identifying and estimating the costs of environment related activities
- identifying and separately monitoring the usage and cost of resources such as water, electricity and fuel and to enable costs to be reduced
- Ensuring environmental considerations form a part of capital investment decisions
- Assessing the likelihood and impact of environmental risks
- Including environment related indicators as part of routine performance monitoring
- Benchmarking activities against environmental best practice.

It is important to have a clear definition of environmental costs as management are often unaware of the extent of environmental costs and cannot identify opportunities for cost savings.

EMA attempts to make all significant costs visible so that they can be considered when making business decisions. The following techniques can be used to identify and allocate environmental costs

- Conventional costs – eg materials, energy costs.
- Potentially hidden costs – usually lost in general overheads.
- Contingent costs – eg costs of cleaning up if a spillage occurs
- Image and relationship costs – eg cost of producing environmental reports

According to Bennett and James (1998), EMA is concerned with gathering data related to the environment (lowest levels), which are converted through techniques and processes (middle level) into information which is useful for managers (top).

This key data is both non-financial and financial and management accounting techniques such as input/output analysis is used for the transformation.

Input/output analysis is a technique that can provide useful environmental information. This technique records material flows with the idea that 'what comes in must go out – or be stored' (Jasch, 2003). The purchased input is regarded as 100% and is balanced against the outputs – which are the produced, sold and stored goods and the residual (regarded as waste).

Materials are measured in physical units and include energy and water. At the end of the process, the material flows can be expressed in monetary units. Process flow charts can help to trace inputs and outputs, in particular waste. They demonstrate the details of the processes so that the relevant information can be allocated to main activities.

Flow management involves not only material flows, but also the organisational structure. Classic material flows are recorded as well as material losses incurred at various

stages of production. EMA can benefit from flow cost accounting because it aims to reduce the quantities of materials, which leads to increased ecological efficiency.

11.3.3 Environmental activity-based accounting

Activity-based costing (ABC) applied to environmental costs distinguishes between environment-related costs and environment -riven costs. The former are attributed to joint environmental cost centres, for example incinerators or sewage plants.

The latter are hidden in the general overheads and do not relate directly to a joint environmental cost centre, eg increased depreciation or higher cost of staff. Nevertheless they vary with the amount of throughput.

Schaltegger and Muller (1998) stated 'the choice of an adequate allocation key is crucial for obtaining correct information'. The four main allocation keys are:

- Volume of emissions or waste
- Toxicity of emission and waste treated
- Environmental impact added (volume × input per unit of volume) volume of the emissions treated
- Relative costs of treating different kinds of emissions.

 **Learn**

EG Learning example 11.1

Briefly explain how the concept of environmental management can be included as part of a total quality management approach.

11.4 The changing business environment

Organisations have faced dramatic changes in their business environment:

- Move from protected markets to highly competitive global markets
- Deregulation
- Declining product life cycles.

To compete successfully in today's environment companies are:

- Making customer satisfaction an overriding priority
- Adopting new management approaches
- Changing their manufacturing systems
- Investing in advanced manufacturing technologies.

EG Learning example 11.2

AJ Travel is sited on the high street and deals with a large number of walk-in customers and is known for giving a personal service. Employees working in the office environment share ideas give each other support and often socialise together after work. However a new initiative is proposed – to remain competitive, but cut costs and sell more holidays over the Internet by working from home, which is being considered as a viable working arrangement for staff.

Briefly evaluate the effects of this decision on employees and explain how management may overcome the concerns of employees.

The impact of change

The changing environment presents new risks and opportunities and these must be monitored and identified as early as possible. It is therefore likely that new measures will be added but consideration must also be given to keeping the mix as uncomplicated as possible and as such old unnecessary measures should be removed.

- Too many measures lead to 'indicator overload'
- If something is measured then the importance of that item is highlighted to staff and as such this is a communication exercise. Remember, if you change the mix, what are you telling people?
- At the same time, when you drop a measure from the mix, you will be communicating that it is no longer appropriate. You must ask yourself if that is what you want to achieve.

Success or failure is determined by how an organisation uses its resources. An accountant's role is the provision of a service to ensure that management and staff use resources in the most economic, efficient and effective manner, consistent with the attainment of organisational goals. By its very nature, accounting is a behavioural process. Management information should be economic, timely, accurate and relevant for the following purposes:

- Formulation of policies
- Planning and controlling activities
- Decision-making on alternative courses of action
- Reviewing and reporting on systems and operations
- Preparation of internal and external reports
- Safeguarding of assets.

Management control system operationalises the goals of the organisation. Effective organisation is one which achieves its goals.

A study of an organisation's goals provides an insight into the management control process which in turn sets out sub-systems for motivating employees, decision-making at various levels and the criteria for performance measurement.

Managerial control and management accounting functions should become familiar with the performance indicators which each functional manager uses on a

day-to-day basis, in the management of the mainstream corporate functions such as manufacturing and production, sales and marketing, people, research and development, accounting and finance.

To enable management to control these critical aspects of business, they must be provided with information, which is reliable, up-to-date and understandable. Financial controllers will need to help managers identify the factors which are critical to their operations, and to help in the design of indicators which allow them to monitor performance — not in isolation or ignorance of the real operational issues confronting the organisation.

Performance measurement is simplified – we tend to select only one yardstick for each activity.

We tend to avoid using multiple indicators of performance because:

- They are difficult to design.
- They may lead to confusion and lead inevitably to ranking among performance indicators.

Why is money measurement used so much?

The information derived from the accounting system is used to measure performance.

Because of the all-pervasive nature of accounting as the language of business, financially based indicators are universally adopted to measure performance.

There is often an obsession with bottom line profit as the sole indicator of performance.

This has resulted in the use or external reporting mechanisms as ongoing management control reports – a role for which they were not designed.

Development of mass production leading to cost accounting practices designed to permit managerial drive towards direct labour and raw material efficiencies

Budgets, standard costs, variances are among the most often used internal indicators of corporate performance.

Financial indicators are strictly one-dimensional in the view they permit of corporate activity:

- Not every corporate activity can be expressed in terms of money
- Many non-financial events precede the translation of corporate activity into money terms.

Peters and Waterman (1982) found that among the excellent companies surveyed in the U.S., their values are almost always stated in qualitative rather than quantitative terms and the companies that seemed most focused are those with the most quantified statements, with the most precise financial targets – had done less well financially than those companies with broader, less precise, more qualitative statements of corporate purpose.

What changes were needed in an organisation's internal measurement and reporting systems to assist management to address the critical success factors of their activities?

- Implementing new performance measurement approach
- Abandon financial measures
- Abandon previous non-financial measures.

Abandoning financial measures does not mean that the company employs no financial reporting. The statements of financial position, profit and loss statements, budget reporting are still required for external reporting and cost control purposes.

What is different is that the non-financial reports become the authoritative measures of performance for control, improvement and decision-making at the operational level within the company.

The day-to-day control of the manufacturing and distribution operations is better handled with non-financial measures.

IE Illustrative example 11.2

Financial measures are not sufficiently meaningful for the control of a production or distribution plant. Factory operators do not by nature think in terms of the financial aspects of their work. Their concern is directed towards production rates, yield quantities, reject rates, schedule changes, stock-outs and on-time deliveries.

The top-level measure concerns itself with the cost of quality.

Harvard professor Robert S. Kaplan (Relevance lost: The Rise and Fall of Management Accounting) draws attention to the inadequacies of current management accounting methods:

"My position is that every time you send a financial report from an operating unit to some level of management) you should also include a set of operating performance measures showing physical rather than financial information. They show much better the company performance and are much more action-orientated than are the usual monthly financial reports."

Changing a company's ethos so that non-financial, world class methods of performance measurement become standard practice requires a thorough understanding of the company's needs, a clear assessment of competitive pressures and leadership at a senior level.

Implications for the management accountant

The role of the management accountant continues to evolve in response to changes in the business environment.

London School of Business & Finance
shaping success in business and finance

Key issues facing the management accountant include:

- Changes in the focus and content of management accounting reports, for example, greater emphasis on external factors and non-financial performance indicators
- The increasing use of activity based techniques, such as activity-based costing and activity-based management
- Strategic analysis techniques which promote a greater understanding of the business such as value chain analysis
- New approaches to accounting such as life cycle costing.

 **Learn**

11.5 Burns and Scapens

Burns and Scapens have studied changes in management accounting and noted particularly how the focus of the management accountant's work has changed from financial control to business support.

The management accountant fulfils less a technical, narrowly defined role and has evolved into a business consultant, providing financially aware expertise to managers. They have named this new role a 'hybrid accountant'. Previously, the accountant was separate from operational management, both physically and in terms of contribution to the business. This distance lent objectivity and emphasised the independent and specialist nature of the accountant's role. Changing information needs and evolving business structures have led to a change in the role of the management accountant and in the relationship between the accounting function and the other parts of the business.

According to Burns and Scapens, there are three main forces for change:

- Technology
- Management structure
- Competition.

 **Principle**

Know about the three main forces for change listed by Burns and Scapens

Technology

As discussed elsewhere in the text, the advances in information technology (IT) has changed the way that managers interact with information and has removed some of the uniqueness in the traditional role of the accountant. Where data input was once strictly controlled and few had access to outputs, now more people in the organisation have access to the IT system and the information generated. Management information systems (MIS) allow staff and managers throughout the organisation to input data and obtain information and analysis in a variety of user-friendly formats.

Management structure
Changes in management structures mean that the accountant is now often providing non-financial reports alongside financial reports and more responsibilities have been devolved away from a central head office.

Competition
In recent years, many organisations have become more focused on strategy and customer interaction and have moved away from a focus on narrowly defined financial measures such as cost or profit. More nuanced and multifaceted performance measures are being used (the balanced scorecard is an example of this approach) and the management accountant is expected to play an active role in the understanding of strategic development and long-term performance management.

Articles in 'Student Accountant' often discuss key current issues and implications for the professional accountant.

11.6 Integrated reporting

11.6.1 Introduction

Definition

Integrated reporting (IR) is defined as a process founded on integrated thinking that results in a periodic integrated report by an organisation about value creation over time and related communications regarding aspects of value creation. (International Integrated Reporting Council, IIRC.)

IIRC is a global coalition of regulators, investors, companies, standard setters, the accounting profession and NGOs, who have a shared interest in long-term value creation and enhancement of reporting value creation. IIRC released the International Integrated Reporting Framework (Framework) in December 2013.

 **Principle**

Understand integrated reporting, its aims, purpose, content and role of the management accountant

11.6.2 Aims of IR

IIRC defines the aims of IR in detail as follows:

- Improve the quality of information available to providers of financial capital to enable a more efficient and productive allocation of capital.
- Promote a more cohesive and efficient approach to corporate reporting that draws on different reporting strands and communicates the full range of factors that materially affect the ability of an organisation to create value over time.

- Enhance accountability and stewardship for the broad base of capitals (financial, manufactured, intellectual, human, social and relationship, and natural) and promote understanding of their interdependencies.
- Support integrated thinking, decision-making and actions that focus on the creation of value over the short, medium and long term.
(*Source:* IIRC)

11.6.3 Purpose and content of an integrated report

Definition

An **integrated report** is a concise communication about how an organisation's strategy, governance, performance and prospects, in the context of its external environment, lead to the creation of value in the short, medium and long term. (*Source:* Framework)

The primary purpose of an integrated report is to explain to providers of financial capital how an organisation creates value over time. An integrated report benefits all stakeholders interested in an organisation's ability to create value over time, including employees, customers, suppliers, business partners, local communities, legislators, regulators, and policy-makers. (*Source:* Deloitte)

IIRC makes the business case for IR in observing that businesses require a reporting environment that is conducive to understanding and articulating their strategy and which helps to encourage improvements in performance. Business investors making economic allocation decisions rely on information which will enable them to understand how the company's strategy creates value.

IR applies principles and concepts that are consistent with enhancing the reporting process. It aims to improve the quality and quantity of information available to investors and lenders to aid financial decision-making which is itself better quality and considers all aspects of business performance. By focusing on value creation and encouraging a long-term, balanced perspective, in contrast to traditional short-term measures of profitability, IR aims to encourage long-term business sustainability.

The Framework gives guidance to preparers of reports by explaining the key principles of IR and establishing the contents of an integrated report.

11.6.4 The role of the management accountant

The management accountant has a key role in providing key performance information for integrated reporting to stakeholders. As such, the management information system must be capable of providing the information on a timely basis. Although IR includes non-accounting information, the strategically important position of the management accountant implies a significant contribution to the decision-making and reporting process.

11.6.5 Quantitative and qualitative information required in IRs

Quantitative KPIs promote comparability and are particularly helpful in comparing actual performance against targets and in setting measurable objectives. The International <IR> Framework describes the characteristics of suitable quantitative indicators as follows:

- Relevant to the circumstances of the organisation
- Consistent with indicators used internally by those charged with governance
- Connected (eg, they display connectivity between financial and other information)
- Focused on the matters identified by the organisation's materiality determination process
- Presented with the corresponding targets, forecasts or projections for two or more future periods
- Presented for multiple periods (eg, three or more periods) to provide an appreciation of trends
- Presented against previously reported targets, forecasts or projections for the purpose of accountability
- Consistent with generally accepted industry or regional benchmarks to provide a basis for comparison
- Reported consistently over successive periods, regardless of whether the resulting trends and comparisons are favourable or unfavourable
  (*Source:* Framework)

Qualitative information provides context and improves understanding of the quantitative information.

11.7 Why does the performance measurement system matter?

Senior managers and directors run a company to meet the needs of its stakeholders. Key amongst these will be the shareholders, who expect:

- Dividends
- Capital gains.

In order to satisfy these needs the company will need to improve profits constantly. To do this the company will need to monitor how it is performing so that it can identify:

- Areas where it is strong
- Areas where it is weak (to try and improve them).

These should follow on from the mission of the organisation.

In addition to this, the performance of each division will be measured. This allows:

- Strongly performing divisions to be expanded through investment
- Average performing divisions to be improved
- Poorly performing divisions to be closed.

As we have seen earlier, methods such as ROI are useful in this respect.

As well as this, managers in each division need to be encouraged to perform well, ie to be motivated.

They will be judged on how well their divisions perform and so will tend to make decisions that make their own division improve, whichever performance measure is used.

We saw with ROI that this can lead to managers making decisions that are poor for the company.

11.7.1 Main principles of performance measurement

Any company should design performance measures around what it considers to be important. This will communicate an emphasis to all parties on what is important and will ultimately influence the behaviour of staff, customers and consumers.

Remember the phrase: 'If it is counted, it counts.'

Companies need to develop measurement mixes to reflect their key performance indicators (KPIs). The mix will consider:

- The objectives of the organisation
- The KPIs of the processes. What are the value adding activities?
- The state of the environment ie in terms of turbulence and unpredictability
- The strategy adopted
- The type of business with regards to service, manufacturing, multinational etc
- The mix often forms the basis for the reward scheme for senior executives and consideration must be given to the issues of sub optimality and short-termist risks.

Determination of the measurement mix

1. Identify the objectives of the process and order them in terms of priority.
2. Identify the Key Performance Indicators (KPIs) of the operation.
3. Perform a position audit to identify the current situation and identify any extra KPIs.
4. With a view of the KPIs, develop a pilot measurement mix, perhaps containing a mixture of financial and non-financial elements. This is often referred to as a 'balanced scorecard' approach.
5. Evaluate the mix in terms of culture and change implications.
6. Deploy and monitor.

11.8 Problems with implementing and getting good value from KPIs

The term Key Performance Indicator (KPI) has become standard jargon for management information which identifies how well an organisation is doing and how it can improve. Many organisations view KPIs as best practice, but many MDs and CEOs have had real difficulties in implementing them.

There is an overwhelmingly powerful argument in favour of the production of the right KPIs and to make use of them in a way that profits everyone. It is about being in control of what you do and being ahead of the game.

11.8.1 Feedback process

There needs to be a two-way feedback process between the frontline of the business and the decision-making/management area. It is important to know what is happening and why, and if something can be improved, people need to know what to do about it.

Even more importantly, good KPIs will motivate people in the frontline because they can see, from the figures, the effect they are having on performance, thereby feeling some sense of achievement in their work.

The three functions of KPIs are:

- To show results across the business
- To provide knowledge of how to improve processes
- To motivate and involve people – therefore to cause action.

These three functions give us a set of rules for implementation. The KPIs must show the results of the process, and indeed of the business. These are known as 'high level' KPIs, which tell us whether we have won or lost. However, they may not tell us much about why, and for that we need to have 'knowledge-bearing' KPIs, which show waste errors and other opportunities for improvement. These have to be of such a nature that they prompt suggestions and actions, plus they have to be more detailed and provide root cause information.

The motivational effect of KPIs comes from the improvement in the indicators, which come from actions agreed by the frontline team. Of course this does call for excellent frontline management and a common and enlightened philosophy towards measurement throughout the business. As a frontline manager, it is important to control the process and improve it.

11.8.2 Method

- Define the outcome of the process in simple measures. Is it working as it should be?
- Frequently measure whether you are hitting that level.
- Raise the target to ensure improvement moves forward.
- Agree actions with the people involved in the process, to produce improvement.
- Log the actions that are agreed.
- Ensure that actions are implemented.
- Review the actions frequently.

There are many examples of processes, depending on the different business types. Examples include:

- Promotion for lead generation purposes to get in front of new customers
- The process of winning a new customer; converting leads to new customer or projects

- Developing new products
- Accepting and specifying an order
- Putting an order into operation or into production
- Holding the correct stocks and maintaining appropriate targets for stockholding
- Packing and distribution
- Collecting debts and preventing bad debts
- Existing Customer Contact Management (CRM)
- The management of any form of installation
- Manufacturing the product
- Managing and developing the brand.

Mapping or modelling a process should make it clear what it is organisations need to measure. The mapping doesn't have to be in great detail; merely enough to show what the processes and responsibilities are, and that you know each process is always working well.

Each business will have different priorities for management focus on certain processes. Organisations need to know what the key areas are, otherwise there is a danger of having too much trivial information that obscures what is really important.

When using KPIs, it is essential to have a picture of what organisations are aiming for, following the (probable) four to six months of implementation. When action is successfully implemented, next comes 'full-on' KPIs. These are reviewed regularly by the people in the process, against improvement targets. They are in a fixed hierarchy of well-run action review meetings and are quantified in annual effect financial terms (pounds per unit or percent of output, resource, waste etc.)

11.8.3 Slick information

Targets should be set high for the implementation of KPIs, so that automatic real-time KPIs provide the greatest possible degree of sub-analysis to 'drill-down' instantly. The production of ongoing information should be slick, efficient and automatic, so as not to make the maintenance process too costly to support on an ongoing basis. There is always going to be an up-front implementation workload.

Problems include:

- management focusing too much on operations;
- doing the job and not having a formal process;
- ad hoc investigations taking up management time;
- not making appropriate use of the software available;
- not fully understanding how beneficial KPIs can be; and, finally;
- standards for the production of KPIs being set too low, with KPIs coming out at monthly intervals, with no process for review or actions.

Many of these problems will have killed the process and robbed the organisation of the overwhelming benefits that could have been won. Therefore, organisations must ensure that the correct management behaviour is implemented, to make use of good KPIs. They must decide upon the right KPIs, at the right frequency and in the right degree of detail for its given functions, in terms of results, knowledge and motivation. Lastly, they must take specific implementation issues into account, for example presentation, software, data capture and primary recording.

KPIs help link goals to targets, and assist reporting against both. The planning and reporting process is to be integrated with the desire that the business achieves its objectives.

But what KPIs should be set? Below is a collection of KPIs suggested for a variety of different industries and functions.

IE Illustrative example 11.3

Manufacturing

- Meeting sales targets
- Achieving target cost prices
- Gross margin rates
- Waste rates
- Achieving budgeted labour rates
- Downtime
- Maintenance budget achieved
- On-time delivery
- Rejection rates
- Warranty claims
- Rework rates

Accounting practice (or similar professional organisations)

- Delivering on time
- Recoverable hours charged
- Achieving billing targets
- New clients introduced
- Value of new work introduced
- Added value work sold
- Number of tax investigations
- Number of complaints
- Turn round time on correspondence
- Returning phone messages (hard to measure though)
- WIP write offs/ons
- Low staff turnover
- CPD (including spending the budget)
- WIP days
- Debtor days

Service organisation

- Sales budget
- Obtaining progress payments on time
- Delivery dates
- Achieving budget

- Agreeing payment for contracting variations
- Customer satisfaction rates
- Down time to repair sites
- Complaints
- Obtaining follow on support contracts
- Number of client visits.

11.8.4 Deciding the right KPIs

The rules or principles involved in deciding the right KPIs, at the right intervals are described below.

Visible control

Firstly, there is the principle of 'coverage'. This means that managers need to have visible control over all areas of the business so that the whole management team can see what is going on in all areas. In other words, all of the major parts or functions of the business (marketing, sales, production, delivery and finance) must have their high-level results on display in a top-level dashboard (also known as an executive information system), a one-page presentation of figures for the period (month or four week periods) and cumulative. This list will cover the most important processes of the business.

From this dashboard it must be possible to see the big picture and to get confirmation of performance on such issues as:

- Numbers of customers trading (or numbers of projects being won).
- Some kind of market trend analysis, if the business is exposed to fluctuation in the market.
- The cost and effect of marketing, maybe in terms of the numbers of enquiries or leads being generated and the cost of those leads.
- The conversion rates from prospects and enquiries to secure new business
- Performance levels in the delivery or fulfilment of that business to the customer. Such statistics as percentage of delivery on time and in full would be typical here.
- Customer satisfaction rating, complaints, returns etc.
- A breakdown of sales levels with value added or gross margin by market sector. This could also be shown by product group.
- Key efficiencies of operations processes.
- Overhead spending vs budget, sometimes broken down into two or three elements or functions.
- Staff/labour turnover figures.
- Key financial management figures such as debtor days, creditor days, stock levels and cash liquidity.
- Return on capital employed and on owners' capital is often desirable if that is not confidential information.

This information needs to be confirmation of the big picture because the lower level information in each of these areas should be coming out at least weekly. Therefore, the period review can ask: "What have we done about this?"

Limitations of high-level KPIs

The most important limitation of top management KPIs is that they cannot themselves be used for shop floor motivation. They do not often make sense to people in the process unless those people are able to relate a change in their performance or their efforts directly to a change in the figures shown in the KPIs. Top-level KPIs contain a number of variables all 'mixed in'.

Again, in themselves, top management KPIs do not provide accurate and incisive enough analysis of what to do to change things. They are not usually about root causes.

Second, there is the principle of 'analysis', which involves the ability to drill down easily to the lowest level of detail, in order to understand what is happening at the operational level in each process.

Lastly, the principle of 'short interval control' means that managers have to look at figures with their team every day or even at hourly intervals in some cases. This is actually where the management control is won or lost.

Two factors are vital in management control and process improvement. Firstly if the information does not quickly indicate 'cause' ie why things are happening or how results can be improved, it is unlikely to lead to action. Secondly, if managers do not find out, in real time, when things are not happening as they wish, then the information is not part of the processes of management, which means the organisation is always looking backwards.

Information needs to be part of the process, so that managers are constantly thinking not only about doing the job but about doing it well and preventing things from going wrong. This then allows major gains in the profit and loss and has a big effect on team motivation.

IE Illustrative example 11.4

A real life example will illustrate the point about timing. In monthly sales meetings, certain organisations have become unhappy with the level of leads generated, the number of sales visits, or the fluctuation in activity levels of different sales people. After exhorting people to do better, they come back a month later and find that they still have a shortfall. Instead of having the review six weeks after the event, they could have known within two days that they were off the targets. This would demand a plan and daily figures, and that is called management.

Tips about focus

The smaller business may be attempting to focus on improving one particular area of its functioning because it is fundamental to the success of its strategy. This area must be well covered in KPIs. An example would be that product quality and value for money is good, but delivery lead time is too long, so the focus will be on the latter.

London School of Business & Finance
shaping success in business and finance

KPIs are essential to motivation and if a management team sees a pre-occupation with trivia, whilst a sore area is relatively neglected, it will reduce their commitment to and trust in the KPIs and the overall management control system. Focus on sore areas.

The right figures

Businesses should look for the right kind of figures for operational managers to use every day to manage their processes. Some examples of the kind of information that must be examined are:

In the management of a production process, root causes of downtime on a machine (daily):

- Electrical breakdown
- Mechanical breakdown
- Planned maintenance
- Operator's error
- Waiting materials
- Waiting operator.

In marketing, sources of leads generated (weekly):

- From exhibitions
- From advertising – analysed by media
- From direct mail – analysed by campaign
- From telephone marketing – by operator
- From website.

In distribution, failure rate to deliver 'on time and in full' by cause:

- Lead time longer than standard quoted
- Delivery after the specific date quoted
- Failure to process order to production within allowed time (turnaround)
- Failure to manufacture within allowed lead time (turnaround)
- Carrier failure
- Warehouse and despatch failure.

Customer complaints:

- Delivery was not on time
- Delivery was not in full
- Packaging damaged (returnable)
- Product damaged (returnable and re-workable)
- Product damaged (returnable and scrapped)
- Wrong product specification
- Wrong price
- Poor quality product.

In every one of the above cases, daily scores can be calculated and there can be discussion about how to do things better, how to stop negative things happening and how to replicate good results more consistently. In every case, if the root cause is verified immediately, the learning curve will be steep and the people in the process will be able to contribute. Unfortunately there could be thousands of other statistics that detract from the focus on the most important ones, so it is important to avoid these.

Blind spots

Where the cause and effect are in different departments and in a different time-frame, there can be great potential for improvement. This could be called a blind spot. An example is poor recording or interpretation of customer specification for bespoke products or services. The fault may come out weeks later in production, or even after delivery, and unless the teamwork is good it is all too easy for no-one to own up to the problem. The answer is to have a process which will investigate, understand, record and quantify, in financial terms, the root causes.

Finally, managers need to translate statistics into annual financial effect. Improvement does not usually come free; it costs money and you cannot expect commitment without being reasonably confident of a pay-off. From time to time, all high level KPIs should be translated into cost or even loss of profits (opportunity cost) to put them into perspective.

11.8.5 KPIs – Common information collection and presentation issues

Many of those who fail or struggle to implement KPIs actually do so because of the practicalities of collecting the information rather than disagreement with the philosophy. If companies complete their analysis on an 'as and when' or 'ad hoc' basis, it is not surprising they find it painful and disruptive.

Managers cannot be positive about getting out KPIs when the majority of their involvement is spent pulling together, consolidating and tabulating the information, instead of looking at it with their people to get ideas and inspiration to improve processes.

For that reason standards should be set high. Build the system so that once the base information is input on a day-by-day basis, the KPI spreadsheets and charts are produced automatically, in whatever detail is required without any consolidation and analysis work. Also, they should be real time as much as possible and up to date.

It is almost certain that around 90% of the information required will already be in the IT system somewhere anyway. There may be a need for some extra primary recording in order to capture the last 10%.

The right KPIs

The right KPIs must be in place before setting up the collection and presentation process. People generally want to do a good day's work, and avoid delays, rework, poor quality outputs, lost customers, hassle and stress. They would much prefer a day's work to go smoothly and to achieve what they set out to do.

Therefore, for each process within the business, managers need to make sure that the information being collected tells the team whether today has been a good day or not and why.

In establishing what KPIs to collect and present, start with a clean sheet of paper and define the information the business must have. This information will be on inputs, outputs, errors and waste and it will be root cause information.

Then find out whether that information is in the network or not. That will tell the management how much new recording has to be done, if any.

It is all too easy to bypass this 'clean sheet of paper' stage and lose objectivity, going instead for information which is easy to obtain. If the ideal KPI spreadsheet can be drawn up, the business will have a good chance of getting the information.

KPIs can offer remarkable potential to improve business performance provided they can be in a positive constructive manner. In almost all, if not all cases, problems can be solved, processes can be improved, people can be motivated, teams can be built and competitive advantage secured - as long as KPIs are approached with the right philosophy.

What are the most common problems?

- Management is focused too much on operations. Improvements are made piece-meal and reactive, rather than part of a formal process.
- There is no process for learning how to do better – no 'Plan, Do, Check, Act' cycle.
- There is no rhythm in the culture ie meetings are irregular or even non-existent. This reduces the potential for successful actions.
- Managers do not understand the benefit of KPIs. KPIs are viewed suspiciously as personal yardsticks to be used by top management to catch lower ranks out.

Getting the right behaviours

- Involve employees in all stages of implementation, from mapping the processes to primary recording of performance, reviewing, setting targets, and then generation and implementation of improvement actions.
- Understand the processes in the business. Map the key ones simply, and include all the people involved in the process. This creates the potential for teamwork and 'all one team' breaking down departmental barriers.
- Don't think of key performance indicators as primarily a means of measuring individuals' performance but as a way of identifying the potential for business improvement – think what's wrong not who's wrong. In truth, certain measures of performance, errors and waste may expose people who are not doing their job well. At that point it is appropriate to ask, 'how can we make sure we do better?' Remember, if employees aren't working efficiently it is up to management to support and train them.

In turn, managers also often feel threatened by KPIs. A manager, who does not forward plan, does not have an overall picture of the business processes in which he is involved and does not know how well his part of the process is performing is unlikely to succeed.

However, a well implemented KPI and review programme is the best way to help a manager improve their performance. It is essential to communicate this to managers and give them permission to get their heads out of the machinery and do their job as a manager.

- People are motivated by results and get real satisfaction out of being part of a winning team, and properly designed and implemented KPIs are the best way of demonstrating to the team that they are winning, gaining ground, solving problems and identifying further potential. Celebrate good results and recognise genuine improvements by giving employees a pat on the back. Good people expect to be told the truth, good or bad.
- Create a formal process, so that improvement is continual. Plan, Do, Check, Act – in other words, plan how the job is to be carried out, stick to the plan, measure how well it has been done and if necessary tweak the process until it operates efficiently. Thousands of business processes miss out the Check > Act stage.

This means they are not learning, not locked into improvement and often not even recognising potential for improvement until it hits them in the face. Regularly review the KPIs with the employees and look for ways to ways to improve. It is vital therefore to produce figures which identify the potential for improvement.

- Show the results of the process but also show what lies behind the results. Showing how the process works on a (large) piece of paper demonstrates the need to measure not only outputs but cause/effect relationships and is great for getting people's minds to work. It is vital to measure not only the results but the dozens of factors and thousands of measures behind the results.
- Measurement of errors and waste of all kinds are particularly useful. Usually these are down to lack of care and attention. Sorting this is out presents an easy option.
- Two different types of meeting are required to make this process work. To monitor KPIs, involve people in the process, and agree actions to follow up on actions agreed or introduced at previous meetings, through regular Action Review Meetings.

This should take place weekly and should be short and slick. It should be used to focus on the KPIs and actions but not used to solve anything other than simple problems. This will keep the meeting short, allow time and opportunity to pat people on the back, and will give the sensation of positive improvement.

It will also ensure actions agreed at the previous meeting have been carried out.

The second type of meeting should be used to solve problems or to discuss further opportunities. The right people should be involved and the appropriate information collected to involve a mapping or analysis process of facts and figures which relates to a process crossing several functions of the business.

- Managers should be trained to run one or both types of meetings, and to encourage and understand figures. They should also be able to lead, innovate and create solutions and to understand and promote the philosophy of 'working constantly on the gap between what is and what could be'.

Targets will set the seal on the need to be proactive and improve continuously. They create reasons for innovation and changes in practice. A target without a method is nonsense, so managers need to know how the process in question should function, so that they can see where improvements can be made. If a particular problem has arisen from the review of KPIs at the action review meeting, it follows that managers will already have the commitment of key people and good knowledge of the problem and its cause and importance.

Key Learning Points

- Understand how current developments and emerging issues affect performance management. (F1a, F2c)
- Appreciate how the role of a management accountant has changed with the introduction of new techniques and how this may affect performance management. (F2a, F2b)
- Learn about environmental management accounting and be able to describe its role in capturing costs. (F1b)

What's the story?

Stop and think through the 'story' of this chapter and how it links with other chapters (use the Overview to help).

Learning example solutions

EG Solution 11.1

Environmental management is increasingly recognised as an essential component of TQM.

Organisations should be striving to achieve an integrated environmental strategy underpinned by the same type of culture that is required for the successful operation of a programme of TQM.

In TQM, the focus is upon 'continuous improvement' and the pursuit of excellence. Such organisations pursue objectives that may include zero complaints, zero spills, zero pollution, zero waste and zero accidents.

Information systems need to be able to support such environmental objectives via the provision of feedback - on the success or otherwise - of the organisational efforts in achieving such objectives.

Many TQM accounting techniques can be modified and effectively adopted to help manage environmental issues.

EG Solution 11.2

Effects of the decision on employees

Positive

- Complete saving of commuting time or time spent travelling to meetings and conferences.
- Freedom from the stresses of travelling to work, thus giving them greater flexibility in working patterns/hours
- Significant reduction in the number of interruptions which should in turn lead to greater productivity in some tasks
- Better quality of life with reduced stress allowing them to be more focused on work effort

Negative

- Space taken up at home with IT equipment
- Loss of social contact and feeling of isolation
- Loss of distinction between home and office
- Issues with health and safety and employment rights
- Overheads – gas/electricity etc

Overcoming staff concerns

- Involve staff completely in the change. Ask for their input in relation to implementation of the change, ie phased changeover.
- Point out the benefits of home working, including stress reduction and better quality of life.

- Have an initial trial period and ask for their feedback, making improvements as necessary.
- Overcome the social aspects with regular meetings at a central location, social events/evenings.
- Provide good IT links via e-mail facility, video or telephone conferencing access to all databases.

Question bank

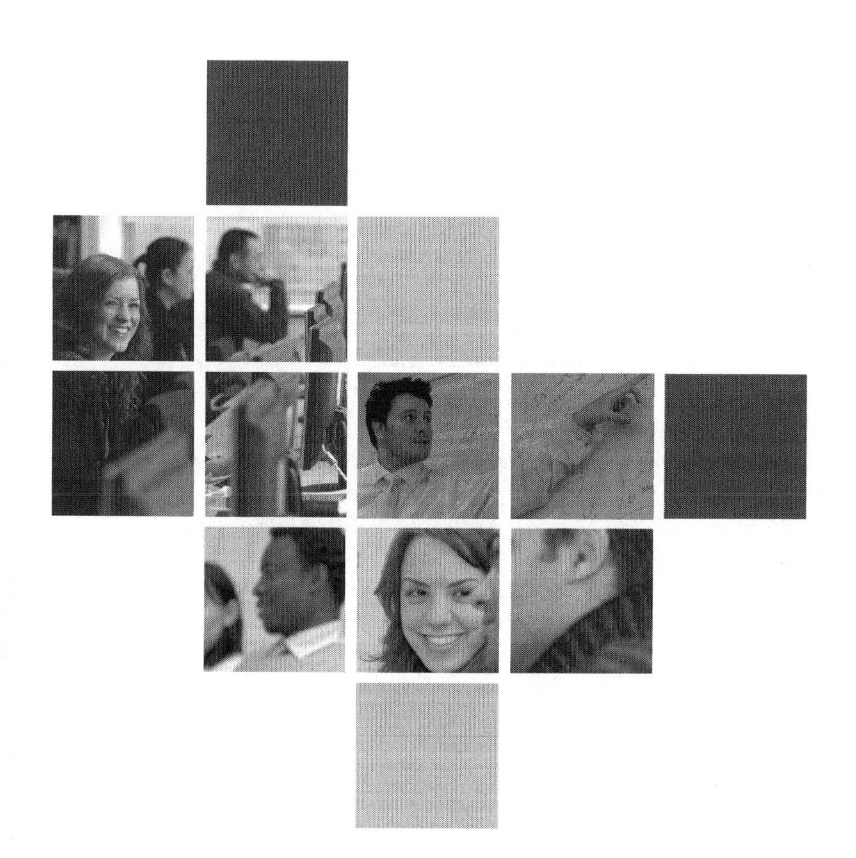

Pilot paper

Please note that the pilot paper is the original ACCA document and is for guidance only. It has not been updated for any subsequent changes in laws and regulations, so some technical details may have changed since the original pilot paper was issued.

Section A: This ONE question is compulsory and MUST be attempted

1. Mackerel Contracting (Mackerel) is a listed defence contractor working mainly for its domestic government in Zedland. You are a consultant brought in to advise Mackerel on a number of issues facing the company. The board need a report from you:

- outlining the external factors affecting the profitability of a potential new contract and how these factors can be built in to the choice of the design budget which is ultimately set,
- advising on a proposed change to the company's information systems and
- advising on suitable performance measures for Mackerel.

Firstly, Mackerel is currently considering tendering for a contract to develop a new armoured personnel vehicle (APV) for the army to protect its soldiers during transport around any future battlefield. The invitation to tender from the government specifies that the APV should take two years to develop and test, and be delivered for a full cost to Mackerel of no more than $70,000 per unit at current prices. Normally, government contracts are approximately priced on a cost plus basis with Mackerel aiming to make a 19% mark-up.

At the last briefing meeting, the institutional shareholders of Mackerel expressed worry about the volatility of the company's earnings (currently a $20.4m operating profit per annum) especially during the economic downturn which is affecting Zedland at present. They are also concerned by cuts in government expenditure resulting from this recession. The Zedland minister for procurement has declared 'In the current difficult economic conditions, we are preparing a wide ranging review of all defence contracts with a view to deciding on what is desirable within the overall priorities for Zedland and what is possible within our budget.' The government procurement manager has indicated that the government would be willing to commit to purchase 500 APV's within the price limit set but with the possibility of increasing this to 750 or 1,000 depending on defence commitments. In the invitation to tender document, the government has stated it will pay $7.5m towards development and then a 19% mark-up on budgeted variable costs.

Mackerel's risk management committee (RMC) is considering how much to spend on design and development. It has three proposals from the engineering team: a basic package at $7.5m (which will satisfy the original contract specifications) and two other improved design packages. The design packages will have different total fixed costs but are structured to give the same variable cost per unit. It is believed that the improved design packages will increase the chances of gaining a larger government order but it has been very difficult to ascertain the relevant probabilities of different order volumes. The RMC need a full appraisal of the situation using all suitable methods.

The risk manager has gathered information on the APV contract which is contained in appendix A. She has identified that a major uncertainty in pricing the vehicle is the price of steel, as each APV requires 9.4 tonnes of steel. However, she has been successful in negotiating a fixed price contract for all the steel that might be required at $1,214 per tonne. The risk manager has tried to estimate the effect of choosing different design packages but is unsure of how to proceed to evaluate the different options.

Secondly, the board is also considering a change to the information systems at Mackerel. The existing systems are based in the individual functions (production, sales, service, finance and human resources). Currently, reports are submitted by each function and then integrated at head office into the board papers that form the main strategic information system of the company. The board are considering the implementation of a new system based on an integrated, single database that would be accessible at any of the company's five sites. The company network would be upgraded to allow real-time input and update of the database. The database would support a detailed management information system and a high-level executive information system.

Finally, the chief executive officer (CEO) of Mackerel believes that this new information system will provide the opportunity for a change in how performance is evaluated within the company. The company's mission is to maximise shareholder wealth and currently, the board use total shareholder return (TSR) as an overall corporate measure of performance. The CEO has asked you consider the general impact of the new information system and also, how profit based measures such as return on capital employed (ROCE) compare to newer measures such as economic value added (EVA) with regard to meeting the overall goals of Mackerel and its external measure of performance.

Appendix A

Budgeted cost for APV

Variable cost per unit

		$	
Steel		11,412	9.4 tonnes at contracted prices
Engine/ transmission		9,500	
Electronics		8,450	
Other		4,810	
Labour		13,800	
Design and development	(fixed total)	$	
Package	Type 1	7,500,000	
	Type 2	8,750,000	
	Type 3	10,000,000	

Risk manager's assessment of likely government order:

	Probability		
Demand	**Type 1**	**Type 2**	**Type 3**
500	85%	25%	20%
750	10%	50%	50%
1,000	5%	25%	30%

Required:

Write a report to the board of Mackerel to:

(i) **Analyse the risks facing the management of Mackerel and discuss how the management team's attitude to risk might affect their response.** (9 marks)

(ii) **Evaluate the APV project using metrics and methods for decision-making under risk and uncertainty and assess the suitability of the different methods used.** (19 marks)

(iii) **Recommend an appropriate choice of method of assessing the project and therefore, a course of action for the APV contract.** (3 marks)

(iv) **Evaluate the potential impact of the introduction of the new executive information system on operational information gathering and strategic decision-making at Mackerel.** (8 marks)

(v) **Assess how profit based measures such as return on capital employed (ROCE) compare to newer measures such as economic value added (EVA) given Mackerel's overall goals.** (7 marks)

Question 1 includes professional marks for the format, style and structure of the discussion of your answer.

(4 marks)

(50 marks)

Section B – Two questions from the three given must be attempted.

2. Albacore Chess Stores (Albacore) is a chain of twelve shops specialising in selling items associated with the game of chess: boards, pieces, clocks, software and books. Three years ago, the company was the subject of a venture capital buyout from a larger group. A new senior management team was put in place after the buyout. They have the aim of running the business in order to maximise profits.

The Chief Financial Officer (CFO) along with the other members of senior management sets the annual budget and uses a standard costing approach with variance analysis in order to control individual shop performance. The head office handles all capital purchases and brand marketing. All inventory purchasing is done centrally and the shop opening times are set as standard across the company. As an illustration of senior management attitude, the CFO had set the budget for 2011 staff costs at $7 per hour for part-time staff and this was rigorously observed in the period.

Each shop is run by a manager who reports their financial results to the operational director at head office. The shop managers recruit and manage the staffing of their shop. They have some autonomy in setting prices locally and have been given authority to vary prices by up to 10% from a master list produced by the CFO. They also have a local marketing budget agreed each year by the shop's manager and the marketing director as part of the annual appraisal process.

The shop managers have approached the Chairman of Albacore to complain about the way that they are managed and their remuneration. They feel that their efforts are unrecognised by senior management. One manager commented 'I have had a successful year in hard economic circumstances. I have run a number of promotions in the shop that have been well received by the customers. However, the budgets that are set are impossible to achieve and as a result I have not been paid any bonus although I feel that I have done everything in my power to bring in good profits.'

The shop managers at Albacore are paid a basic salary of $27,000 with bonuses of up to 30% of basic salary dependent on two factors: performance above budget and the operational director's assessment of the manager's performance. The budget for the next year is prepared by the CFO and presented by the operational director at the shop manager's annual appraisal.

The Chairman has come to you to ask if you can consider the system of performance assessment for the shop managers and give an independent perspective on the reward systems at Albacore. She has heard of variance analysis but is unsure as what would be relevant in this situation. She has provided the following illustrative branch report from the previous year for one shop:

Albacore Chess Stores

Tunny Branch Year to Sept 2011

		Budget	Actual	Variance
		$	$	$
Sales		266,000	237,100	-28,900
Cost of sales		106,400	94,840	11,560
Gross profit		159,600	142,260	-17,340
Marketing		12,000	11,500	500
Staff costs	Manager	27,000	27,000	0
	Part-time staff	38,000	34,000	4,000
Property costs		26,600	26,600	0
Shop profit		56,000	43,160	-12,840

Notes:

Property costs includes heating, lighting and rental.

Positive variances are favourable.

End of report

The manager of this shop commented at the appraisal meeting that she felt that the assessment was unfair since her failure to make budget was due to general economic conditions. The industry as a whole saw a 12% fall in revenues during the period and the budget for the period was set to be the same as the previous period. She was not paid a bonus for the period.

Required:

(a) Evaluate the suitability of the existing branch report as a means of assessing the shop manager's performance and draft an improved branch report with justifications for changes. (13 marks)

(b) Analyse the performance management style and evaluate the performance appraisal system at Albacore. Suggest suitable improvements to its reward system for the shop managers. (12 marks)

(25 marks)

3. Pharmaceutical Technologies Co (PT) is a developer and manufacturer of pharmaceuticals medical drugs in Beeland. It is one of the 100 largest listed companies on the national stock exchange. The company focuses on buying prospective products drugs from small bio-engineering companies that have shown initial promise in testing from small bio- engineering companies. PT then leads these through three regulatory stages to launch in the general medical market. The three stages are:

1. to confirm that the safety of the drug product (does it harm humans?), with small scale trials;,
2. to test the efficacy of the product (does it help cure?), again in small scale trials; and
3. finally, large scale trials to definitively decide on the safety and efficacy of the product.

The drugs are then marketed through the company's large sales force to health care providers and end users (patients). The health care providers are paid by either health insurance companies or the national government dependent on the financial status of the patient.
The Beeland Drug Regulator (BDR) oversees this testing process and makes the final judgement about whether a product can be sold in the country.
Its objectives are to protect, promote and improve public health by ensuring that:

- medicines have an acceptable balance of benefit and risk;,
- the users of these medicines understand this risk-benefit profile; and
- new beneficial product development is encouraged.

The regulator is governed by a board of trustees appointed by the government. It is funded directly by the government and also, through fees charged to drug companies when granting licences to sell their products in Beeland.
PT has used share price and earnings per share as its principal measures of performance to date. However, the share price has underperformed the market and the health sector in the last 2 two years. The chief executive officer (CEO) has identified that these measures are too narrow and is considering implementing a balanced scorecard approach to address this problem.

A working group has drawn up a suggested balanced scorecard. It began by identifying the objectives from the board's medium term strategy:

- Create shareholder value by bringing commercially viable drugs to market
- Improve the efficiency of drug development
- Increase shareholder value by innovation in the drug approval process

The working group then considered the stakeholder perspectives:

- Shareholders want an competitive return on their investment
- Payers Purchasers (governments, insurers and patients) want to pay a reasonable price for the drugs
- Regulators want an efficient process for the validation of drugs
- Doctors want safe and effective drug products
- Patients want to be cured

Finally, this leads to the proposed scorecard of performance measures:

- Financial – share price and earnings per share
- Customer – number of patients using TTPT products
- Internal business process – above exceed industry-standard quality of on design and testing; time to regulatory approval of a product
- Learning and growth – training days undertaken by staff; time to market of new product; percentage of drugs bought by TTPT that gain final approval.

This balanced scorecard now needs to be reviewed to ensure that it will address the company's objectives and the issues that it faces in its business environment.

Required:

(a) Evaluate the performance measures proposed for PT's balanced scorecard.
(10 marks)

(b) Briefly describe a method of analysing stakeholder influence and analyse the influence of four different external stakeholders on the regulator (BDR).
(8 marks)

(c) Using your answer from part (b), describe how the application of the balanced scorecard approach at BDR would differ from the approach within PT. (7 marks)

(25 marks)

4. PLX Refinery Co is a large oil refinery business in Kayland. Kayland is a developing country with a large and growing oil exploration and production business which supplies PLX with crude oil. Currently, the refinery has the capacity to process 200,000 barrels of crude oil per day and makes profits of $146m per year. It employs about

2,000 staff and contractors. The staff are paid $60,000 each per year on average (about twice the national average in Kayland).

The government of Kayland has been focussed on delivering rapid economic growth over the last 15 years. However, there are increasing signs that the environment is paying a large price for this growth with public health suffering. There is now a growing environmental pressure group, Green Kayland (GK), which is organising protests against the companies that they see as being the major polluters.
Kayland's government wishes to react to the concerns of the public and the pressure groups. It has requested that companies involved in heavy industry contribute to a general improvement in the treatment of the environment in Kayland.
As a major participant in the oil industry with ties to the nationalised oil exploration company (Kayex), PLX believes it will be strategically important to be at the forefront of the environmental developments. It is working with other companies in the oil industry to improve environmental reporting since there is a belief that this will lead to improved public perception and economic efficiency of the industry. PLX has had a fairly good compliance record in Kayland with only two major fines being levied in the last eight years for safety breaches and river pollution ($1m each).
The existing information systems within PLX focus on financial performance. They support financial reporting obligations and allow monitoring of key performance metrics such as earnings per share and operating margins. Recent publications on environmental accounting have suggested there are a number of techniques (such as input/output analysis, activity-based costing (ABC) and a lifecycle view) that may be relevant in implementing improvements to these systems.
Currently, the refinery has the capacity to process 200,000 barrels of crude oil per day and makes profits of $146m per year. It employs about 2,000 staff and contractors. The staff are paid $60,000 each per year on average (about twice the national average in Kayland). PLX has had a fairly good compliance record in Kayland with only two major fines being levied in the last eight years for safety breaches and river pollution ($1m each).
PLX is considering a major capital expenditure programme to enhance capacity, safety and efficiency at the refinery. This will involve demolishing certain older sections of the refinery and building on newly acquired land adjacent to the site. Overall, the refinery will increase its land area by 20%.
Part of the refinery extension will also manufacture a new plastic, Kayplas. Kayplas is expected to have a limited market life of five years when it will be replaced by Kayplas2. The refinery accounting team have forecast the following data associated with this product and calculated PLX's traditional performance measure of product profit for the new product:

All figures are $m's

	2012	2013	2014	2015	2016
Revenue generated	25.0	27.5	30.1	33.2	33.6
Costs					
Production costs	13.8	15.1	16.6	18.3	18.5
Marketing costs	5.0	4.0	3.0	3.0	2.0
Development costs	5.6	3.0	0.0	0.0	0.0
Product profit	0.6	5.4	10.5	11.9	13.1

Subsequently, the following environmental costs have been identified from PLX's general overheads as associated with Kayplas production.

	2012	2013	2014	2015	2016
Waste filtration	1.2	1.4	1.5	1.9	2.1
Carbon dioxide exhaust extraction	0.8	0.9	0.9	1.2	1.5

Additionally, other costs associated with closing down and recycling the equipment in Kayplas production are estimated at $18m in 2016.
The board wishes to consider how it can contribute to the oil industry's performance in environmental accounting, how it can implement the changes that this might require and how these changes can benefit the company.

Required:

Write to the board of PLX to:

(a) Discuss and illustrate four different cost categories that would aid transparency in environmental reporting both internally and externally at PLX. **(6 marks)**

(b) Explain and evaluate how the three management accounting techniques mentioned can assist in managing the environmental and strategic performance of PLX. **(9 marks)**

(c) Assess the impact of implementing an input/output analysis on the information systems used in PLX. **(3 marks)**

(d) Evaluate the costing approach used for Kayplas's performance compared to a lifecycle costing approach, performing appropriate calculations. **(7 marks)**

(25 marks)

Present Value Table

Present value of 1 ie $(1 + r)^{-n}$

Where

r = discount rate

n = number of periods until payment

Discount rate (r)

Periods

(n)	1%	2%	3%	4%	5%	6%	7%	8%	9%	10%	
1	0·990	0·980	0·971	0·962	0·952	0·943	0·935	0·926	0·917	0·909	1
2	0·980	0·961	0·943	0·925	0·907	0·890	0·873	0·857	0·842	0·826	2
3	0·971	0·942	0·915	0·889	0·864	0·840	0·816	0·794	0·772	0·751	3
4	0·961	0·924	0·888	0·855	0·823	0·792	0·763	0·735	0·708	0·683	4
5	0·951	0·906	0·863	0·822	0·784	0·747	0·713	0·681	0·650	0·621	5
6	0·942	0·888	0·837	0·790	0·746	0·705	0·666	0·630	0·596	0·564	6
7	0·933	0·871	0·813	0·760	0·711	0·665	0·623	0·583	0·547	0·513	7
8	0·923	0·853	0·789	0·731	0·677	0·627	0·582	0·540	0·502	0·467	8
9	0·914	0·837	0·766	0·703	0·645	0·592	0·544	0·500	0·460	0·424	9
10	0·905	0·820	0·744	0·676	0·614	0·558	0·508	0·463	0·422	0·386	10
11	0·896	0·804	0·722	0·650	0·585	0·527	0·475	0·429	0·388	0·350	11
12	0·887	0·788	0·701	0·625	0·557	0·497	0·444	0·397	0·356	0·319	12
13	0·879	0·773	0·681	0·601	0·530	0·469	0·415	0·368	0·326	0·290	13
14	0·870	0·758	0·661	0·577	0·505	0·442	0·388	0·340	0·299	0·263	14
15	0·861	0·743	0·642	0·555	0·481	0·417	0·362	0·315	0·275	0·239	15

(n)	11%	12%	13%	14%	15%	16%	17%	18%	19%	20%	
1	0·901	0·893	0·885	0·877	0·870	0·862	0·855	0·847	0·840	0·833	1
2	0·812	0·797	0·783	0·769	0·756	0·743	0·731	0·718	0·706	0·694	2
3	0·731	0·712	0·693	0·675	0·658	0·641	0·624	0·609	0·593	0·579	3
4	0·659	0·636	0·613	0·592	0·572	0·552	0·534	0·516	0·499	0·482	4
5	0·593	0·567	0·543	0·519	0·497	0·476	0·456	0·437	0·419	0·402	5
6	0·535	0·507	0·480	0·456	0·432	0·410	0·390	0·370	0·352	0·335	6
7	0·482	0·452	0·425	0·400	0·376	0·354	0·333	0·314	0·296	0·279	7
8	0·434	0·404	0·376	0·351	0·327	0·305	0·285	0·266	0·249	0·233	8
9	0·391	0·361	0·333	0·308	0·284	0·263	0·243	0·225	0·209	0·194	9
10	0·352	0·322	0·295	0·270	0·247	0·227	0·208	0·191	0·176	0·162	10
11	0·317	0·287	0·261	0·237	0·215	0·195	0·178	0·162	0·148	0·135	11

12	0·286	0·257	0·231	0·208	0·187	0·168	0·152	0·137	0·124	0·112	12
13	0·258	0·229	0·204	0·182	0·163	0·145	0·130	0·116	0·104	0·093	13
14	0·232	0·205	0·181	0·160	0·141	0·125	0·111	0·099	0·088	0·078	14
15	0·209	0·183	0·160	0·140	0·123	0·108	0·095	0·084	0·074	0·065	15

Annuity Table

Present value of an annuity of 1 i.e. $\frac{1 - (1+r)^{-n}}{r}$

Where

r = discount rate

n = number of periods

Discount rate (r)

Periods

(n)	1%	2%	3%	4%	5%	6%	7%	8%	9%	10%	
1	0·990	0·980	0·971	0·962	0·952	0·943	0·935	0·926 77	2·531	2·487	3
4	3·902	3·808	3·717	3·630	3·546	3·465	3·387	3·312	3·240	3·170	4
5	4·853	4·713	4·580	4·452	4·329	4·212	4·100	3·993	3·890	3·791	5
6	5·795	5·601	5·417	5·242	5·076	4·917	4·767	4·623	4·486	4·355	6
7	6·728	6·472	6·230	6·002	5·786	5·582	5·389	5·206	5·033	4·868	7
8	7·652	7·325	7·020	6·733	6·463	6·210	5·971	5·747	5·535	5·335	8
9	8·566	8·162	7·786	7·435	7·108	6·802	6·515	6·247	5·995	5·759	9
10	9·471	8·983	8·530	8·111	7·722	7·360	7·024	6·710	6·418	6·145	10
11	10·368	9·787	9·253	8·760	8·306	7·887	7·499	7·139	6·805	6·495	11
12	11·255	10·575	9·954	9·385	8·863	8·384	7·943	7·536	7·161	6·814	12
13	12·134	11·348	10·635	9·986	9·394	8·853	8·358	7·904	7·487	7·103	13
14	13·004	12·106	11·296	10·563	9·899	9·295	8·745	8·244	7·786	7·367	14
15	13·865	12·849	11·938	11·118	10·380	9·712	9·108	8·559	8·061	7·606	15

(n)	11%	12%	13%	14%	15%	16%	17%	18%	19%	20%	
1	0·901	0·893	0·885	0·877	0·870	0·862	0·855	0·847	0·840	0·833	1
2	1·713	1·690	1·668	1·647	1·626	1·605	1·585	1·566	1·547	1·528	2
3	2·444	2·402	2·361	2·322	2·283	2·246	2·210	2·174	2·140	2·106	3
4	3·102	3·037	2·974	2·914	2·855	2·798	2·743	2·690	2·639	2·589	4
5	3·696	3·605	3·517	3·433	3·352	3·274	3·199	3·127	3·058	2·991	5
6	4·231	4·111	3·998	3·889	3·784	3·685	3·589	3·498	3·410	3·326	6
7	4·712	4·564	4·423	4·288	4·160	4·039	3·922	3·812	3·706	3·605	7

8	5·146	4·968	4·799	4·639	4·487	4·344	4·207	4·078	3·954	3·837	8
9	5·537	5·328	5·132	4·946	4·772	4·607	4·451	4·303	4·163	4·031	9
10	5·889	5·650	5·426	5·216	5·019	4·833	4·659	4·494	4·339	4·192	10
11	6·207	5·938	5·687	5·453	5·234	5·029	4·836	4·656	4·486	4·327	11
12	6·492	6·194	5·918	5·660	5·421	5·197	4·988	4·793	4·611	4·439	12
13	6·750	6·424	6·122	5·842	5·583	5·342	5·118	4·910	4·715	4·533	13
14	6·982	6·628	6·302	6·002	5·724	5·468	5·229	5·008	4·802	4·611	14
15	7·191	6·811	6·462	6·142	5·847	5·575	5·324	5·092	4·876	4·675	15

End of Question Paper

Other exam-standard questions

1. Osthollow is a large, industrial manufacturer operating within the automotive industry. The company is based in Europe and has around twelve different manufacturing sites. Over recent years Osthollow has come under pressure from smaller competitors that can produce some of the component parts which Osthollow produces at lower cost. Osthollow has only recently concluded a strategic review of the business and the board of directors decided to increase the autonomy of local managers to make investment decisions which will increase return on investment and contribute to efficiency savings. All twelve manufacturing plants are now treated as investment centres in order to try to improve the quality and speed of decision-making, to increase the motivation of local managers and to allow the board of directors to concentrate their own resources on strategic issues.

   Currently, local investment centre managers are appraised on divisional return on investment and residual income. However, the Chief Executive Officer of Osthollow is concerned that these measures might be manipulated by local managers or may lead to short-term decision-making based on the impact of a decision on this year's key performance indicators rather than long-term shareholder wealth maximisation. The Financial Director of Osthollow has responded: 'By using two different performance measures (return on investment and residual income) the chance of sub-optimal behaviour can be minimised. It is much more difficult to manipulate two different measures than one.'
   One of the non-executive directors has suggested that the board consider adding 'Economic Value Added' as a performance measure and has commented:
   'EVA can be used as a single top level financial measure and actually solves the problem of having multiple objectives leading to conflicting behaviours. EVA shows whether the management are adding or destroying value over a period of time. It is adaptable to measure performance at all levels, for example, it was originally used to assess the performance of companies quoted on the stock exchange but can also be used across all levels of management.'
   Wellpond is an investment centre within Osthollow and the manager of Wellpond is considering an investment in a new piece of equipment which will generate cash savings over the next five years. The machine would cost £100,000 and the estimated effect on net cash flows is equal to savings of £29,000 per year for the machine's estimated life of five years.
   Osthollow has an estimated cost of capital of 10%.

Required:

As an independent consultant, produce a report for the board of directors of Osthollow which includes:

(a) a brief discussion of what considerations should be included in deciding on what performance measures should be used for the investment centres in Osthollow;

(6 marks)

(b) an explanation of the problems with using return on investment and residual income as performance measures for divisions within Osthollow; (10 marks)
(c) an explanation and appraisal of 'Economic Value Added' as a divisional performance measure for Osthollow; (14 marks)
(d) calculations, with comments, in respect of the proposed investment for Wellpond which show:
   (i) the net present value of the investment
   (ii) the EVA for year 1 assuming straight-line depreciation
   (iii) the EVA for year 1 assuming annuity depreciation, and; (11 marks)

(e) a discussion of how business process re-engineering may be of use to Osthollow.

(9 marks)

(50 marks)

2. Fieldmarsh plc is a large, international group of companies in the travel industry, organised into strategic business units. Fieldmarsh has identified that it is losing market share in a number of markets and countries and wishes to use benchmarking to improve its performance in key markets.

Required:

(a) Explain what types of benchmarks Fieldmarsh could identify and explain what the benchmarking process is likely to involve. (7 marks)
(b) Discuss the benefits and difficulties involved in benchmarking. (10 marks)
(c) Discuss what factors Fieldmarsh should consider when deciding on performance measures for individual divisions and managers. (8 marks)

(25 marks)

3. Whitesummer is a clothing company which uses only fair-trade and natural materials. Over the past year, the company has grown significantly, mainly due to the pop-up shops it has opened around the country. Due to this, 80% of the sales are through shops and only 20% of sales are online at present. The Management Accountant at Whitesummer recently attended a seminar about the importance of setting SMART objectives based on core competencies and existing identified strengths of the business.

   The Management Accountant has suggested two objectives for next year and is planning to present them to the Board of Directors:

   - Evaluate how successful the pop-up shops have been to business activity this year and to expand this for the coming year.
   - Focus upon frequent customers to ensure they stay loyal to the firm over the next 24 months.

   You are working as the assistant management accountant and you have been asked to help evaluate these objectives for the company and explain how they could be implemented.

Required:

(a) Prepare notes which summarise the key strengths and weaknesses of Whitesummer's current business model and which identify one or two key opportunities and threats. (10 marks)

(b) Explain how each of the objectives above could be implemented by Whitesummer. (12 marks)

(c) Suggest alternative possible objectives that the board of directors might consider. (3 marks)

(25 marks)

4. Wildehall is a small airline business operating mainly business flights between secondary airports, using small aircraft. The company's mission statement is 'to connect communities'. Prices are set at premium levels to reflect the convenience of direct flights and the quality of service provided. The average passenger load factor (the proportion of seats occupied, on average, across all operated flights) in 2012 was 65%, which is lower than that of most of Wildehall's larger competitors but around the same as its principal competitor in this sector of the market. Wildehall has a good record for reliability and punctuality and generally receives positive feedback from individual and corporate clients.

   Recently, Wildehall has increased its passenger load factor by offering a limited number of seats for advance purchase at lower fares. These fares have been designed to appeal to more price sensitive leisure and business travellers who can book in advance. The fares are non-refundable and on-exchangeable and Wildehall has not noticed any significant reduction in sales of its more usual flexible tickets. Passenger load factor is 2013 increase to an average of 73% thanks to these new fares and more refined revenue management. Wildehall also measures performance using revenue per available seat kilometre (RASK). Available seat kilometre is a compound unit based on multiplying the total distance of all flights operated by the number of seats on that flight (for example, an aircraft with 50 seats operating a single flight of 200km would result in 50 × 200 = 10,000 available seat kilometres). RASK is total revenue divided by the number of seat-kilometres flown. RASK in 2013 was 7% higher than in 2012.
   One of Wildehall's large corporate clients, Westerloch, has pointed out that Wildehall should consider offering more favourable rates to its largest customers and has asked Wildehall to match its low fares offered to the public with the bulk-buy price offered to Westerloch, though Westerloch also wishes to keep the flexibility offered by the changeable tickets as part of its corporate contract.

Required:

(a) Explain the relevance of Porter's generic strategies of 'cost leadership' and 'differentiation' to Wildehall. (15 marks)

(b) Discuss the significance to Wildehall of performance measures such as 'load factor' and 'revenue per available seat kilometre'. (6 marks)

(c) Briefly explain the relevance of a mission statement to strategic planning in Wildehall. (4 marks)

(25 marks)

5.

(a) Evaluate the contribution made by environmental management accounting systems to meeting the information needs of managers. (14 marks)

(b) Explain how the concept of Environmental Management can be included as part of a Total Quality Management approach. (5 marks)

(c) Briefly explain and evaluate a quantitative model which can be used for predicting corporate failure. (6 marks)

(25 marks)

6. Rockmead is a large telecoms distributor and retailer, based in Europe. The company has around 2,300 stores and retail outlets across seven countries in mainland Europe, some of which are owned outright and some of which are franchised. It also has significant sales over well established and marketed online channels. Rockmead has recently committed to significant investment in highly trained sales consultants, planning to try to benefit from the evolution of smartphones, tablets, Internet-enabled household goods and other areas of complex technology.

Rockmead has also recently started to open concessions in bigger stores owned by third parties in order to benefit from the opportunity to sell specialist connected products and services on behalf of non-expert retailers with larger store formats with significant custom. Rockmead is aware that there is intense global competition in this market and that they are facing increasingly knowledgeable and demanding customers and competitors and this has changed the competitive environment from competition based on ability to invest in and manage physical (or tangible) assets to competition based on knowledge and the ability to exploit intangible and soft assets (like human capital, information systems, intellectual capital, brand development, research and development etc.).
The directors of Rockmead are concerned that the current performance measures used are not appropriate reflections of the company's future strategy and are unsure if the current management accounting system is capable of supplying information needed to establish and use new performance measures which would be designed to facilitate increased divisional autonomy at the same time as promoting local behaviour consistent with corporate objectives.
In particular, Rockmead is concerned that too much emphasis is being placed on short-term financial results and not enough attention is paid to the implications

of inefficient internal business processes and the value that could be generated by staff development and innovation.
Summary financial information is shown below:

Year ended 31 December	2009	2010	2011	2012	2013
	€m	€m	€m	€m	€m
Revenue	25.0	35.5	61.1	60.8	65.0
Operating expenses	-4.8	-6.0	-8.7	-5.4	-7.9
Operating profit	20.2	29.5	52.4	55.4	57.1
Finance income/ (expense)	-3.2	-1.6	3.9	2.9	1.9
Profit before tax	17.0	27.9	56.3	58.3	59.0
Tax	1.0	0.4	-1.6	-0.6	-0.9
Profit for the period	18.0	28.3	54.7	57.7	58.1

Required:

(a) Based on the financial information shown above, calculate and comment upon growth in revenues and profits over the 5 years to 31 December 2013. (8 marks)

(b) Explain the concept of the balanced scorecard in the context of performance measurement. (10 marks)

(c) Evaluate how useful the balanced scorecard would be to Rockmead's concerns about over-reliance on short-term financial performance measures and lack of innovation. (12 marks)

(d) Explain and discuss how Fitzgerald and Moon's system of non-financial performance indicators for service industries based on the concepts of Dimensions, Standards and Rewards could be used by Rockmead. (10 marks)

(e) Discuss the reasons why the Rockmead's information needs are changing and why its management accounting system may need to be improved. (10 marks)

(50 marks)

7. Summerglass is a medium-sized provider of office services and facilities management. Most of Summerglass's divisions are cost centres and managers are allowed only a minimal amount of autonomy in setting intra-divisional transfer prices.

   Managers in each division are given a cost budget each year which is designed to encourage savings on avoidable fixed costs and are rewarded based on achievement of cost budgets.
   Cleardale supplies office space to another division within Summerglass, Drival, but not to any external customers.

Forecast sales for Cleardale for the next year are as follows:

Net selling price per unit of space	Quantity sold
(£)	Units
100	15,000
90	30,000
80	45,000
70	60,000
60	75,000
50	90,000

The variable costs per unit of office space for Cleardale are £11 and Cleardale has fixed costs of £0.9m per year. Drival has fixed costs of £1.35 million per year and estimates the additional cost per unit at £7.
The transfer price of the service provided to Drival by Cleardale this year was set at £35 per unit of space, based on a full cost plus mark-up.

Required:

(a) Calculate the profit generated by both divisions at each output level and suggest an optimal transfer price that could be set in order to maximise company profit. (12 marks)

(b) Explain the general features of an effective transfer pricing system. (5 marks)

(c) Explain the arguments in favour of zero-based budgeting and suggest possible problems which may arise as a result of implementing a zero-based budgeting system. (8 marks)

(25 marks)

8. Westerloch is a government-owned local healthcare provider responsible for providing primary care to around 120,000 residents and employees of local businesses.

   The managers of Westerloch often have difficulty in obtaining reliable information about the cost of providing such healthcare and there is some resistance among junior managers and individual financial managers in doctor's practices to provide detailed financial information. Although Westerloch is not profit-making, it is expected to operate within a value-for-money framework and has been given efficiency and cost targets which the managers think are quite challenging.

Required:

(a) Explain, in general terms, the strategic importance of a management information system. (9 marks)

(b) Discuss the main considerations for Westerloch, as a not-for-profit organisation, when preparing budgets. Suggest practical solutions to how best to prepare budgets which meet Westerloch's objectives. (16 marks)

(25 marks)

9.

(a) Explain the relationship between strategic corporate planning and operational decision-making. (9 marks)

(b) Discuss possible sources of conflict between strategic business plans and short-term business plans for parts of the organisation and explain the implications for strategic planning. (10 marks)

(c) Explain how the three levels of strategy identified by Johnson and Scholes can be used in corporate planning. (6 marks)

(25 marks)

10.

(a) Discuss and evaluate the relevance of benchmarking to financial performance measurement. (15 marks)

(b) Explain the practical difficulties involved with benchmarking exercises.

(10 marks)

(25 marks)

Pilot paper answers

1.

To:	Board of Mackerel Contracting
From:	A Accountant
Date:	XX XX 20XX
Subject:	APV contract, new information system and performance measurement

Introduction

Mackerel has to make a decision on which level of design expenditure and so on which type of APV to tender. This choice will be dictated by the objectives of the business and its appetite for risk.

(a) Risks and risk appetite for APV contract

It is natural to assume that the main objective of a business is the maximisation of shareholder wealth and in the context of the APV project the main measure of performance will be the profit made on the contract as this will drive the earnings over which the institutions are concerned.

However, in a decision where there is risk and uncertainty, the company also has to decide on its appetite for risk. Risk appetite is usually divided into three categories:

- risk averse individuals tend to assume the worst outcome and seek to minimise its effect
- risk seekers are interested in the best outcomes and seek to maximise their returns under these circumstances
- risk neutral individuals are interested in the most probable outcome

The risks for Mackerel arise from uncertainties in its external environment. The key stakeholders in this situation are the government (the customer) and Mackerel's shareholders. The other factor giving rise to uncertainty is the forecast price of steel, the main raw material in the APV's construction.

The shareholders have indicated a concern over earnings volatility and so seem to be risk averse. This is commercially sensible in a recessionary situation where the company's survival could be placed at risk if a large project (such as the APV) were to fail. The project can be seen to be large for Mackerel as the expected profit is $5m if package 1 is chosen and this is material when compared to the current operating profit of $20.4m.

A risk averse approach might also be called for where winning the bid could lead to additional future work so that securing a deal is more important than optimising profit. This appears to be the case here as the government is the major customer of Mackerel.

The demand level for the APV is also uncertain as the recession could lead to cuts in government expenditure. Defence spending is often considered more discretionary than spending on public services (such as pensions) especially if there is not an immediate threat of conflict. Thus, it has been difficult to predict the probabilities of the different demand levels. Given that there are significant fixed costs of design and development, these different levels have a material impact on the return from the project.

These problems in quantifying the level of risk will affect the choice of method of analysing the return from the contract. Mackerel should evaluate the contract using different methods and come to a conclusion based on the most appropriate one for its objectives and risk appetite.

A further source of risk is the danger of cost over runs. If successful in its tender, Mackerel will be working towards a fixed price for the contract ($7.5 m + budgeted variable cost per unit plus 19%). Any over runs of actual cost as compared to budget will reduce the profit margin earned.

A major cost risk is the cost of the primary raw material of production (steel). However, this has been fixed by the forward purchase of the steel for the contract. This has eliminated the risk of price fluctuations during the contract.

(b) Risk evaluation methods and results

As was stated earlier, it is natural to assume that the main objective of the business is the maximisation of shareholder wealth and in the context of the APV project the main measure of performance will be the profit made on the contract. Although discounted cashflow would be a superior approach, there is insufficient data available here to calculate it.

The first priority is to ensure that the contract complies with the government requirement of a maximum per unit cost of $70,000 to Mackerel. The results per the Appendix 2 are:

Cost per unit	**Demand**		
	500	750	1,000
Package			
1	62,972	57,972	55,472
2	65,472	59,638	56,722
3	67,972	61,305	57,972

This complies with the contract specifications.

The total profit for each design package under the different demand levels is calculated at the Appendix 2 as:

Profit ($)	**Demand**		
	500	750	1,000
Package			
1	4,557,302	6,835,953	9,114,604
2	3,307,302	5,585,953	7,864,604
3	2,057,302	4,335,953	6,614,604

There are four possible approaches to selecting a package. The methods depend on the information available and the risk appetite of the decision-maker.

If we assume that there is insufficient information to make an estimate of the probabilities of the different demand levels then we are making a decision under uncertainty and there are three common methods of approach which depend on the risk appetite of the decision-maker (maximax, maximin and minimax regret). I have calculated payoff and regret tables in Appendix 1. The results can be summarised as follows:

Risk seekers and the risk averse will use profit under the different demand scenarios to make the appropriate choice.

Risk seekers will aim to maximise the possible returns from the different demand scenarios. The maximax method would be appropriate in this situation and here the company would be advised to choose design package 1 which will have a maximax profit of $9.1m.

Risk averse decision-makers will aim to maximise the minimum possible returns from the different demand scenarios. The maximin method would be appropriate in this situation and here the company would be advised to choose design package 1 which will have a maximin profit of $4.6m.

Pessimistic decision-makers will choose to focus on the lost profit (regret) compared to the best choice under that demand scenario. They aim to minimise the maximum level of regret that they can suffer under any demand scenario. This minimax regret method shows the company would be advised to choose design package 1 which will lead to no regret.

These conclusions should not be surprising as design package 1 has considerably lower fixed costs and yet is scalable to cope with all levels of demand.

A risk neutral manager does not take an optimistic or pessimistic stance. They will choose the option that yields the maximum expected value. This method depends on the use of probabilities for each of the outcomes. The risk manager has attempted to quantify the probabilities of the different levels of demand given the different design packages employed. It would be wise to involve both the design and sales teams in these estimates as such estimates are usually highly subjective and a broad canvassing of opinion may help to gain more accurate values.

The estimated probabilities allow the calculation of an expected profit for each choice of design package. Appendix 2 shows that the maximum expected profit of $5.6m arises if design 2 is chosen. This is due to the much greater likelihood of higher demand in that case. Design 3 does not seem to increase the chances of higher demand sufficiently to outweigh the extra fixed cost of $1.25m compared to design 2.

(c) Recommendation

In this situation, the choice of method will depend on the risk appetite of Mackerel, whether this type of decision is likely to be repeated many times and the accuracy of the probability estimates. As Mackerel shareholders seem risk averse, the profit under the contract is significant compared to the operating profit of the whole company and the economic environment is difficult so the low risk method of maximin seems appropriate. The use of expected values appears questionable as the probability estimates have not been widely debated and in the current economic circumstances, the company's survival may be at risk and so the repeated trials necessary to make this method valid may not arise.

Design package 1 should be chosen as with unknown probabilities, it carries the least risk. The company could seek to sharpen the probability estimates and review the implications for company survival before considering the use of expected values although there is the potential to make an additional expected profit of $573k if we could justify choosing design 2 over design 1.

The risk over steel prices has been removed by using forward (advance) contracts to cover the purchase of the material required. As steel is used in many of the company's products, this should be investigated as a general risk management technique for the company.

(d) New information system

The executive information system (EIS) will bring a number of benefits in decision-making at the strategic level at Mackerel but at certain costs and with certain problems at the operational and strategic levels. The key danger is that the tangible increase in costs is not balanced by the intangible (and difficult to quantify) benefits of the new system.

At the operational level, the data gathering will generate new costs as the expectations of users for immediate update of the system drive demand for less batch input of data. This problem represents an opportunity to automate the input of data in order to fully benefit from real-time data availability.

At the strategic level, the benefits relate to improved decision-making as the EIS should allow drill-down access to the more detailed operational records but the initial presentation of data should be based on the key performance indicators for the company. This system should also be linked to external data sources so that senior management do not fall into the trap of only looking inwards in the organisation at the risk of ignoring wider issues in the business environment (for example, the risks associated with the APV contract such as the effect of the recession and the attitude of government). These will represent new data sources and so again increase the cost of the system.

The new system will increase the amount of information and analysis that it will be possible for senior managers to perform. It will present opportunities for better decision-making using the more up-to-date information. However, it may present the problem of information overload for senior managers. Therefore, the system will need to be designed to give access to only those areas that it is appropriate for any given manager to see.

The data used in decision-making will be more robust as a single database will reduce the problem of redundancy where multiple copies of the same data are held on different systems. This will remove the danger of inconsistencies and reduce the storage required by the company. This benefit will be felt at the tactical level of the company were such data consistency will aid inter-functional communication.

The EIS would allow access to decision support systems such as large spreadsheet models built in order to pull data out of the database for use in forecasting and appraising projects (for example, demand forecasting and risk modelling of the APV contract).

The EIS will also give access to tactical information such as budgets in order to help the executive control the business.

In order to gain the maximum benefit from the new system, executive managers will need to be trained and this training should occur just before the new system is available so that they are in a position to use it immediately.

(e) Performance measures at Mackerel

The proposed new performance measures should be judged against the overall mission which is to maximise shareholder wealth and so optimise total shareholder return (TSR). It should be noted that TSR reflects both dividend returns and capital gains and so deals with both the current performance of the business (current dividend payments) and its expected future performance (as this dictates the share price).

The return on capital employed (ROCE) is calculated on profit before interest and tax divided by capital employed in a project or at the company as a whole. ROCE is a simple, commonly used measure of performance. However, it can encourage delays to investment in new assets since this measure improves as assets are depreciated with age. ROCE has the disadvantage of being based on profit measures of performance rather than cash. Measures such as NPV use cash flows which are less subject to the interpretation of accounting rules and are more directly aligned with shareholder interests. It is unclear that ROCE will align with the overall performance measure of TSR since TSR depends on share price and dividends paid. In particular, the fact that share price is based on a long-term

view of dividend prospects makes the use of short period-based measures (such as profit) less valuable.

EVA is an absolute performance measure. It involves a more complex calculation than ROCE with many adjustments to the accounting figures of profit and net assets, such as the use of replacement costs for asset values and economic depreciation rather than accounting depreciation.

Many of the EVA adjustments are intended to avoid distortion of results by accounting policies that are present in ROCE. EVA has the advantage that by treating certain costs as investments it encourages appropriate capital expenditure.

However, EVA depends on historical data while shareholders will be focused on future performance. Thus, while EVA is more directly aligned with the objective of increasing shareholder wealth, it too falls short of measuring shareholders' expectations which are present in the share price.

Conclusions

Given the current risk appetites of key stakeholders and economic environment, it is recommended that the design package 1 for the APV be chosen, as it carries least risk.

The new EIS represents an opportunity to gain considerable strategic advantage provided the costs of the new system are properly understood and controlled.

Neither ROCE nor EVA represent a perfect match to the company's main external measure of performance (TSR) due to their backward looking nature. However, EVA may be closer to the spirit of TSR in measuring increased shareholder wealth.

Appendix 1
Variable cost

Steel	11,412	9.4 Tonnes at $1,214
Engine/ transmission	9,500	
Electronics	8,450	
Other	4,810	
Labour	13,800	
	47,972	

Payoff table

Demand	**500**	**750**	**1,000**	**Max payoff**	**Min payoff**
Design package					
1	4,557,302	6,835,953	9,114,604	9,114,604	4,557,302
2	3,307,302	5,585,953	7,864,604	7,864,604	3,307,302
3	2,057,302	4,335,953	6,614,604	6,614,604	2,057,302
Maximum of the maximum payoffs =	9,114,604	Package 1			
Maximum of the minimum payoffs =	4,557,302	Package 1			

Regret table

Demand	**500**	**750**	**1,000**	**max regret**
Design package				
1	0	0	0	0
2	1,250,000	1,250,000	1,250,000	1,250,000
3	2,500,000	2,500,000	2,500,000	2,500,000
Minimum of max regret Package 1	0			

Appendix 2

Demand	**500**	**750**	**1,000**
Variable cost	23,985,800	35,978,700	47,971,600
Fixed cost			
Package			
1	7,500,000	7,500,000	7,500,000
2	8,750,000	8,750,000	8,750,000
3	10,000,000	10,000,000	10,000,000
Total cost			

Package				
1	31,485,800	43,478,700	55,471,600	
2	32,735,800	44,728,700	56,721,600	
3	33,985,800	45,978,700	57,971,600	
Cost per unit				
Package				
1	62,972	57,972	55,472	
2	65,472	59,638	56,722	
3	67,972	61,305	57,972	
Revenue $7.5M + (Budgeted variable cost × 1.19)				
	36,043,102	50,314,653	64,586,204	
Profit ($)				
Package				
1	4,557,302	6,835,953	9,114,604	
2	3,307,302	5,585,953	7,864,604	
3	2,057,302	4,335,953	6,614,604	
Expected profit				Total
Package				
1	3,873,707	683,595	455,730	5,013,032
2	826,826	2,792,977	1,966,151	5,585,953
3	411,460	2,167,977	1,984,381	4,563,818

2.

(a) The branch information appears to be inadequate on a number of levels to appraise the shop manager's performance. The manager should only be held responsible for those areas of performance that they can control.

The branch manager should be appraised on a realistic sales budget. The overall market fall of 12% suggests that the original budget of no change on previous year was not realistic. It is possible to analyse this by calculating planning and operational variances as follows:

	$
Revised budgeted sales given market fall	234,080
Budgeted gross margin	60%
Revised budgeted gross margin	140,448

Original budgeted gross margin	159,600	
Planning variance	19,152	A
Actual sales	237,100	
Revised budgeted sales	234,080	
	3,020	F
Budgeted gross margin	60%	
Operational variance	1,812	F

The operational variance reflects more accurately the manager's work and from this we can see the manager has done well by limiting the fall in gross profit by $1,812.

This analysis could be extended to other areas of the performance report. For example, if the breakdown of sales prices and volumes for individual product lines were given together with details of market volumes and price movements then the sales price variance could be broken down into operational and planning elements to reflect the manager's use of the limited discounting power that she has. Overall at the Tunny branch, the gross margin has remained constant (at 60%) which indicates that the manager may not have made use of the sales price discounting authority.

There are a number of other non-controllable costs in the branch information. It is unlikely that the branch manager can affect the price variance of heating and lighting costs as the prices are set through central purchasing although they will have some control over usage. The rental cost will reflect head office property management and is not controllable. The manager's own wages are not controllable although the staff costs will reflect the fact that the manager can choose to work longer hours and so save on part-time staff, therefore a labour efficiency variance would be appropriate.

A revised report would split the costs into two groups (controllable and on-controllable) so that a controllable profit would be shown as well as the overall shop profit. This would be the basic measure of performance of the store. A more detailed understanding of responsibility for the variances would be given by a breakdown of the operational (controllable) and planning (non-controllable) elements of each variance.

It might look like this:

Revised performance report

Albacore Chess Stores

Tunny branch Year to Sept 2011

	Budget	Actual	Planning Variance	Opera-tional Variance	Variance
	$	$	$	$	$
Sales	266,000	237,100	-28,900		
Cost of sales	106,400	94,840	11,560		
Gross profit	159,600	142,260	-17,340	-19,152	1,812
Controllable costs:					
Marketing	12,000	11,500	500		
Staff costs					
Part-time staff	38,000	34,000	4,000		
Controllable profit	109,600	96,760	-12,840		
Non-controllable costs:					
Staff costs					
manager	27,000	27,000	0		
Property costs	26,600	26,600	0		
Shop profit	56,000	43,160	-12,840		

Notes:

Property costs includes heating, lighting and rental.

Positive variances are favourable.

Summary

The manager's performance has been good in difficult general economic circumstances since if we exclude the gross margin planning variance ($19,152A) and allow that the part-time staff costs and marketing costs are controllable then we see that there is a favourable variance in controllable profit of $6,312 ($19,152-$12,840).

As indicated, additional variances that could be reported include operational and planning price variances for sales; part-time labour efficiency variances in operational variances; part-time labour rate variances in planning variances; and some price and usage variances for property costs. There is insufficient data to calculate examples of these variances here.

(b) The management style at Albacore is highly budget-constrained (Hopwood). It is driven by financial performance to meet the needs of the venture capitalist owners who have probably highly geared the business at the time of purchase. The cost control attitude is illustrated by the focus on achieving budget in the reward system and the enforcement of staff pay rates. This management style leads to stress for employees and difficult working relationships – as illustrated by the unhappiness of the shop managers. It also can motivate manipulation of performance reports although given the centralised nature of Albacore this appears unlikely at the shop level. It does however focus attention on achieving budget. This could be desirable in difficult economic circumstances.

Alternative styles are:

- profit-conscious where the performance is evaluated on longer-term effectiveness of the business unit in question (plausible here given Albacore's aim of profit maximisation)
- non-accounting where the budget is of low importance in performance evaluation

The performance appraisal system at Albacore reflects this cost-conscious, budget constrained approach. The shop managers are instructed as to their objectives and there appears to be no discussion of this target between the appraiser and the shop manager. For the branch given, it is striking that the failure to make budgeted profit (by $12,840) has led to no bonus being paid although the shop made an operating profit of $43,160 and the operating margin of the shop has held up at 18% compared to 21% per the budget.

The branch information needs to reflect the areas that the manager can control as mentioned in part (a) to this answer. Using the analysis of revised controllable profit, we have seen that the manager has returned a good performance $6,312 ahead of budget. The increased use of operational and planning variances should help to motivate the managers and reduce the friction with senior staff.

The current contract between the manager and Albacore could be described as coercive as it is imposed. The budget should be agreed between the manager and their appraiser using the detailed knowledge of both parties to improve the budget estimates. Although for Albacore, the likely budget will reflect the expectations of the senior management in order to achieve the business' overall financial objectives.

The reward system could move to a more calculative basis where the manager is paid a percentage of the profit above a certain level, usually this bonus is capped to a maximum as in the current system. The senior management will need to assess the trigger level based on head office costs (administrative support and financing costs). Therefore, the operational director's assessment would become more objective and this could remove lack of clarity in how performance is assessed.

Performance appraisal could also recognise longer-term and non-financial factors in the manager's performance such as innovative marketing ideas and customer feedback on their shopping experience. Additionally, as the branch manager handles the shop's staff development, recognition could be given for branch staff who progress from part-time to shop manager.

3.

(a) Evaluation of proposed performance measures

The financial perspective has not been altered from the existing measures of strategic performance. These are appropriate to address the objectives of enhancing shareholder wealth although it has been argued that measures such as economic value added or shareholder value added are better long long-term measures of this topic. Also, it is more common to use share price and dividend per share to reflect total shareholder return. Additionally, measures of survival (cashflows) and growth (in eps) could also be considered.

The customer perspective mainly seems to address the patient (end user) viewpoint. However, it should also reflect the concerns of those paying for the products (the government and insurers). Therefore, measures of cost in comparison to competitors would be appropriate.

The internal process perspective reflects appropriate measures of manufacturing excellence and efficiency in the testing process. This directly addresses the second of the board's objectives.

The learning and growth perspective would appear to be an obvious area to address the third objective on innovation. Again, the ranking of the measures is unclear and it would be surprising if training days were considered the principal measure. From the learning perspective of learning, it would be the improvement in the time to market from product to product that would better indicate learning and the improvement in percentage of drugs finally approved that would indicate learning. It may be appropriate to benchmark these measures against industry competitors as well as internally.

It is not clear if the points in the proposed scorecard are already prioritised and it may be appropriate to reconsider the order of measures, for example, in the internal perspective, the measure of time to gain approval seems to be more directly relevant to the objective of efficiency of the development process.

The suggested scorecard does not consider the difficulty of collecting data on some of the non-financial measures. For example, the measurement of above-industry standard design and testing is likely to be subjective unless the company undergoes a regular quality audit which can be scored.

(b) Stakehlders and their influence

The key stakeholders of BDR are the government, the drug companies being tested, the healthcare providers and their funders, and the patients.

A measure of influence of different stakeholders could be obtained by considering the degree to which they have power to affect decisions in the company and the likelihood that they would exercise their power (their degree of interest in the decisions). (Mendelow's matrix would be a suitable technique to perform this analysis.)

The government is an influential stakeholder on this basis as they have power over senior appointments and the funding of BDR. They are unlikely to use this power having delegated authority to the trustees, unless they are provoked by some financial or medical scandal.

The drug companies will be highly interested in the day-to-day workings of BDR as it sets the testing environment without which the drug companies will not have products. However, they will have little influence in the decisions within BDR as BDR must be seen to be independent of them. Nevertheless, it is in BDR's interest to have a successful drug development industry in order to achieve its goal of encouraging new drug development.

The healthcare providers will have interest principally in the quality of the approval process so they can have confidence about the cures that they dispense. They will have limited influence mainly through the pressure that they can bring to bear through the government.

The patients will be concerned that there is innovation as new cures are quickly and safely brought to market. They have limited secondary influence on decisions decision-making in BDR, as for the healthcare providers. Their influence will mainly be felt by affecting the actions of the government.

(c) Differences in the application of the balanced scorecard

The objectives at BDR are less obviously financial than at PT. The use of the balanced scorecard approach will be of great use to BDR as it emphasises non-financial performance which fits with BDR's objectives relating to quality of drugs and the relationship with key stakeholders. This can lead to difficulty in setting quantifiable measures due to the soft issues involved, eg measuring the level of user understanding of the risk/benefit profile of products. There is also the danger of setting quantifiable measures which are then obsessively pursued without regard to the softer aim of the organisation. An example could be the need to encourage drug innovation at the expense of making sure that each new product was a material improvement on existing drug products.

BDR will have a more complex balanced scorecard than PT due to the diverse nature of important stakeholders. As a public service organisation, the customer perspective may be more significant. The principal stakeholder is the government and so there will be a complex, political dimension to measuring performance.

The primary objective at PT is financial while at BDR there are several key objectives among which there is no clear ranking. Stakeholders may have conflicting objectives, for example, patients want effective drugs but the same individuals as taxpayers/insurance premium payers may not be willing to foot the bill if the price is too high. This will lead to difficulties in setting priorities among the various measures identified on the balanced scorecard.

4.

(a) Environmental cost categories

PLX will need to identify existing and new cost information that is relevant to understanding its environmental impact.

There are conventional costs such as raw material costs and energy costs which should be broadened to include the cost of waste through inefficiency. These and other conventional costs (such as regulatory fines) are often hidden within overheads and therefore will not be a high priority for management control unless they are separately reported.

There are contingent costs such as the cost of cleaning industrial sites when these are decommissioned. These are often large sums that can have significant impact on the shareholder value generated by a project. As these costs often occur at the end of the project life, they can be given low priority by a management that is driven by short-term financial measures (eg annual profit) and make large cash demands that must be planned at the outset of the project.

There are relational costs such as the production of environmental information for public reporting. This reporting will be used by environmental pressure groups and the regulator and it will demonstrate to the public at large the importance that PLX attaches to environmental issues.

Finally, there are reputational costs associated with failing to address environmental issues when consumer boycotts and adverse publicity lose sales revenue.

(b) Explanation and evaluation of techniques

A lifecycle view consists of considering the costs and revenues of a product over the whole life of the product rather that one accounting period. For an oil refinery, this might be taken to be the useful life of the refinery. A lifecycle view may take profit or discounted cashflow as the principal measure of performance. This is particularly relevant for PLX given the planned redevelopment programme at the refinery which will highlight the decommissioning costs of such plant. This will aid future long-term investment planning at PLX.

Activity-based Costing (ABC) is a method of detailed cost allocation that when applied to environmental costs distinguishes between environment-related costs and environment-driven costs. At PLX, related costs would include those specifically attributed to an environmental cost centre such as a waste filtration plant while driven costs are those that are generally hidden in overheads but relate to environmental drivers such as additional staff costs or the shorter working life of equipment (in order to avoid excess pollution in the later years of its working life). This will assist PLX in identifying and controlling environmental costs.

Input/output analysis (sometimes called mass balance) considers the physical quantities input into a business process and compares these with the output quantities with the difference being identified as either stored or wasted in the process. These physical quantities can be translated into monetary quantities at the end of the tracking process. Flow cost accounting is associated with this analysis as it reflects the movement of physical quantities through a process and will highlight priorities for efficiency improvements.

These techniques are not mutually exclusive and all can assist PLX in improving performance. However, cost/benefit analysis will need to be undertaken for each of the systems. This will be difficult, as benefit estimates will prove vague given the unknown nature of the possible improvements that may accrue from using the techniques. The non-financial benefits will include a better public image and reduced chance of protest by environmental groups and an improved relationship with the government who is likely to be a key supplier of crude oil to the business. Additionally, ABC and input/output analysis will require significant increases in the information that the management accounting systems collect and so incur increased costs. As a result, the decision to use these techniques is likely to be based on the balance between known costs and estimated strategic benefits of non-financial factors.

(c) Impact of input/output analysis on information systems

Input/output analysis will require the information systems to collect not just monetary but also physical measurements of the materials being processed through the refinery. This may require additional records and costly changes to company's existing database structures. Systems will have to be put in place to monitor physical volumes of raw materials, waste and recycled material within the refinery's processes. The collection and use of such information may present a challenge to PLX with its culture of focussing on financial performance measures. The information that will be generated will help to identify efficiency improvements and so drive the profit margin and earnings of the company.

(d) Lifecycle costing

A traditional analysis of the costs of Kayplas might yield the product profit given in the original data. However, this ignores capital costs, environmental costs and the cost of decommissioning. A lifecycle analysis aims to capture the costs over the whole lifecycle of the product and it would show

Costs

Production costs	82.3
Marketing costs	17
Development costs	8.6
	107.9

Environmental costs

Waste filtration	8.1
Carbon dioxide exhaust extraction	5.3
	13.4

Other costs

Decommissioning costs	18
Total costs	139.3

This should be compared to revenues of $149.4m and leaves only a small overall return on investment (surplus of $10.1m). It should be noted that the decommissioning costs are estimated at $18m in 5five years. It is likely that given the difficulty in dealing with specialised equipment and the fact that environmental legislation may get stricter, this could easily be a significant underestimate. This could destroy all of the added value of the product.

The value of lifecycle costing often lies in the visibility it gives to costs that are determined in the early stages of the design of the product and in this case, it emphasises the need to minimise the cost of decommissioning. This should be done in the design phase of the refinery extension.

The traditional product profit analysis shows a surplus of $41.5m over the life of the product failing as it does to capture the environmental and decommissioning costs.

Additionally, if volumes of production can be ascertained then a cost per unit of Kayplas could be calculated and this would assist in price setting.

Marking scheme

				Marks
1.	**(i)**	Appropriate metrics		1
		Risk appetites 3 × 0.5		1.5
		Identify key stakeholders and risks		3
		Risk appetite		3
		Demand risk		1
		Cost overrun risk		2
		Other 1 mark per point made		
		Maximum		**9**
	(ii)	Comment on metric used: profit v DCF		1
		Variable cost per unit		1
		Total cost under each package		2
		Cost per unit contract check		2
		Revenue		1
		Profit total table		2
		Maximax	calculation	1
			Conclusion	0.5
		Maximin	calculation	1
			Conclusion	0.5
		Minimax regret	calculation	2
			Conclusion	0.5
		Expected value	calculation	1.5
			Conclusion	0.5
		(Working rounded to thousands is acceptable.)		
		Describe different methods 4 × 0.5		2
		Evaluate methods		4
		Maximum		**19**
	(iii)	Recommend method		2
		Final recommendation on contract		1
		Other risk reduction comments		1
		Maximum		**3**
	(iv)	New information system impacts		

		Operation information gathering up to 3 marks		
		Strategic decision-making		
		Benefits	up to	4
		Problems	up to	3
		Maximum		**8**
	(v)	Comments on TSR	Up to	2
		Comments on ROCE	Up to	3
		Comments on EVA	Up to	3
		Maximum		**7**
		Up to 4 professional marks.		
	Total			**50**
2.	**(a)**	**Variances**		
		Calculations:		
		Flexed budget		1
		Operation and planning (1 mark per point up to 4)		4
		Controllable profit		1
		Revised performance report	up to	8
		Comments:		1
		Structure		
		Revenue budget unrealistic		1
		Controllable costs		3
		(general 1 specific justifications 2)		
		Controllable profit		1
		Other variances	up to	5
		Maximum		13
	(b)	Management styles (1 mark per point up to 6)		6
		Performance appraisal system (1 mark per point up to 6)		6
		Improvements (1 mark per point up to 3)		3
		Maximum		12
		Total		**25**

3. (a) 1 mark per point. There is a wide range of good answer points to be made. Points should be made about the measures suggested (whether they cover the perspective intended) and also, if there are other suitable measures. Other marks are for linking the measures to the stated company objectives, commenting on the difficulty of collecting appropriate data and ranking the measures. Maximum of 10 marks.

(b) Up to 2 marks on method of analysis. Up to 2 marks on each stakeholder. Answers must display a consideration of both the power and the likelihood of exercising it in order to score full marks. Maximum of 8 marks.

(c) 1 mark per point. In order to score highly, a candidate must give examples that are relevant to the scenario. Maximum of 7 marks.

(25 marks)

4. (a) Up to 2 marks per cost area discussed. Points must include examples of relevance to the scenario to score full marks. Maximum of 6 marks.

(b) Up to 2 marks per technique – an explanation and its link to environmental performance. 3 marks for an evaluation of the techniques. Maximum of 9 marks.

(c) 1 mark on need for more non-financial information (physical units). 2 marks for comments on sources and difficulties of collecting such information. Maximum of 3 marks.

(d) 2 marks for calculation of lifecycle costs. Up to 2 marks for calculating the product profits of the two approaches. Up to 4 marks for discussion of improvements and issues identified by lifecycle costing. Maximum of 7 marks.

(25 marks)

Answers to other exam-standard questions

1.

(a) Possible considerations when deciding what performance measures to use include the following.

The size, complexity and diversity of the organisation will affect its performance and the way in which performance can be measured.

Any difference between costs / revenues controllable by the manager and attributable to the division is important (ie a consideration what is being assessed: the manager or the division). There are strong arguments for producing two measures of divisional profitability —one to evaluate managerial performance and the other to evaluate the economic performance of the division.

Senior management will base their decisions on these measures - if they do not accurately reflect what the division is doing then the wrong decisions will be made.

Measures should motivate division managers – if they do a better job, then this will be good for the entire company and its shareholders motivate the manager of the investment centre, and the team, to achieve the goals of the group.

Provide the right incentive for the manager and the team to make decisions that are consistent with the goals of the group's management.

(b) Return on Investment

ROI is calculated in exactly the same way as Return on Capital Employed and shows how much profit has been made compared to the investment. It is widely used because it is based on financial information in statutory accounts. In particular it is one of only a few measures which can be used to ascertain divisional performance.

However, there are several problems with using ROI in the context of decision-making and divisional performance measurement.

- It can highlight the different motivations of investors and managers.
- It can provide a disincentive to invest or force the sale of assets in order to better the return on capital irrespective of whether they are working efficiently for the organisation. This helps to create a short-term focus rather than a long-term focus.
- ROI may also motivate managers to make incorrect asset disposal decisions – as assets depreciate the ROI will improve, encouraging managers to keep older equipment rather than invest in new. It also encourages the use of leasing rather than buying.
- Comparison across divisions is difficult as a manufacturing division will have a greater level of fixed assets than a marketing division and thus a lower ROI.
- As a result of the above problems it can be seen that a manager may attempt to 'massage' the ROI to make their performance look better.

Residual Income (RI)

This is an alternative way of measuring the performance of an investment centre. Residual income is calculated as Profit less Imputed Interest (Investment × Required Return) = Residual Income

Firstly, RI will increase if new profitable investments are taken on and a cost of capital which is individual to each project may be used to give greater flexibility. This will allow for different risks by using different costs of capital when calculating imputed interest. Secondly, this method is more consistent with the overall objective of increasing shareholder wealth. The residual income is calculated by deducting an annual charge for financing assets from the profit.

However, it is not widely used. The calculations are not as intuitive as those for ROI (and not as familiar as, say, ROCE). The use of RI requires knowing an exact cost of capital and applying this consistently over time and making decision based on RI is still not consistent with the overall goal of shareholder value maximisation. Applying RI and NPV to the same investment would not always lead to the same decision.

There are a number of general problems which will exist whether ROI or RI is used as a measure, including:

- Calculation of profit - There is always some scope for manipulating the profit figure used to conduct the calculation.
- Asset measurement - The treatment should be consistent.
- Conflict with investment decisions - These should be made on the basis of DCF calculations which are designed to give a long-term view. It is possible to alter the effects of depreciation to make both ROI and RI more consistent with DCF.

(c) The concept of EVA was developed as an accounting measure by the consulting firm of Stern Stewart & Co. during the 1990's who refined RI and patented it as EVA.

EVA is an estimate of the amount by which earnings exceed or fall short of the required minimum rate of return that shareholders and debt holders could get by investing in other instruments of comparable risk. It is calculated as:

Operating profit after tax less capital charge (weighted average cost of capital × net assets).

Another way of expressing this is:

Conventional divisional profit based on IFRS after making specific accounting adjustments less cost of capital charge on divisional assets.

Value based performance management is an approach which is based on the principle that an organisation's strategy should be measured on whether it adds value to shareholders, rather than looking at other objectives such as growth in turnover or market share.

The primary measure used is economic value added (EVA). Other measures which have been developed are market value added (MVA) and shareholder value added (SVA).

EVA has been proposed as a single top level financial measure in order to avoid problems caused by having a number of conflicting objectives.

A number of advantages are put forward for the use of EVA:

- It is simple to translate into financial objectives.
- It reflects the performance of the organisation in monetary terms rather than as a ratio.
- It helps managers to link accounting information to decision-making.
- It takes into account the cost of capital in assessing whether an organisation is adding value for its shareholders.
- It is less easy to manipulate than accounting figures.
- EVA makes managers accountable not just for the results but also for the resources used in achieving those results and is more likely to lead organisations towards achieving a higher company value and hence a higher share price.
- If linked to incentives and divisional performance measures it will promote behaviours which add value to the organisation rather than destroy it – a positive EVA indicates value creation while a negative one indicates destruction. A series of negative EVAs could be a signal that a company needs to take corrective action, possibly involving restructuring.

EVA however has a number of disadvantages:

- Calculations can sometimes be complex and involve numerous adjustments to accounts.
- EVA is an absolute number – it will be bigger for larger divisions.
- EVA is usually computed on the basis of historical numbers: sometimes this produces distortions in incentives, and incorrect analysis.
- EVA measures can be difficult to understand, particularly for non-finance managers.
- As with other new approaches, for success EVA needs an implementation programme which includes raising awareness and educating staff.

EVA shows whether the management are adding or destroying value over a period of time. It is adaptable to measure performance at all levels, for example, it was originally used to assess the performance of companies quoted on the stock exchange but can also be used across all levels of management. It can also be used to aid in capital budgeting decisions in conjunction with NPV and payback.

In summary, financial performance measures can encourage managers to become short-term oriented and seek to boost short-term profits at the expense of long-term value.

To reduce the effect of short-termist outlooks, Osthollow can use divisional performance evaluations based on economic income (PV of future cash flows) by using EVA. Osthollow also needs to bear in mind that it is unwise to rely exclusively on financial measures, rather, it could incorporate non-financial measures that measure those factors that are critical to the long-term success of the organisation (ie adopt a balanced scorecard approach).

(d) Net present value

Time	Description	Cashflow	DF	PV
0	investment	(100,000)		(100,000)
1-5	efficiency gains	29,000	3.791	109,939
				9,939

The positive NPV shows that the investment is worthwhile and should be accepted.

EVA for year 1 using the straight-line method of depreciation

Time	Description		
1	Annual cash inflow		29,000
1	Less Depreciation	20,000	
1	Interest on capital		
	(10% × £100,000)	10,000	
			(30,000)
			(1,000)

There is a danger that this project will be rejected on the basis of the first year's EVA calculation if the straight-line method of depreciation is used.

The annuity method of depreciation sets the annual depreciation expense constant, and equal to the capital element of an annuity required to repay £100,000 borrowed at 10% over five years.

This can be calculated as £100,000/3.791 = £26,380.

London School of Business & Finance
shaping success in business and finance

EVA for year 1 using the annuity method of depreciation

Time	**Notional re-payment**	**Interest**	**Capital**		**Closing balance on capital**
1	26,380	10,000 *(10% × 100,000)*	16,380		83,620
Time	Opening balance	Cash inflow	Deprecia-tion	Interest on capital	EVA
1	100,000	29,000	16,380	10,000	2,620

Approaches for reducing this short-term orientation can include:

- Divisional performance evaluated on the basis of economic income (PV of future cash flows).
- Adopt EVA incorporating many accounting adjustments.
- Lengthen the measurement period.
- Do not rely excessively on financial measures and incorporate non-financial measures that measure those factors that are critical to the long-term success of the organisation (ie adopt a balanced scorecard approach).

(e) Business Process Re-engineering (BPR) is the fundamental rethinking and radical redesign of business processes to achieve dramatic improvements in critical, contemporary measures of performance, such as cost, quality, service and speed. Improved customer satisfaction is often the primary aim.

BPR draws on the work of Porter's value chain by viewing the organisation as a set of value adding processes rather than as a segmented structure of activities. The value chain is commonly used in BPR as a method to identify and analyse processes that are of strategic significance to the organisation.

The following are common features of the BPR process

- Several jobs are combined into one
- Workers make real decisions
- Work is performed where it adds most value
- Checks and controls are reduced
- Reconciliation processes are reduced
- Case managers provide points of contact

As such BPR may be of use to Osthollow as it could help the organisation to generate efficiency savings, including those obtainable from restructuring, and help to address the threat of new entrants with lower cost bases and different ways of working. BPR would be consistent with the increasing autonomy offered to local managers and savings would be reflected in divisional performance measures such as ROI, RI and EVA.

Advantages of BPR

- BPR revolves around customer needs and helps to give an appropriate focus to the business.
- BPR provides cost advantages that assist the organisation's competitive position.
- BPR encourages a long-term strategic view of operational processes by asking radical questions about how things are done and how processes could be improved.
- BPR helps overcome the short sighted approaches that sometimes emerge from excessive concentration on functional boundaries. By focusing on entire processes the exercise can streamline activities throughout the organisation.
- BPR can help to reduce organisational complexity by eliminating unnecessary activities.

Criticisms of BPR

- BPR was sometimes seen (incorrectly) as a means of making small improvements in existing practices. In reality, it should be a more radical approach that questions whether existing practices make any sense in their present form.
- BPR was often perceived (incorrectly) as a single, once for all cost cutting exercise. In reality, it is not primarily concerned with cost cutting (though cost reductions often result), and should be regarded as ongoing rather than once for all. This misconception often creates hostility in the minds of staff who see the exercise as a threat to their security.
- BPR requires a far reaching and long-term commitment by management and staff. Securing this is not an easy task, and many organisations have rejected the whole idea as not worth the effort. In many cases business processes were not redesigned but merely automated.
- To make BPR work requires a focus on integrated processes (as discussed above) that often involves obliterating existing processes and creating new ones.
- Some companies became so focussed on improving internal processes that they failed to keep up with competitors' activities in the market.

2.

(a) There are three types of benchmarks.

Internal: This is where another department of the organisation is used as the benchmark because conformity of service is the critical. Although easily arranged it is unlikely to provide innovative solutions

Competitor: Uses a direct competitor with the same or similar process because the competitor is the threshold benchmark. The problem is whether the competitor will be willing to hand over their basis for success.

Process or activity: Focuses upon a similar process in another company which is not a direct competitor to look for new innovative ways to create advantage as well as solving threshold problems. Such an approach takes time, is expensive but resistance is likely to be less and can provide the new basis for advantage.

A typical benchmarking process is likely to include:

- Identifying what is wrong within the current organisation; and the criteria that will be used to assess success, selecting the approach and type of benchmarking and identifying best practice elsewhere.
- Collecting data and information developing with partners a mutual understanding and benchmarking protocol, agreeing terminology and performance measures to be used, undertaking information and data collection, collation of findings.
- Analysing the findings review of findings, gap analysis, seeking explanation for the gaps in performance, ensuring comparisons are meaningful and credible, communicate the findings and identify realistic opportunities for improvement.
- Implement recommendations examine the feasibility of making improvements with respect to organisational constraints and preconditions, obtain the support of key stakeholders for making the changes needed, implement action plans, monitor performance, keep stakeholders informed of progress.
- Monitoring and reviewing evaluate the benchmarking process and the results of improvement initiatives against business objectives, document the lessons learnt, periodically reconsider the benchmarks in the light of changes.

(b) The potential benefits to be obtained from a benchmarking exercise are:

- identifying gaps in performance by comparing an organisation's own performance with the performance of the organisation acting as the benchmark
- putting the company's resources and performance into perspective, reflecting the fact that it is the relative position of a company which matters in assessing its capabilities
- learning and applying best practices
- learning from the success of others
- minimising complacency with your own performance
- encouraging continuous improvement

There are a number of difficulties and issues facing organisations wishing to undertake a benchmarking exercise.

- Benchmarking exercises can be costly and time consuming – it is necessary to consider whether the value of the exercise is sufficient to justify its cost
- Other organisations may be unwilling to share information
- It may be difficult to obtain information, particularly non-financial information about competitors
- The business functions being benchmarked must be similar enough to allow meaningful comparison

- Companies need to be as specific as possible when identifying areas to benchmark. For example, if a company is interested in studying customer service, it needs to determine what specific area or activity within customer service needs to be examined.
- Success will hinge on the level of commitment from top managers who must be prepared to make changes in response to the results of benchmarking.
- Benchmarking information must be interpreted carefully to ensure that organisations are being compared on a similar basis, and account must be taken of differences in the way data is produced, such as differences in accounting treatment, and external factors which influence performance in the area being benchmarked.
- Organisations should concentrate on areas that: tie up most cash, significantly improve the relationship with customers and impact on the final results of the business.

(c) A significant issue for large, decentralised companies such as Fieldmarsh is what performance measures should be used in assessing divisions and managers in charge of them.

The first factor to be considered is that of whether it is the divisional performance or the divisional manager's performance that is being measured.

If the purpose is to evaluate the manager then the measures must be based on items over which the manager has control.

Determining which assets should be included in a division's asset base is also an important issue when using financial performance measures, as is the impact of inflation and depreciation.

There are a number of considerations when considering what measures to use:

- Senior management will base their decisions on these measures - if they do not accurately reflect what the division is doing then the wrong decisions will be made
- Measures should motivate division managers – if they do a better job, then this will be good for the entire company and its shareholders motivate the manager of the investment centre, and the team, to achieve the goals of the group
- Provide the right incentive for the manager and the team to make decisions that are consistent with the goals of the group's management

There are strong arguments for producing two measures of divisional profitability —one to evaluate managerial performance and the other to evaluate the economic performance of the division.

3.

(a)

Strengths	Weaknesses
• Significant growth in the past year, indicating higher profits.	• Only 20% of Whitesummer's sales are online. The growth in interest sales has been very large; therefore Whitesummer could be missing-out on further sales.
• Pop-up shops, which are not permanent meaning lower costs for the company.	
• As there is a growing demand for fair-trade and natural ingredients, Whitesummer are ahead of many of their competitors.	• Pop-up shops means there is not a fixed site in many cities for the shop if it is doing well in that area.
Opportunities	**Threats**
• Pop-up shops are becoming a more preferable way of clothing companies to sell their goods. Whitesummer could expand the amount of these which travel at time.	• Pop-up shops are becoming more popular, meaning Whitesummer may lose its unique way of selling.
• The Internet is a large hub for activity and therefore Whitesummer should try to expand the sales of this.	• More companies are becoming aware of customers' demands for natural and fair-trade materials, meaning Whitesummer may need to promote its products in a different way.

(b) *Objective I:*

– To evaluate how successful the pop-up shops have been to business activity this year and to expand this for the coming year.

Specific – This objective is specific to the revenue of the company to assess how much of an impact these shops have on the sales.

Measurable – This could be measured by using simple ratios and a comparison to previous figures to evaluate how much the business has grown due to these pop up shops.

Achievable – This objective will affect all employees and will need to be evaluated to ensure that the objective is achievable by all. The finance and account division will be responsible for the calculations and the evaluation; however for the shops to be expanded it will involve all staff from designers and material buyers to installation fitters and employees running the shop.

Relevant- The objective will be relevant as the shops have had a significant increase in revenues and therefore evaluating just how successful they have been would be a string building point if expansion where to take place.

Time bound – The objective states the time-period in which this will cover. The objective is to evaluate the previous year's figures and to focus and expand on the upcoming year sales.

Objective 2:

- Focus upon frequent customers to ensure they stay loyal to the firm over the next 24 months.

  Specific – This objective is specific to the customers of the business.

  Measurable – The Internet sales are probably customers who have visited the pop-up shop and then further bought items online. The interest sales can be monitored easily and if customers have to create a log-in when placing an order online, this is an easy way to be able to monitor customer's frequency of buying. This can then lead to Whitesummer being able to give discounts and other such offers to returning customers to retain them.

  Achievable – This objective is specific in terms of retaining customers to the business and is achievable by keeping a focus on the customers as the number one priority.

  Relevant – The objective is relevant as Whitesummer has seen an increase in sales over the past year and usually, especially in the fashion industry many customers will return if they were satisfied with the items they bought originally.

  Time-bound – This objective shows the exact time period in which Whitesummer will be looking at and it will give Whitesummer a chance to analyse, if sales do increase, how to handle the increase in material buying and production etc.

(c) Other possible objectives:

- To focus on increasing online-sales in a certain time-frame.
- To keep a focus on competitors in the upcoming year to see whether it will comprises Whitesummer's niche in the market.
- To assess whether there is one area of the country where a high proportion of sales occurs and evaluate whether it could be better to have more permanent shops.
- Over the next five to ten years, could consider expanding the business from just clothing to other items, such as accessories and home ware items.

4.

(a) Two 'generic' strategies that are frequently distinguished are 'price leadership' and 'differentiation'. 'Price leadership' implies low prices combined with a standardised offering. The strategic effort goes into developing a customer proposition that appeals to large numbers of customers and can be provided at low

cost. Product variation or even tailoring products to individual customers' wishes is then not usually part of the product offering.

Budget airlines are a good example of this strategy. By contrast, 'differentiation' emphasises the satisfaction of individual customers' wishes as closely as possible, be it with respect to quality of manufacture, ease of use, flexibility of application or delivery, product variety, reliability or any combination of these. An example would be luxury motor vehicle manufacturers. Product cost is also a concern for organisations that pursue this strategy but not to the same extent as for those that pursue price leadership.

Even though the strategy literature often portrays price leadership and differentiation as strategic opposites, in practice one usually finds combinations of the two, for example, in the various markets for electronic consumer goods.

There are different reasons for this. In large organisations some divisions may tend towards one strategy and some towards the other. During their life cycle, certain products may start out as differentiated products that are tailored towards the high price segment (perhaps because they are innovative), and later they may be marketed to compete mainly on price (perhaps because many competitors have entered this market, production volumes have increased and high quality is no longer a differentiating factor).

The strategic relevance of management accounting would depend on the extent to which it supports management in finding out which strategy is most promising for an organisation. Here one would expect management accountants to prepare alternative scenarios together with marketing, product, and production managers who assess the long-term profitability of operating in different markets, offering different price–value combinations to different customer segments.
In target costing, value engineering and life cycle costing, the experience has been that such efforts are best placed in the development and design stages of a new product because here a large percentage of a product's cost is built into its design.

The role of management accountants can be to advise on the cost implications of certain design choices and calculate the added revenue that can be expected from additional product attributes (eg reliability, functionality, appearance, etc).

Michael Porter also poses the question about the enterprise's relative position within its industry. The question of position is important because it influences the ability of a business to generate profits greater or less than the industry average. Above average returns may be achieved by sustainable competitive advantage. This is achieved by three basic generic strategies.

Cost leadership
An enterprise aims at being the lowest cost producer in the industry. This is achieved by economies of scale, capitalising on experience curve effects, tight cost control and cost minimisation in such areas as R&D, service, and advertising.

This is also known as a "no frills" strategy adopted because the enterprise deals in

- Commodity-like products or services
- Price-sensitive customers
- High buyer power and/or low switching costs
- Small number of providers with similar market shares
- Avoiding the major competitors

Differentiation
An enterprise seeks to offer some different dimension in its products/services that is valued by its customers and may command a premium price. This can be achieved by image, superior customer service solutions, dealer network and support and product design.

Enterprises adopting this strategy operate within highly competitive markets where customer attrition rates are high. The key to delivering this competitive strategy is supporting high level of customer service and marketing through quality and a detailed system of target setting in place to ensure compliance. When choosing a differentiation strategy, an organisation will take into account the following factors – reputation, size, financing ability, command of technology, economies of scale and the ability to deliver geographical coverage.

(b) Wildehall is operating in a niche market to the extent that it is not competing directly with larger airlines on a route specific basis. The convenience and premium quality of the product, supported by premium pricing, means that pressure on costs is not as significant as it would be if Wildehall were competing primarily on price.

A significant proportion of Wildehall's costs will be fixed (fleet costs, airport charges) and even variable costs (for example fuel, staff costs) are unlikely to increase proportionately with passengers carried on a given flight.

Load factor effectively represents how many passengers are carried on a given flight, relative to the number of seats available. By focussing on load factor, Wildehall's managers are focussing on increasing the number of passengers (and therefore total revenue) in a way which will not result in a proportionate increase in costs. Revenue per available seat kilometre (RASK) also reflects the fixed nature of many costs and the desire to maximise the revenue generated by resources already in place. Wildehall's strategy appears to recognise that extra seats, that would otherwise go unsold, can be sold at lower than average price and still generate extra profits.

Wildehall is, however, facing problems with a corporate client who has realised that it is discounting and is starting to put pressure on price. So Wildehall needs to ensure that the strategies for different market places and products is clear and that appropriate market segmentation is in place.

(c) A statement of corporate mission is inextricably linked with the organisation's goals and objectives.

The organisational objectives comprise the specific targets of the company and the goals comprise its broad aims, the mission encapsulates the reason that the entity exists in terms of the service and utility provided to meet specific needs of society.

Before the preparation of a strategic plan the management should consider the mission of an organisation.

Many commentators have suggested that consideration and determination of the mission and its articulation into a statement of corporate mission constitutes the first stage in the strategic planning process and that therefore it is central to the whole planning process. Johnson and Scholes have suggested that 'the mission of an organisation is the most generalised type of objective and can be thought of as an expression of its raison d'être'.

To enable an organisation to fulfil its mission, the mission must be translated into strategic plans and objectives, tactical plans and objectives, and detailed operational plans and targets.

5.

(a) In the early stages of its development, EMA focused on finding the 'hidden' costs related to the treatment of generated pollutants. However, it now focuses even more on the other costs of pollution that are 'hidden' in production costs, such as those associated with the costs of raw materials, energy that goes wasted and the value that is added from the process but which does not enter into the final product.

EMA is concerned with the accounting information needs of managers in relation to corporate activities that affect the environment as well as environment related impacts on the corporation. This includes:

- Identifying and estimating the costs of environment related activities
- Identifying and separately monitoring the usage and cost of resources such as water, electricity and fuel and to enable costs to be reduced
- Ensuring environmental considerations form a part of capital investment decisions
- Assessing the likelihood and impact of environmental risks
- Including environment related indicators as part of routine performance monitoring
- Benchmarking activities against environmental best practice

It is important to have a clear definition of environmental costs as management are often unaware of the extent of environmental costs and cannot identify opportunities for cost savings.

EMA attempts to make all significant costs visible so that they can be considered when making business decisions. The following techniques can be used to identify and allocate environmental costs

- Conventional costs – eg materials, energy costs.
- Potentially hidden costs – usually lost in general overheads.
- Contingent costs – eg costs of cleaning up if a spillage occurs
- Image and relationship costs – eg cost of producing environmental reports

According to Bennett and James (1998), EMA is concerned with gathering data related to the environment (lowest levels), which are converted through techniques and processes (middle level) into information which is useful for managers (top).

Experience with EMA has shown that, on average, hidden production-related costs can be ten to twelve times higher than obvious transaction-based waste and emissions treatment costs, such as the operational and investment costs associated with pollution treatment equipment and the transport of waste and its disposal at a dumping site.

For example, the costs associated with the disposal of packaging discarded by distributors or customers, or, the additional costs borne by customers when they use products that produce pollution or waste energy. There are also the costs that customers pay (directly or indirectly) when they dispose of the products: the disposal cost itself and the shadow cost related to the value of the materials in the product that could be reused but are not.

(b) Environmental management is increasingly recognised as an essential component of TQM.

Organisations should be striving to achieve an integrated environmental strategy underpinned by the same type of culture that is required for the successful operation of a programme of TQM.

In TQM, the focus is upon 'continuous improvement' and the pursuit of excellence. Such organisations pursue objectives that may include zero complaints, zero spills, zero pollution, zero waste and zero accidents.

Information systems need to be able to support such environmental objectives via the provision of feedback – on the success or otherwise – of the organisational efforts in achieving such objectives.

Many TQM accounting techniques can be modified and effectively adopted to help manage environmental issues.

(c) Qualitative and quantitative models exist to predict corporate failure. Quantitative models focus on particular values and ratios which are said to be indicative of future financial health, whereas quantitative models identify particular risk factors and, often, assigns scores and weightings to these risk factors.

The Altman Z-score formula, first published in 1968, is used to predict debt defaults by companies within a 2 year period and is based on financial ratios that are key to measuring the overall level of financial distress of a company. The models attraction is that a number of financial ratios our combined, using weightings, to produce a single score. The score can then be interpreted as a prediction of the likelihood of insolvency.

The calculation is as follows:

$Z = (1.2 \times T1) + (1.4 \times T2) + (3.3 \times T3) + (0.6 \times T4) + (0.999 \times T5)$

where

T1 = Net current assets/Total assets

T2 = Retained earnings/Total assets

T3 = Earnings before interest and taxes/Total assets

T4 = Market value of equity/Total liabilities

T5 = Sales revenue/Total assets

A Z score of 3 or above indicates a safe company, a score of 1.8 or below indicates a company in significant danger of insolvency.

The limitations of quantitative models such as the Altman Z score include:

- they can be over simplistic, trying to capture the complexity of an entire business in a single number
- the values of individual variables are open to manipulation such as window dressing
- they focus on short-term performance

6.

(a)

Year ended 31 December	**2009**	**2010**	**2011**	**2012**	**2013**
	€m	**€m**	**€m**	**€m**	**€m**
operating profit margin	81%	83%	86%	91%	88%
growth in operating profit		46%	78%	6%	3%
growth in revenue		42%	72%	0%	7%

The table shows high profit margins and significant growth in revenues and operating profits in 2010 and 2011, slowing to much lower growth rates in 2012 and 2013.

(b) The concept of 'Balanced Scorecard' was first introduced in the journal "Harvard Business Review" (January- February, 1992) by Robert S. Kaplan and David P. Norton. The basic idea behind the introduction of the Balanced Scorecard was that the traditional financial measures (like ROI, EPS etc.) alone cannot provide a clear and comprehensive performance target or focus attention on all the critical areas of the business that bear significant impact on its long-term survival, growth and development, rather it requires a balanced presentation of financial as well as operational measures.

The concept of balanced scorecard is relevant in the present era of emerging intense global competition where the organisation s are facing increasingly knowledgeable and demanding customers and activist shareholders which has changed the competitive environment from competition based on ability to invest in and manage physical (or tangible) assets to competition based on knowledge and the ability to exploit intangible and soft assets (like human capital, information systems, intellectual capital, brand development, research and development etc.). In this changed business paradigms, the Balanced Scorecard throws an insight into an organisation's performance by integrating financial measures with other key performance indicators around customer perspectives, internal business processes and organisational growth, learning and innovation, and enables organisations to track short-term financial and operating results while monitoring progress for future growth, development and success.

The Balanced Scorecard is an organisational framework for implementing and managing strategy at all levels of an enterprise by linking objectives, initiatives and measures to an organisation's strategy. The Balanced Scorecard is a strategic management system (not only a measurement system) that enables organisations to clarify their vision and strategy and translate them into action. When fully deployed, the Balanced Scorecard transforms strategic planning from an academic exercise into the nerve centre of an enterprise. The scorecard provides an enterprise view of an organisation's overall performance. The scorecard integrates financial measures like ROI, RI, Dividend yield, EPS etc. with other key performance indicators around customer perspectives, internal business processes and organisational growth, learning and innovation.

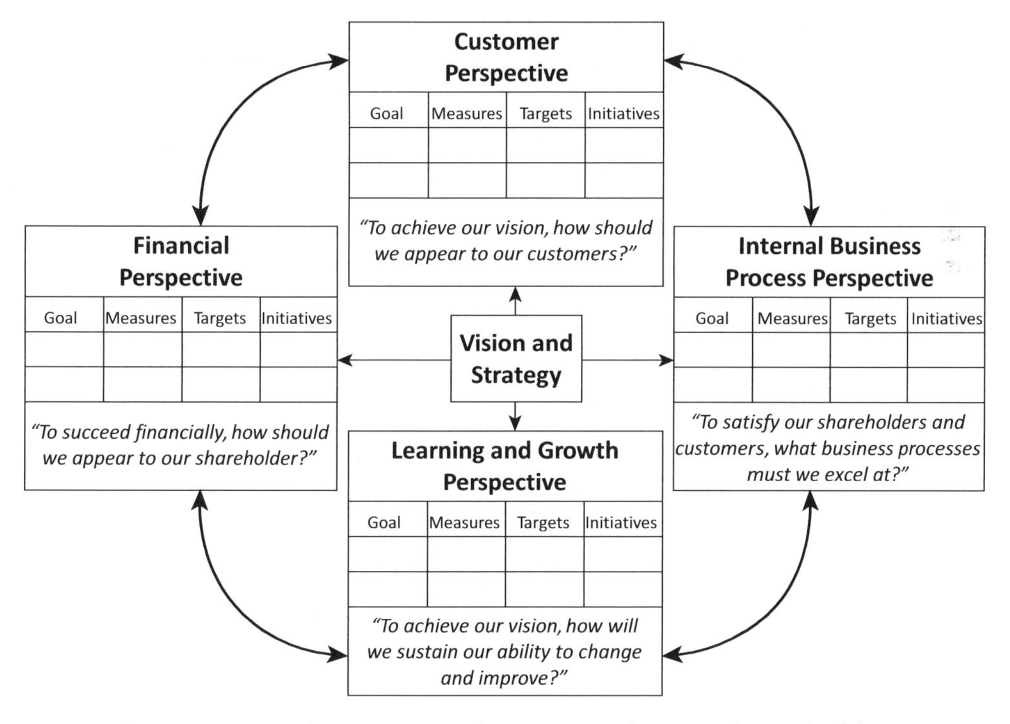

To measure overall corporate performance, goals are set for each of these perspectives and then specific measures for achieving such goals are determined.

Each of these perspectives is critical and must be considered simultaneously to achieve overall efficiency and effectiveness and to succeed in the long-run. If any area is either overemphasised or underemphasised, performance evaluation will become 'unbalanced'. In this way, the aim of the concept is to establish a set of measures-both financial and non-financial through which a company can control its activities and 'balance' various measures to effectively track performance.

Thus, the balanced scorecard represents a fundamental change in the underlying assumption about performance measurement and strikes a balance between short-term and long-term objectives, between financial and non-financial measures, between outcome and process measures, between lagging and leading indicators and between internal and external perspectives.

(c) The traditional financial measures of corporate performance like ROI, EPS etc. are based exclusively on past performance and results have little predictive value to the management of an organisation. But an effective performance measurement system must encompass a blend of both results and process measures so that organisations can not only keep score but also can more reasonably predict what the score will look like. The lagging indicators of performance worked well for the industrial era but they have now become inadequate and often misleading in tracking complex management challenges posed by competitive and rapidly changing business arena.

Conventional financial performance measures focus on creation of shareholders value. But, placing too much importance on shareholder value for measurement of management's performance can jeopardise a company's long-term growth and success. The shareholders can reasonably expect maximum return on their risky investment. Before the commencement of taxation on dividends, this return on investment primarily consisted of dividends but after that commencement appreciation of share price assumed a greater role in providing return on investment because of the favourable tax treatment on capital gains. But the appreciation of share price as a criterion for measuring management performance has some major weakness. Firstly, stock price can rise or fall for reasons other than earnings such as competitive advantage, industry structure, stock market exuberance etc. Secondly, stock market is volatile and inconsistent in its judgement. Moreover, by focusing on shareholder value, the long-term potential and prospects of the business are sacrificed to short-term results. If the firm wants to maximise shareholder value in short-run it has to sacrifices its long-term prospect. In fact, most of the financial measures are rigid targets to be achieved, which discourage alternative action opportunities, no matter how promising they are.

Furthermore, the conventional performance measurement systems generally don't communicate or explain the factors that drive performance. But once the drivers of performance can be identified performance achievement would be easier.

Again, traditional performance measurements systems measure the tangible and financial assets but an organisation has to measure and respond to intangible assets of value to the organisation because of their substantial effect on the bottom-line.

A serious shortcoming of the traditional management systems is their inability to link a firm's long-term strategy with its short-term actions. Most companies' operational and management control system are designed on the basis of financial measures and targets which have little relation to the companies' progress in achieving long-term strategic objectives.

The concept of Balanced Scorecard overcomes these drawbacks and inadequacies of the conventional financial measures and measures corporate performance both from financial and operational perspectives of an organisation.

(d) Fitzgerald and Moon designed a system of non-financial performance indicators specifically for service industries and developed an approach to performance measurement that is based on the three building blocks of Dimensions, Standards and Rewards

- Dimensions are those aspects of performance that need to be measured. These are determined by the key factors that determine the success of the organisation in achieving its objectives.
- Standards are the benchmarks or targets for the measures identified for the different dimensions.
- Rewards are the incentives given to managers who achieve the standards.

The Dimensions of Performance

In developing this model 6 generic dimensions of performance were identified:

- Competitiveness
- Financial performance
- Quality of service
- Flexibility
- Resource utilisation
- Innovation

Questions in relation to each area are:

- What has happened?
- Why has it happened?
- Is it going to continue?
- What are we going to do about it?

Performance measurement is traditionally used to provide an answer to the first of these questions, but it can be developed to give insights that help answer the other three questions.

Measures can be developed to provide appropriate impressions for each of these 6 dimensions.

The first two are considered to relate to 'downstream results' – that is they describe what has actually been achieved in the past while not giving material insights into what might happen in the future.

The other four dimensions might be considered to relate to 'upstream determinants' in that they provide indicators for the ability to achieve results in the future.

The selection of performance measures to be used for a business, business sector or manager should be determined by the nature of the organisation and an identification of the key factors that determine the success of the organisation in achieving its objectives.

Standards
Consideration of standards involves:

- Ownership – managers who participate in the setting of standards are more likely to accept and be motivated by the standards than managers on whom standards are imposed.
- Achievability – an achievable standard is a better motivator than an unachievable one
- Equity – when setting standards across an organisation, care should be undertaken to ensure that all managers have equally challenging standards

Rewards
Consideration of rewards involves:

- Clarity – goal clarity contributes to motivation, eg a standard of achieving X number of product innovations per year may be a more effective motivator
- Motivation – the actual means of motivation may involve performance related rewards
- Controllability – managers will be better motivated if they actually control the factors contributing to achievement of the measures and standards on which their rewards are based

(e)

- Information needs (on competition, customers etc.) are becoming more important
- Change inside organisations is generally regarded as positive and Rockmead is considering organisational changes
- Technology has allowed more information to be processed in more complex and flexible ways
- Responsibilities in Rockmead have been devolved to an extent resulting in more people having responsibilities, but each being involved in narrower areas of the business
- Realisation that focussing solely on short-term financial measures is not adequate and need to obtain information about different aspects and measures of performance

(Details should be added for full marks.)

7.

(a)

Whole company profit computations

Output level (units)	Total revenues	Company variable costs	Company fixed costs	Company profit/(loss)
15,000	1,500,000	270,000	2,250,000	−1,020,000
30,000	2,700,000	540,000	2,250,000	−90,000
45,000	3,600,000	810,000	2,250,000	540,000
60,000	4,200,000	1,080,000	2,250,000	870,000
75,000	4,500,000	1,350,000	2,250,000	900,000
90,000	4,500,000	1,620,000	2,250,000	630,000

Cleardale division (Supplying division)

Output level (units)	Transfer price revenues	Variable costs	Fixed costs	Total profit/(loss)
15,000	525,000	165,000	900,000	−540,000
30,000	1,050,000	330,000	900,000	−180,000
45,000	1,575,000	495,000	900,000	180,000
60,000	2,100,000	660,000	900,000	540,000
75,000	2,625,000	825,000	900,000	900,000
90,000	3,150,000	990,000	900,000	1,260,000

Drival division (Receiving division)

Output level (units)	Total revenues	Variable costs	Total cost of transfers	Fixed costs	Total profit/(loss)
15,000	1,500,000	105,000	525,000	1,350,000	−480,000
30,000	2,700,000	210,000	1,050,000	1,350,000	90,000
45,000	3,600,000	315,000	1,575,000	1,350,000	360,000
60,000	4,200,000	420,000	2,100,000	1,350,000	330,000
75,000	4,500,000	525,000	2,625,000	1,350,000	0
90,000	4,500,000	630,000	3,150,000	1,350,000	−630,000

Setting a £35 transfer price does not motivate optimum output level for the company as a whole.

To ensure overall company optimality the transfer price must be set equal to the marginal cost of the intermediate product (ie the variable cost of £11 per unit).

At a transfer price of £11 Cleardale will choose to expand output to 5,000 units and Drival will choose to produce 4,000 units.

There is no external market so Cleardale's manager has little bargaining power.

(b) A good transfer pricing policy should meet the following criteria:

- It should provide motivation for divisional managers
- It should allow divisional autonomy and independence to be maintained
- It should allow divisional performance to be assessed objectively
- It should ensure that divisional managers make decisions that are in the best interests of the divisions and also of the company as a whole (goal congruence).

Its two overriding features should be simplicity in calculation and implementation and robustness (ie not requiring frequent adjustment)

Although different approaches will result in different figures, the limits within which the transfer price should fall can be summarised as follows:

- Minimum: The sum of the selling division's marginal cost and the opportunity cost of the resources used.
- Maximum: The lowest market price at which the buying division could acquire the goods or services externally, less any internal cost savings in packaging and delivery.

The difference between the two limits represents the savings made by producing internally as opposed to buying in from outside.

(c) ZBB is a method of budgeting that requires each cost element to be specifically identified and justified, based on a default assumption of no cost (in other words, as though the activity or process were taking place for the first time and the manager were justifying the expense ab initio),

The process necessitates a review of all activities associated with the budget along the lines of how essential it is, whether the cost is at the right level and if there are alternative ways to achieve the same effect?

It is especially useful for:

- Service departments such as stores, maintenance, marketing, finance which pursues different projects each year
- Discretionary costs such as research and development (R&D)
- Public sector organisations such as local authorities

There are four distinct stages in the implementation of ZBB and starts with the idea that each manager begins with a zero base of resources. The manager only receives resources if they can be justified.

(i) Managers should specify for their responsibility centres those activities that can be individually evaluated
(ii) Each of the individual activities is then described in a decision package. The decision package should state the costs and revenues expected from the given activity. It should be drawn up in such a way that the package can be evaluated and ranked against other packages
(iii) Each decision package is evaluated and ranked usually using cost/benefit analysis
(iv) The resources are then allocated to the various packages

Strengths

- Responds to changes in the environment so that resources should be allocated efficiently and economically
- Should result in more efficient use of resources as inefficient or obsolete operations can be identified and discontinued
- Managers are forced to consider alternative methods of achieving their objectives
- ZBB leads to increased staff involvement at all levels. This should lead to better communication and motivation
- Attention is focused on outputs in relation to value for money
- Knowledge and understanding of the cost behaviour patterns of the organisation will be enhanced

Weaknesses

- Requires a lot of management time and cost involved in preparing the budget each year
- Involves participation by managers so needs a suitable culture and managers and employees may feel threatened
- It may emphasise short-term benefits to the detriment of long-term benefits
- The rankings of packages may be subjective where the benefits are of a qualitative nature
- It is difficult to compare and rank completely different types of activity
- Incremental costs and benefits of alternative courses of action are difficult to quantify accurately
- The budgeting process may become too rigid and the company may not be able to react to unforeseen opportunities or threats

8.

(a) Management is reliant on Information Systems in order to get the information needed to make organisational decisions. The structure, characteristics and quality of the Information Systems therefore affect the information available for decision-making. A management information system will record and collate information from individual transactions and events, in order to produce reports allowing managers to control the business.

The nature of the information system will depend partly on the size and structure of the organisation. A large business with a complex structure will need a sophisticated management information system, whereas a smaller simpler business would require a simpler, cheaper management information system.

Other characteristics of the business are also relevant, for example a high number of transactions between different business units or a high level of integration between different business units will introduce a requirement for a management information system which facilitates communication between different managers and analysis of the interdependencies of business units.

A larger, more complex or more diverse business is likely to have a greater number of strict financial targets in place, since otherwise it is too difficult to manage the large quantity of information and the diversity of business activities. The management information system will be required to enable managers to measure financial targets such as profitability, revenue growth, cost control etc. In large complex businesses, business units will be able to measure their performance independently of each other and so measures such as divisional return on investment or residual income may be used.

The development of the management information system over time will be influenced not only by the objectives and characteristics of the organisation but also by the system itself. A more flexible, expandable system will be better able to respond to changes in requirements.

(b) The main features of importance when preparing budgets in NFP organisations are:

- No profit motive, but they still need to control costs.
- Many of the benefits arising from expenditure by these bodies are non-quantifiable

So how can measurable budgets be prepared which meet the organisation's objectives?

- Often revenue is not generated and there is a fixed budget for spending within which they have to keep (ie a capital rationing problem). 'Value for money' is often quoted as an objective here but it does not get round the problem of measuring 'value'.
- Multiple stakeholders give rise to multiple objectives so there is a need to prioritise/compromise (eg hospital – patients, staff, government, taxpayers, local community, society at large, contractors, management, donors/contributors, etc.).
- Objectives may be difficult to define, may change as a result of the political process and may be achievable in different ways.

A budget in the public sector:

- Establishes income as well as expenditure

- Authorises expenditure
- Acts as a control on expenditure
- Communicates plans to staff

Budgets tend to concentrate on planning for one year ahead. Attempts have been made to link expenditure in the longer term.

Incremental budgeting is traditionally used. This focuses on the change at the margin and reflects the size, complexity and internal power of public sector bodies in setting budget targets.

Other budgeting approaches such as ZBB and planned programme budgeting systems (PPBS) have been used. PPBS breaks work down into programmes designed towards achieving various objectives.

Several departments may contribute towards a single programme and budget targets may spread over more than one year which means used to achieve programmes should be efficient and cost effective.

There are a number of issues that arise from budgeting in the public sector:

- Some organisations are legally prevented from borrowing money.
- It may be difficult or impossible to move funds from one part of an organisation's budget to another (making them inflexible).
- Most public sector budgets simply focus on the coming fiscal year – rather than a longer timescale.
- Incremental budgeting (with all its inherent problems) is still widely used.

9.

(a) Strategic planning vs local decision-making

The distinction between strategic planning (long-term) and localised decision-making can create conflicts.

In summary, a strategic business plan:

- Supports major business changes through a programme of projects.
- Tends to have a relatively long time scale over several years or financial periods.
- May require a specific strategy support team reporting to high level management and the coordination of many staff in different geographic locations, departments and projects.
- Required budgets may be expressed in forecast outline terms.
- Objectives may be expressed in wide terms perhaps reflecting aspirations rather than specific targets eg maximising shareholder wealth.
- Is likely to be reported on half yearly or yearly cycles, although monthly reporting is not uncommon.

Whereas a short-term business plan:

- Tends to support a specific business process over a short timescale perhaps no longer than one financial year.

- Usually focused on the activity of a specific location, department, cost centre or project.
- Likely to be expressed in measurable specific objectives or targets.
- Likely to be managed by a single manager with supporting staff.
- Likely to have to be reported on monthly, weekly and perhaps even daily.

(b)

- Departments or cost centres may not be financed or resourced to meet the need of the overall strategic business plan.
- Lack of alignment of local business objectives with strategic objectives and local objectives may not support the strategic business plan.
- Departmental or cost centres may not be designed to deliver the strategic business plan.
- Localised decisions by managers are likely to maximise results to meet their localised objectives rather than support the strategic business plan.
- Meeting the strategic business plan might only be through the removal of aspects of the business that will deliver it eg through planned redundancy leading to reduced commitment to deliver the strategic plan.
- Strategic business plan may not be designed to solve local problems or support local processes.
- The purpose of the strategic business plan may not be communicated clearly to lower level managers leading to confusion eg higher level management may not be prepared to release commercially sensitive information to lower level managers.

Implications for decision-making:

- Organisations must developing consistent strategies. Overall strategic objectives should be broken down into compatible objectives at local level, so that conflicts can be avoided. The strategic planning process has to be multi-layered.
- Managers need to decide objectively between strategic options. Strategic business plans should be carefully evaluated and the impact of unintended consequences considered.
- Managers also need to develop and use appropriate performance measures.

(c) Corporate strategy

This looks at the industries in which the organisation operates. This may mean deciding to leave existing areas or enter new ones. This is particularly true if the organisation has a number of divisions. Activities supporting strategic development at this level include portfolio analysis, environmental and industry analysis and decision-making about: diversification, business structure, business expansion etc.

Business strategy
This looks at how the organisation (or subsidiary/division) competes.

Operational strategy
This looks at how resources are used to carry out the strategies noted above.

Corporate planning refers to the formal process which facilitates the 3 stage strategic planning framework described above.

Corporate planning supports senior management in making decisions to ensure corporate objectives are met. Its main roles are to:

- Manage the business planning process through which the objectives of individual departments and support services are agreed
- Compile and publish the annual plan for the organisation
- Monitor performance against the targets set in the business planning process
- Monitor performance compared with other similar organisations
- Undertake specific strategic projects

10.

(a) Financial performance is often assessed in relation to benchmarks.

Benchmarking requires gathering information that can be used to generate targets so that current levels of performance can be evaluated and improved. Benchmarking can particularly help organisations to improve the performance of aspects of their business which are currently under performing.

Benchmarking targets can be based on data from within the organisation (internal benchmarks) or from outside the organisation, for example from other businesses in the same industry, competitors, or other businesses which engage in the same or similar processes (external benchmarks).

External benchmarks might include:

- targets based on the market performance of comparable companies
- industry averages

Internal benchmarks might include:

- the best-performing divisions within the company
- targets based on improvements from last year's performance

Benchmarking is also useful in helping a business to assess its current strategic position, by assessing its strengths and weaknesses against those of other businesses.

Advantages of using benchmarks

- improvements in processes
- cost reduction and efficiency savings
- delivers products and services to specified standards
- provide information about sources of competitive advantage and competitive disadvantage
- provide assurance that targets are reasonable, achievable unsuitable
- can be effective as a way of implementing changes in business processes

Disadvantages of using benchmarks

- assumes that there is a single best standard to achieve or a single best way of carrying out an activity
- based often on historic performance and so may not be relevant for future strategic development
- depends on the availability of accurate information
- may create unwanted side-effects and dysfunctional behaviour (managers focus on the measure rather than the long-term objectives of the business)

(b) There are a number of difficulties and issues facing organisations wishing to undertake a benchmarking exercise.

- Benchmarking exercises can be costly and time consuming – it is necessary to consider whether the value of the exercise is sufficient to justify its cost
- Other organisations may be unwilling to share information
- It may be difficult to obtain information, particularly non-financial information about competitors
- The business functions being benchmarked must be similar enough to allow meaningful comparison
- Companies need to be as specific as possible when identifying areas to benchmark. For example, if a company is interested in studying customer service, it needs to determine what specific area or activity within customer service needs to be examined.
- Success will hinge on the level of commitment from top managers who must be prepared to make changes in response to the results of benchmarking.
- Benchmarking information must be interpreted carefully to ensure that organisations are being compared on a similar basis, and account must be taken of differences in the way data is produced, such as differences in accounting treatment, and external factors which influence performance in the area being benchmarked.
- Organisations should concentrate on areas that: tie up most cash, significantly improve the relationship with customers and impact on the final results of the business.

Index

Index

O

P

R

S

T

V

Z

Publishing Feedback

We want your feedback! Our aim is to develop the best possible material in order to give you and other students the best chance of passing. We would appreciate your feedback on our material so we can help you be successful in your studies.

Your feedback will take a short time and covers important areas such as your learning, your revision and your preparation for the exam.

Learning

Please rate any of the following that you used 1 (Poor), 2 (Fair), 3 (Good), 4 (Very Good) by ticking the appropriate boxes:

	1	2	3	4
Study Manual				
Interactive Videos				
Class Notes				

If you have any comments and suggestions on how to improve the material please let us know:

Revision

Please rate any of the following that you used 1 (Poor), 2 (Fair), 3 (Good), 4 (Very Good) by ticking the appropriate boxes:

	1	2	3	4
Revision Kit				
Revision Cards				
Interactive Videos				

If you have any comments and suggestions on how to improve the material please let us know:

Preparation for the exam

How well prepared for your exam were you? 1 (Poor), 2 (Fair), 3 (Good), 4 (Very Good) by ticking one of the boxes:

	1	2	3	4
Study Manual				
Interactive Videos				
Class Notes				

How else could we have helped you be prepared for the exam? Please consider our current package of material to help you pass as well as what else we could offer to you in the future. These could include different ways to study (eg via iPad or other tablet), different products to study from (eg ebooks) or anything else that you would consider useful.

Finally, would you recommend us to your colleagues? Yes No

Name

Employer

Thanks for your feedback, it is much appreciated! Good luck for your exam and future studies.

If it helps then please email PublishingFeedback@lsbf.org.uk with your comments and grades. Otherwise please post your completed form to Clive Bullen, Sceptre Court, 40 Tower Hill, London EC3N 4DX.